# Praise for *The Real Jaw*

"*The Real Jaws* is a captivating, fast-paced investigation into the shark attacks that plagued New Jersey vacationers in the summer of 1916. Perez takes the reader through the horror and confusion of that summer step-by-step, showcasing how experts and city officials failed to adequately warn beach goers of the dangers that lurked beneath the water's surface. This is an incredible look into a sometimes mythologized part of our past and one that offers a fresh perspective on the influence one chaotic summer had for decades to come."
— Alycia Asai, Historian and Founder of *Civics & Coffee* Podcast

"A thrilling read, *The Real Jaws* brings the horrific but enthralling story of the 1916 shark attacks to life in a way that even the brightest stars of cinema could not. Proof that fact is often more interesting than fiction."
— Chloe Gardner, PhD Candidate and Author of *Women Against the Raj*

"Blood so thick it was mistaken for a red canoe, media frenzy, denial by experts, and the harrowing details of the victims' last words, makes this a gripping and visceral story full of intrigue. Perez brings this all to life by blending history and sensationalized journalism."
— Kelsie Brook Eckert, Author, Professor, and Executive Director of the *Remedial Herstory Project*

"The excitement of the Jaws movie, the information of a textbook, and the heart-wrenching narrative of a novel all rolled into one. Rachel Lee Perez has truly combined all these aspects to create the perfect book for anyone wishing to dip and then dive into the history and humanity behind the 1916 New Jersey shark attacks."
— Tehya Nakamura, History Educator and Creator of *For the Love of History* Podcast

# The Real Jaws

**Disclaimer:**

*Peter Benchley, the author of the Jaws novel, always denied that the 1916 shark attacks inspired the book. Steven Spielberg, the director of the Jaws film, however, never denied the inspiration and even included references to the attacks in the movie. One character in the movie directly mentions the 1916 attacks that occurred on the Jersey beaches. Additionally, the number of deaths, as well as the city's response to these attacks, appears to coincide with true events. But because Benchley always maintained that he did not draw inspiration for his book from the 1916 shark attacks, it is important to note that upfront.*

# The Real Jaws

## The Attacks that Inspired the Movies

Rachel Lee Perez

First published in Great Britain in 2025 by
White Owl
An imprint of Pen & Sword Books Limited
Yorkshire – Philadelphia

Copyright © Rachel Lee Perez 2025

ISBN 978 1 03613 261 3

The right of Rachel Lee Perez to be identified as
Author of this Work has been asserted by her in accordance
with the Copyright, Designs and Patents Act 1988.

A CIP catalogue record for this book is
available from the British Library.

All rights reserved. No part of this book may be reproduced, transmitted, downloaded, decompiled or reverse engineered in any form or by any means, electronic or mechanical including photocopying, recording or by any information storage and retrieval system, without permission from the Publisher in writing. NO AI TRAINING: Without in any way limiting the Author's and Publisher's exclusive rights under copyright, any use of this publication to "train" generative artificial intelligence (AI) technologies to generate text is expressly prohibited. The Author and Publisher reserve all rights to license uses of this work for generative AI training and development of machine learning language models.

Typeset by Mac Style
Printed in the UK by CPI Group (UK) Ltd, Croydon, CR0 4YY.

The Publisher's authorised representative in the EU for product safety is Authorised Rep Compliance Ltd., Ground Floor, 71 Lower Baggot Street, Dublin D02 P593, Ireland. www.arccompliance.com

For a complete list of Pen & Sword titles please contact

**PEN & SWORD BOOKS LIMITED**
47 Church Street, Barnsley, South Yorkshire, S70 2AS, England
E-mail: enquiries@pen-and-sword.co.uk
Website: www.pen-and-sword.co.uk
or
**PEN AND SWORD BOOKS**
1950 Lawrence Road, Havertown, PA 19083, USA
E-mail: uspen-and-sword@casematepublishers.com
Website: www.penandswordbooks.com

*To Alex,*
*Because I've got you.*

# Contents

*Acknowledgments* ix
*Chronological List of Events* xv
*Introduction* xix

**Part I** 1

**Chapter 1**  An Ancient Fear  3
**Chapter 2**  Beach Haven: The Beginning of the Horror  21
**Chapter 3**  Spring Lake: 'The Most Likeable Employee'  39
**Chapter 4**  Matawan Creek: A Highly Unusual Location  51
**Chapter 5**  Cliffwood: The Forgotten Victim  69
**Chapter 6**  'The Largest Scale Animal Hunt in History'  73
**Chapter 7**  This Vicinity Will Be Alive with Sharks  87
**Chapter 8**  The Rogue Shark Theory  101

**Part II**  111

**Chapter 9**  Shark Attacks 101  113
**Chapter 10**  What Modern-Day Shark Attacks Can Tell Us About 1916  125
**Chapter 11**  Sharks, Infantile Deaths, and the First World War  137
**Chapter 12**  The Jaws Effect  147

*Epilogue: The Fiftieth Anniversary of* Jaws  163
*Notes*  169
*Resources*  167
*Bibliography*  185
*Index*  195

# Acknowledgments

First, I must thank Pen & Sword Books for the wonderful opportunity to write this book. Writing a history book has truly been a lifelong dream and I am so thrilled that my first history book is about a much neglected, underwritten, but incredibly important event in history. Not only was it so important for me to talk about this event and the ways in which it quite literally changed and shaped the human perception of sharks; it was also so important to me to highlight sharks as the amazing creatures that they are and the ways in which they have unfortunately become the prey and humans have become the predators over the last several decades. I could not have found a publisher whose mission to 'bring you closer to the past' could have aligned better with my own and whose vision and understanding for where I wanted to go with this book was so well understood. I have had such a wonderful experience through the entire proposal, writing, and publishing process, and am eternally grateful to the whole team at Pen & Sword for taking a chance on me and making my first traditional publishing experience an amazing one. I am looking forward to many exciting partnerships in the future.

This book could not be written without the dedicated work of people like Dr Richard G Fernicola, Michael Capuzzo, and Allan Savolaine, without whom the world would not know nearly as much as we do about the 1916 shark attacks. Thank you for your extensive investigative work in interviewing people there at the time of the attacks, combing through archives and newspapers and photographs, and providing your own thorough analysis and expertise.

In the same vein, I am especially thankful for world-leading shark experts, Richard Ellis (who sadly passed away as I was writing this book) and George Burgess, for all that you have both done to educate the world so thoroughly on sharks over the last several decades. Both of you have dedicated your lives to this research and I am so in awe of your commitment to the study of sharks and your commitment to sharing the knowledge you learn with the world.

Something I was not expecting when I first embarked on this journey was how many wonderful and helpful people I would meet along the way. I want to extend special thanks to all the people that assisted in my search for historical source material, such as *The New York Times*, *The Matawan Journal*, and *The Evening Star*. I am especially thankful to the Monmouth County Historical Association, the Matawan Historical Society, the Bronx Historical Society, and the New Jersey State Archives.

Thank you endlessly to Matawan historian Kurtis Roinestad for meeting with me and offering his extensive knowledge about the Matawan attacks. Your passion for the topic and impressive research forced me to reevaluate some of my own previous opinions and really helped shape some of the theories in this book. A heartfelt thanks again to Matawan historian and author Allan Savolaine for sharing so much with me about Stanley Fisher and his bravery. It reminded me that studying history is about studying real people and putting ourselves in their shoes and the shoes of their loved ones.

An overwhelming thanks to Dr Blake Chapman, the author of *Shark Attacks: Myths, Misunderstandings and Human Fear*, who graciously reviewed portions of Chapter One and provided such helpful feedback and understanding when it comes to shark basics. I truly cannot thank Dr Chapman enough for her time and expertise!

Thank you also to my dear friends and brilliant historians who served as advance readers and provided such thoughtful reviews of my early work: Kelsie Brook Eckert, Alycia Asai, Chloe Gardner, and Tehya Nakamura.

I would not be here with the opportunity to write about history without the avenue that first allowed me the chance to dive into the history world professionally: The *Hashtag History* podcast. It is because of the podcast that I have had the opportunity to write for various history publications and had the credibility to make my pitch to Pen & Sword in the first place. The podcast began as a passion project and a way for me to 'tickle' the history funny bone that I have had for as long as I can remember. This passion project has been going on for nearly six years now and has received hundreds of thousands of downloads. It is only because of the dedicated listeners and supporters that we have had the opportunity to go on this beautiful journey. It is because of you that I was able to write this book, and for that, I am eternally grateful.

Above and beyond anyone else, I would not have been able to write this book without my husband, Alex. Alex, you are the most supportive, compassionate, and patient person I have ever met. Every day, you encourage me to achieve my dreams and are always there, cheering me on from the sidelines. Your constant listening ear, intelligent contributions, and direct assistance with some of the graphics for this book cannot be overstated. I could not have done any of this without you. I love you forever.

Charlotte and Olivia, you are my joy and my reason. I love you both from the core of my being. The best part of every day is seeing your sweet, sleepy faces each morning. Being your mom is my most favorite thing and something I would never trade for anything else in the world.

To my mom who watches our baby girls every day, I am so grateful. It simply would not have been possible for me to have the time to write and research without your support and care for our girls. Thank you for everything you do.

And to the rest of our families: Thank you always for all of your support of me and Charlie and Liv. I could not do any of this without you.

And finally, to my sister Leah, who never leaves my mind. Your memory bleeds through everything I do. You are woven in and out, all around, above and in between every word on every page. I miss you more than I could ever express, and I express how much I miss you constantly.

*'Assuredly the accidents of the present summer will linger with great vividness in popular memory through many a quiet season to come.*

*Few things endure as long
as a substantial shark story.'*

*John Nichols and Robert Murphy
Brooklyn Museum Quarterly
October 1916*

# Chronological List of Events

**725 BCE:** First known drawing of a shark attack found on a vase from Ischia, Italy, in which the shark is shown attacking a shipwrecked human.

**493 BCE:** 'Sea monsters' devour twenty thousand men whose ships had been wrecked during the war (according to Greek historian Herodotus).

**336 BCE:** Unprovoked shark attack of a man washing a pig in preparation for a religious event (according to Greek philosopher and historian Plutarch).

**214 BCE:** Unprovoked shark attack on a diver in the Ionian Sea (according to Greek poet Leonidas of Tarentum).

**1580:** The oldest shark attack investigated and documented by the International Shark Attack File occurs this year. A Portuguese sailor fell off his boat while traveling to India. He was then seen being attacked and killed by a surprise shark.

**1841:** Publication of Johannes Müller's *Systematische Beschreibung der Plagiostomen*.

**1891:** Multimillionaire Hermann Oelrichs advertises a $500 reward in the *New York Sun* to anyone that can prove that a shark attacked a human along the East Coast.

**July 28, 1914:** The First World War begins (though Americans were not yet involved).

**May 7, 1915:** A German U-boat launches a torpedo into the *Lusitania*, a passenger's ship carrying 1,959 passengers and crew members. This attack caused the ocean liner to sink within just twenty minutes, leading to the drowning deaths of 1,198 people, 128 of which were innocent American citizens.

**April 24, 1916**: Dr Frederic Lucas, Dr John Nichols, and Robert Murphy publish a piece in the *Brooklyn Museum Science Bulletin* in which they contend that sharks are 'not particularly strong in the jaws.'

**June 17, 1916:** The first official announcement about the 1916 polio epidemic is made in Brooklyn, New York.

**Late-June 1916:** The German U-boat, the *Deutschland*, makes its maiden voyage, eventually making its way to Baltimore, Maryland.

**July 1, 1916:** Charles Vansant is killed by a shark in Beach Haven, New Jersey.

**July 6, 1916:** Charles Bruder is killed by a shark in Spring Lake, New Jersey.

**July 6th–11th, 1916:** Several sightings of sharks are reported all along the Jersey coast, even stretching as far out as Connecticut, Florida, and Alabama.

**July 8, 1916:** A press conference is held at the American Museum of Natural History in Manhattan, New York. Those presenting on the panel are Dr Frederic Lucas, Dr John Nichols, and Robert Murphy.

**July 8, 1916:** Lifeguard captain Benjamin Everingham beats a shark with an oar in Asbury Park, New Jersey.

**July 8, 1916:** A group of kids spot a shark in the water in Bayonne, New Jersey.

**July 11, 1916:** Esterbrook Carter, the nephew of Charles Evan Hughes (the Republican candidate running in opposition to Woodrow Wilson for the presidency in 1916), reports a shark swimming underneath his boat while he is out to sea.

**July 12, 1916:** Lester Stillwell is killed by a shark in the Matawan Creek in Matawan, New Jersey.

**July 12, 1916:** Stanley Fisher is killed by a shark in the Matawan Creek in Matawan, New Jersey, while attempting to recover Stillwell's body.

**July 12, 1916:** Joseph Dunn is attacked by a shark in Cliffwood, New Jersey.

Chronological List of Events    xvii

**July 13, 1916 (on or about):** United States President Woodrow Wilson calls for an all-day meeting with his Cabinet to address the terrifying shark attacks and what the government could do to bring them to a halt.

**July 14, 1916:** Lester Stillwell's body surfaces roughly 150 feet from where the attacks took place.

**July 14, 1916:** Barnum & Bailey Circus animal trainer Michael Schleisser captures and kills a shark that is later dubbed to be *the* 'Jersey man-eater.'

**July 19–20, 1916:** Schleisser places the shark he captured on display at the office of the *Bronx Home News,* located at 155 W 125th Street, New York.

**October 1916:** Experts Dr John Nichols and Robert Murphy issue a revised statement about the capabilities of sharks and the probability of shark attacks in the *Brooklyn Museum Quarterly.*

**November 1916:** President Woodrow Wilson wins re-election by a narrow margin of 277–254 electoral votes.

**February 24, 1917:** British intelligence agents provide the US government with a secret telegram that they intercepted between Germany and Mexico. This telegram, named after the German Foreign Minister who sent it, Arthur Zimmermann, promises an alliance between the two countries if Mexico joins the Central Powers.

**April 4, 1917:** The US Senate votes to declare war on Germany, officially marking the entrance of the United States in the First World War.

**1917–1918:** Thousands of German Americans are held in internment camps.

**April 5, 1918:** Robert Prager is lynched by an angry mob as a result of anti-German sentiment.

**1918:** An influenza pandemic – known as the 'Spanish flu' – hits the country, killing approximately fifty million people.

**1920:** The 19th Amendment to the United States Constitution is ratified, granting women the right to vote.

**July 30, 1945:** The USS *Indianapolis* is struck with torpedoes by the Japanese Army, forcing hundreds of men into the ocean. Somewhere between a dozen and 150 men later become victim to surrounding sharks in what is considered one of the worst shark attacks in history.

**December 18, 1957–April 5, 1958:** Nine shark attacks – six of which are fatal – occur off the coast of KwaZulu-Natal, South Africa. This series of shark attacks are so dark and disquieting that they are often referred to as 'Black December.'

**August 1960:** New Jersey experiences a 'second wave' of shark attacks, but many of these are written off by officials.

**1974:** New Jersey resident and freelance writer Peter Benchley publishes his breakthrough novel titled *Jaws* about a great white shark that wreaks havoc in the fictional seaside resort town of Amity.

**1975:** The *Jaws* film is released, becoming an immediate success. The movie breaks the $100 million box office record and becomes the standard for 'summer blockbusters.' It goes on to win three Academy Awards.

**July 17, 1988:** The first Shark Week airs on the Discovery Channel. It is so successful that the Discovery Channel continues to air this program every year for the next thirty-plus years (and continues to this day).

**Summer of 2001:** *Time Magazine* dubs this summer the 'Summer of the Shark' due to a string of shark attacks that takes place and causes mass media attention.

**December 2010:** In a singular week in December of 2010, four people are attacked by a shark, and another is killed, in Sharm el-Sheikh, Egypt.

**May–July 2015:** Over the span of just two months, eleven people are attacked by sharks in North and South Carolina. To this day, 2015 remains the year with the highest number of recorded shark attacks since the International Shark Attack File first began recording such encounters.

**July 9–17, 2016:** Matawan hosts a centennial commemoration for the 1916 shark attacks which draws in more than 3,000 visitors worldwide.

**July 2025:** Fiftieth Anniversary of the *Jaws* movie.

# Introduction

It was a beautiful day in Beach Haven, New Jersey. It was the Summer of 1916, and it was hot. New Jersey is often hot in the summertime, but this was an unprecedented heat. The temperature rose to the low nineties, a stark contrast to the typical seventies-degree weather of summers past. This heatwave was unlike any other, causing thousands of locals and tourists alike to flock to the Jersey Shore. More people than ever crowded the New Jersey beaches, perhaps making themselves a greater target for a danger that, unbeknownst to them, lurked just below the sparkling surface of the Atlantic Ocean.

The Jersey Shore has long been a popular location for tourists, and this summer was no exception. One family in particular, the Vansant family, had traveled from Philadelphia to New Jersey to enjoy a few days at the Engleside Hotel, a beautiful resort huddled within Beach Haven, a resort town filled with restaurants and hotels that sit right along the beach. One of the family members, 23-year-old Charles Epting Vansant, decided to take a quick swim in the ocean before having dinner at the hotel's scheduled serving time of 6:30 PM. He swam about fifty yards out to chest-deep water. Witnesses along the shore spotted a dorsal fin gliding just above the ocean's surface and called out to Vansant to warn him, but he did not hear them.

Not long after, the peaceful sound of the waves crashing on the sand was replaced by Vansant's horrifying screams.

Those nearby initially ignored him. He had jumped into the water along with a Chesapeake Bay retriever and it was assumed by onlookers that he was simply shouting at the dog. They quickly learned, however, that this was not the case, and that Vansant was being viciously attacked by a large mass just below the water's surface.

A lifeguard by the name of Alexander Ott and two bystanders rushed to the water and created a human chain to rescue the struggling Vansant, all while Vansant's family stood along the shore, watching in horror as their loved one was dragged out of the ocean. Some nearby witnesses reported that the beast that had attacked him – presumably, a shark – had followed him all the way up to the shore during his rescue! There on the shore, the horrified crowd saw the extent of Vansant's injuries, which included a left leg that had been mangled and stripped entirely of its flesh. Vansant was brought inside the Engleside Hotel and placed on the hotel manager's desk where he would tragically bleed to death. He was dead by 6:45 that evening. The Vansant family had only just arrived in the resort town that very day and, before nightfall, their eldest son was gone.

This attack would be the first in a two-week long series of vicious shark attacks along the Jersey coast. Vansant's death, initially considered to be an isolated event, was quickly swept under the rug by the tourism industry, motivated by fear that an attack by a dangerous sea monster would dissuade potential clients from traveling to the beachfront resorts and spending their hard-earned money. This incident was so severely underreported that the *New York Times* only briefly mentioned it in a short article titled 'Dies After Attack by Fish,' buried on the eighteenth page of the newspaper days after the event.

But by the end of this catastrophe, the front page of the *New York Times* would be plastered with full-length coverage of the 'man-eating species' wreaking havoc on the beautiful Jersey Shore. By the end of this horrific two-week nightmare, four people would be dead, and one other would be severely injured. Beaches would be closed with safety nets placed along the ocean, hotels would shut down completely, and New Jersey officials would issue a reward for anyone that could kill 'the ferocious man-eating sharks' in what would be dubbed 'the largest scale animal hunt in history.'

By the end of this two-week killing spree, that innate fear of sharks that humans have felt since the beginning of time would officially be cemented, establishing our modern-day misconstrued perception of these beautiful beasts as evil, man-eating monsters.

# PART I

Chapter One

# An Ancient Fear

*'…there is practically no danger of an attack from a shark about our coasts.'*

Dr Frederic Lucas

A fear of sharks has existed since the days of Greek mythology. The Greeks built legends about sharks as a way of providing understanding about these mysterious creatures. In Ancient Greece, the mythological figure Ceto (whose name is derived from the word *ketos*, meaning 'sea monster') is a shark-like monster who was sent after Cassiopeia for bragging that her daughters were more beautiful than the daughters of the sea god, Poseidon. This myth depicted the shark-like figure as a monstrous beast, intent on destroying life. In fact, throughout much of Greek mythology, there are representations of sharks as terrifying creatures, with some exhibiting children-eating behaviors.

Stories of shark attacks on humans extend beyond just mythological legends in Greek history, however, with Greek historians writing of real-life encounters with the beasts of the sea. In perhaps one of the greatest stories of a shark attack in Greek history, Greek historian Herodotus wrote of 'sea monsters' that devoured twenty thousand men whose ships had been wrecked during the war in 493 BCE. In 336 BCE, Greek philosopher and historian Plutarch also wrote of an unprovoked shark attack, this one on a man who was washing a pig in preparation for a religious event. While doing so, 'a shark seized him, bit off all his lower parts up to the belly and devoured them.'[1] In 214 BCE, Greek poet Leonidas of Tarentum wrote of an unprovoked shark attack on a diver that occurred in the Ionian Sea. It is written that the shark 'bit [the diver] in two.'[2]

Polynesian culture tells of a shark-god named Kauhuhu who lived inside of a cave where, if one entered, they never returned.[3] Australian Aboriginal culture has a legend about a shark named Bangudja that killed a man and left a blood-red stain along the Chasm Island rocks, still visible today.[4]

Other ancient depictions of sharks continue to perpetrate the narrative of sharks as human-devouring beasts. In fact, the very first known drawing of a shark attack can be found on a vase from Ischia, Italy, dated 725 BCE, in which the shark is shown attacking a shipwrecked human.[5]

Even in cultures where sharks are not necessarily feared – such as in Fijian and Hawaiian legends – sharks are still treated with a god-like reverence. In Fijian legend, there is a warrior god named Dakuwaqa that is half-man/half-shark and is believed to protect fishermen from the evil creatures living within the sea.[6] Sharks are so revered in this culture that offerings are made to ancestral sharks at events such as weddings, deaths, and births, as a way of requesting their blessing. In more modern-day Fijian culture, sharks continue to be respected, and efforts are made to protect their livelihood. In Fiji, there are certain areas of the ocean where one is not allowed to fish in order to maintain protected areas for the local sharks.[7]

In ancient Hawaiian culture, it was believed that sharks possessed a connection to the spiritual world and our passed loved ones. Sharks were referred to as aumākua, spiritual creatures that had once been humans.[8] If the aumākua belonged to your family – for example, if a shark possessed the soul of your passed-on grandmother – it was common to take special care and attention of that shark in order to protect it. To this day, Hawaiians maintain a healthy respect for sharks and have implemented laws to protect them. In fact, they were the first state in the United States to ban trade on shark fins.[9]

These cultures acknowledged that sharks were dangerous creatures, but they exhibited this fear more as an expression of respect and reverence, perceiving sharks to be god-like. In contrast, Western culture has often depicted sharks simply as dangerous (without the labels of respect attached).

An Ancient Fear  5

*Watson and the Shark* by John Singleton Copley. (*Public Domain*)

An early example of this can be seen in 1778 when artist John Singleton Copley first exhibited his painting titled *Watson and the Shark* at the Royal Academy in London.

This oil painting depicts the real-life story of a 14-year-old English boy named Brook Watson. Watson was attacked by a shark off the Havana Harbor in Cuba in 1749. Watson miraculously survived the attack, but not before losing his right leg to the shark from the knee down. While the extent of Watson's injury cannot be seen in the painting, you can spot blood pooling in the water. What is of particular importance to note about the painting is how unrealistic the shark is portrayed. Copley, who had likely never seen a shark in real life, painted the creature with features such as lips and forward-facing eyes, features that no shark possesses.

For indeed, when it comes to our fear of sharks, so much of this is derived from the fear of the unknown. So much of the lore of sharks

6   The Real Jaws

exists simply because so little was known about them for so long. Still, to this day, there are gaps in our understanding of sharks. Sharks have never fared well in captivity, meaning that scientists have never had the ability to study them completely.

This lack of knowledge was particularly prevalent in early histories, though the world did receive a more modern study of sharks in the early-1800s with the publication of Johannes Müller's *Systematische Beschreibung der Plagiostomen*. Translated into English, 'Systematic Description of the Plagiostomi' is an extensive scientific journal explaining the class *Plagiostomi*, a class of cartilaginous fish which includes sharks and rays. While this book was critical in providing information about sharks, like the fact that their skeletons are made up of cartilage and not bones, there was still a large gap in the human understanding of these mysterious creatures. For example, look at the very human-like eyes drawn on the sharks in the illustrations included in this book.

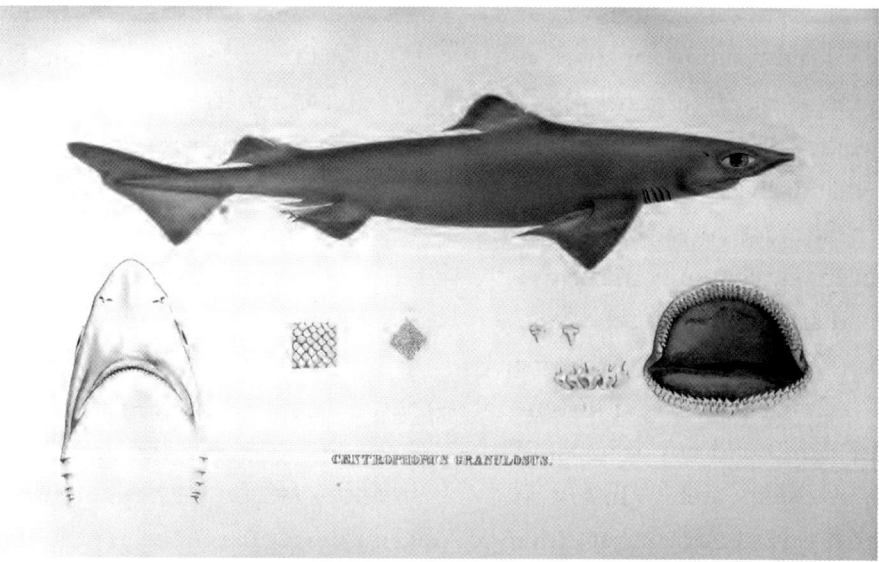

*Centrophorus granulosus* illustration from Johannes Müller's *Systematische Beschreibung der Plagiostomen*. (*Public Domain*)

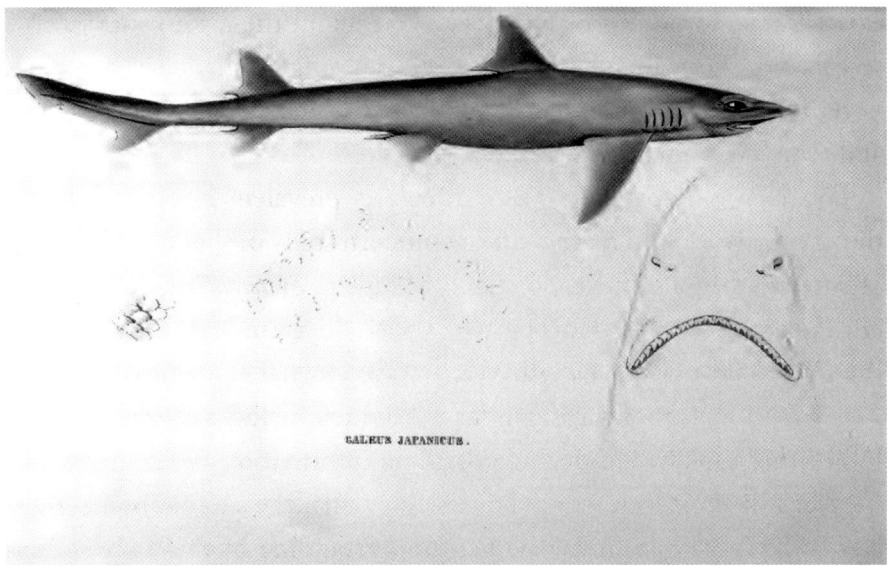

*Galeus japanicus* illustration from Johannes Müller's *Systematische Beschreibung der Plagiostomen*. (*Public Domain*)

It wasn't until roughly the mid-twentieth century that scientists finally received funding for shark research. Prior to that, scientific funding for marine research generally supported sea creatures like tuna or cod or salmon. Why would this be the case? The answer is rather simple: Because what really drove marine studies was money and what ultimately benefited the average consumer. Because sharks did not directly contribute to the everyday economy in the way that largely consumable fish like tuna and cod and salmon do, the funding for shark research simply did not exist for marine biologists to pursue.

Arguably, 'the first serious attempt to collect and utilize knowledge of sharks' did not occur until after 1945, the direct result of one of the worst shark attacks in history.[10] On July 30, 1945, an incident occurred that was so alarming that it urged society to reexamine the gaps in our comprehension of sharks and forced the government to allocate funds to help us better understand their behaviors.

It was the final months of the Second World War and American soldiers onboard the USS *Indianapolis* had just completed their top-secret mission of delivering critical components for the first ever nuclear weapon used in wartime, set to be used approximately one week later in Hiroshima, Japan.[11] Just after midnight, the Japanese Navy launched two torpedoes into the USS *Indianapolis*, causing the ship to sink in a matter of twelve minutes. Close to 300 of the 1,196 men onboard went down with the ship. The remaining 900 were forced to do their best to survive for nearly five days in the open water which threatened death by starvation, dehydration, exposure…and sharks. Not long after the men were stranded in the water, hundreds of sharks swarmed the site and began picking at the dead. After feeding on the drowned humans, they began attacking the living. Stories from survivors tell terrifying tales of sharks popping up 'like lightning' to take a sailor down with them.[12] Men huddled in groups with those on the outskirts knowing it was only a matter of time before they became the shark's next victim. Ultimately, when the crew was rescued days later, just 316 had survived.[13] Despite the fact that it was later determined that only between a dozen and 150 men had become victims to the sharks, the stories of the attacks overshadowed the reality. It was the perceived need to protect oneself from sharks that ultimately led the government to establish funding to study them further.[14] The team of government officials assembled to complete this task, however, were surprised to find the existing lack of knowledge pertaining to sharks. They also found, in the course of their mission, that sharks proved to be particularly difficult creatures to study.

The elusiveness and scarcity of sharks has most certainly played into our limited knowledge of them. Most people have never seen a shark in real life, outside of those you may have observed behind a glass wall at a public aquarium. This elusiveness is by design. To explain how the shark's elusiveness and scarcity is fundamental to its existence, author Michael Capuzzo wrote of the great white shark species (a major character in our study of the 1916 shark attacks), it 'must consume such massive quantities of flesh to survive, it would be unthinkable for them to be numerous…it is, quite simply, too dangerous for there to be more than a limited number of its kind.'[15] The way in which a shark lives, the behaviors it exhibits, and the prey that it eats forces it to be a scarce breed.

Because of these many factors, humans have historically had very limited knowledge when it comes to sharks. And where knowledge is limited, the human mind grasps to fill in the gaps. And the gaps exposed by the lack of knowledge of sharks have oftentimes been filled with fear, myths, and legends.

This is the way the human brain works. It is wired to fear the unknown. Evolution has taught us to prioritize our safety above all else; any unknown, potential risks could very well jeopardize that hard-earned safety. When humans have a lack of knowledge or understanding, fear and anxiety are a natural response. In fact, a fascinating study about how humans respond to unpredictability proved exactly that. In this study, participants were hooked up to electrodes that were set to deliver 'harmless, but slightly painful' electric shock to the participants.[16] The participants were observed closely by the researchers conducting the experiment to determine if they were exhibiting tell-tale signs of fear, such as sweating or pupil dilation.[17] Amazingly, this study revealed that it was not the actual electric shock that caused stress and anxiety in the participants, but rather, the unknown possibility of it. This study revealed that participants exhibited higher levels of stress when there was a fifty percent chance that they *might* be shocked, versus the situations in which they knew without a doubt that they would be shocked. Ema Tanovic, a psychologist for the Boston Consulting Group said it best when she concluded, 'If we think in purely rational terms, this does not make sense: a 50 percent chance of a shock should be half as anxiety provoking as a 100 percent chance if all we care about is the threat itself. But this is not how our minds work.'[18]

The human mind has been trained, by evolution, to either avoid uncertainty at all costs or to force our bodies into this heightened, anxiety-provoking state to prepare us to face an unknown fear. Historically speaking, responding otherwise could quite literally result in death.

There are ways that we can gradually reframe our way of thinking – and thus, reprogram our brains – to cope with uncertainty and unpredictability.

There are things we can do to help us accept that our response to uncertainty is purely natural and to embrace that uncertainty is a natural part of life. One method to overcome a debilitating fear of the unknown is to boldly dive straight into it.

Perhaps you have a fear of roller coasters. So, in preparation for the big family vacation to Six Flags Magic Kingdom next summer, you download every YouTube video, consume every library book, and listen to every podcast about roller coasters that you can find. You learn about the mechanics of roller coasters, you study the safety precautions in place, and you analyze the statistics about how much more likely you are to die by falling out of your own bed than you are to die from falling off a roller coaster (yes, this is a real statistic).[19]

Metaphorically speaking, once you have learned more about the monster hiding under your bed, you may find that there was no reason to be fearful of the monster in the first place.

But when we think about sharks and the severe lack of knowledge that existed until arguably the mid-twentieth century, the method of diving headfirst into your fear and learning all you can simply was not an option. There were virtually no books to study or scientific research to consume that could help one understand these majestic beasts that roam the ocean waters. The human mind had to do what it has done since the dawn of time when faced with uncertainty: It had to fill in the gaps.

Fortunately, the extensive amount of research conducted post-1945 has taught us so much of what we know today about sharks. We now know that sharks are one of the oldest species to still exist. In fact, scientists have discovered shark fossils dating back more than 450 million years! This means that sharks have existed longer than trees! Some of today's species of sharks were around at the time dinosaurs roamed the Earth; some existed even before dinosaurs. While more than 500 species of sharks are known to exist, and have been formally described, there are likely many others. The number of shark species continues to grow as more and more species are discovered.[20] And each species is wildly unique, though all sharks share similar features.

All sharks have what is called a cartilaginous skeleton. This means that sharks do not have bones. Rather, their bodies are made up of cartilage (similar to a human nose or ears) that allows their bodies to be incredibly flexible. Cartilage is also significantly lighter than bone which means that sharks can swim more quickly and exert less energy in doing so.

All sharks have fins, though the type of fin may differ. Most sharks, with few exceptions, have five different types of fins: a dorsal fin, pectoral fins, pelvic fins, anal fin, and a caudal fin. Each type of fin serves a different function with the overall intention of helping the shark balance, steer, lift, or even create propulsion.

All sharks have scales, also known as dermal denticles. As you will see later in this book, the feel of these denticles is rather rough to the touch when going against the grain with many describing the

A Close-Up View of the Mouth of a Mako Shark Showing Its Multiple Rows of Teeth. (*David J. Shuler | Adobe Stock Photo*)

sensation like brushing against sandpaper. These denticles cover the surface of a shark's body and help the shark to glide through the water quickly, as well as serve as a protective layer. A shark's denticles allow some shark species to swim through the ocean at a remarkable rate of speed. The optimized aerodynamics of their denticles is so impressive that modern-day engineers are actively studying them in an effort to replicate their structure for wings on airplanes and helicopters.[21] Pretty incredible!

All sharks have gills. These gills allow the shark to receive the water that enters the gills and convert it into oxygen. Gills also allow sharks to filter and remove carbon dioxide from their blood.

Most sharks have rather large livers in relation to the rest of their bodies. In fact, the average shark liver takes up somewhere between five and twenty-five percent of its body weight and, in some cases, can even take up ninety percent of the space inside its body! There is a major reason for this. Sharks, unlike many other species of fish, do not have swim bladders. Swim bladders are an organ that is filled with gas that helps a fish not sink. Because sharks, like all other cartilaginous fish, do not have swim bladders to keep them afloat, their enlarged livers compensate for this.

Finally, perhaps the two most well-known – and also most over-sensationalized – features that the majority of sharks have in common are, of course, their teeth and their sense of smell.

In relation to their teeth, sharks have multiple rows of them that are constantly and continuously being replaced. Known as a process called revolver dentition, if a shark loses a tooth, one of the teeth behind it will shift forward and into place so that the shark is never without a tooth. This allows a shark to continue to hunt and eat as needed. If this isn't incredible enough, consider the fact that the process of revolver dentition can take as little as twenty-four hours to complete! Because sharks are constantly losing and replacing teeth, this means that a single shark can go through thousands of teeth in one lifetime!

> And finally, the last trait that all sharks have in common is their remarkable sense of smell. A shark's cerebrum contains olfactory tracks which are what the shark uses to smell. Across shark species, somewhere between three and eighteen percent of the brain is dedicated to their sense of smell which means that 'the shark is perpetually enshrouded in a world of scents.'[22] For the great white shark, for example, eighteen percent of its brain weight is made up by the olfactory bulb![23] Compare this to the human brain which dedicates approximately 0.01% to the olfactory bulb.[24] A shark's sense of smell is so great, in fact, that it is one of the best in the entire animal kingdom. This sense of smell has led to sharks receiving the nickname of 'swimming noses.' It is a common misconception that sharks can smell blood from miles away; that if you enter the ocean with so much as a paper cut, a shark from fifty miles away will sniff you out and chase you down in a heartbeat. While this myth has long since been debunked, there is evidence to suggest that a shark *can* smell blood up to a quarter of a mile away. A shark's sense of smell is so incredible that it can detect one-part blood even when diluted by one million parts water.[25] To better visualize this measurement, this is the equivalent of one teaspoon of blood diluted in the amount of water it would take to fill an average-sized swimming pool.[26]

We also now know that sharks are not man-eating monsters with an appetite for human blood, despite what ancient legends may have alleged. In fact, the truth is quite the contrary. Research shows that, in the rare cases in which a shark does attack a human, it is generally thought to be the case of mistaken identity in which the shark intended to attack and feed on a different large mammal, such as a seal or dolphin.[27] Further evidence that supports this hypothesis, more formally known as the Mistaken Identity Hypothesis (MIH), can be seen in the fact that sharks rarely consume humans after attacking them, as opposed to how they would behave if they had captured, for example, a seal. This leads credence to the belief that, once a shark realizes its mistake in attacking a human, it forgoes the attack and disappears.[28] This type of behavior in sharks is referred to as a 'hit-and-run.'

The likelihood of a shark attacking a human is one in 11.5 million. Here is a short list of accidents or injuries that are more likely to occur during a human lifetime than an attack by a shark:

- Lightning strike (one in 161,856 chance)[29]
- Ladder fall (more than 300 occur in the US every year)[30]
- Food poisoning (approximately 3,000 fatalities in the US each year)[31]
- Even a falling coconut is thirty times more likely to kill you than a shark (with coconuts causing approximately 150 deaths a year)![32]

Considering these statistics, why is it that humans have such an intense fear of sharks? Why is it that a 2015 study found that thirty-eight percent of Americans are terrified to swim in the ocean for fear of an attack by a shark?[33]

A series of shark attacks along the Jersey coast in 1916 is what would officially instill our modern-day fear and misconstrued belief that sharks are 'man-eating monsters.' It was these events that cemented the long-standing underbelly of fear of the ocean, the fear of the unknown, and the fear of the dark monsters that swim just below its surface. This series of attacks would then go on to inspire one of the most successful movies in history, *Jaws*, which further perpetuated the narrative of sharks as 'man-killers,' solidifying the false perception that many people have of sharks to this day.

Now, of course, there had been several shark attacks prior to 1916. According to the Global Shark Attack File, there were close to 800 documented fatal shark attacks worldwide between the years of 4000 BCE and July 1916.[34] In fact, roughly thirty fatal shark attacks occurred across the world in just the five years leading up to 1916.[35] But not much information is known about these incidents. The most recent fatal shark attack in the United States to occur prior to the 1916 attacks was in September of 1914. This incident involved a 17-year-old boy who was attacked by a shark while swimming in Lake Pontchartrain, Louisiana. He struggled to fight off the shark for some twenty minutes before eventually succumbing to his injuries.

Now despite these commonalities that exist across all species of sharks, it is important in the context of the 1916 shark attacks to discuss in detail the features unique to four particular species of sharks that will become rather relevant as this story unfolds: the great white shark, the bull shark, the tiger shark, and the sand bar shark.

**The great white shark** (*Carcharodon carcharias*) is most commonly associated with shark attacks. This is the species featured in the *Jaws* films and will also make several appearances throughout this book. Adult great whites are generally between twelve and fifteen feet long, weighing anywhere from 1,500 pounds to 2,400 pounds. There are

Great White Shark. (*Shane Myers | Adobe Stock Photo*)

certainly exceptions to this, however, with some of the largest known great whites measuring up to twenty feet in length and over 4,000 pounds in weight.[36] Some of their most common features are their grey skin, which starkly contrasts with their white underbellies. They feed on varying sizes of prey with some of the largest sea creatures they devour being sea lions, dolphins, whales, seals, turtles, and even other sharks. They swallow their small prey whole and rip apart their larger prey with their hundreds of teeth. A great white shark, on average, has roughly three hundred teeth at a time, layered in multiple rows. These teeth are sharply serrated and can reach a length of 2.5 inches each. As previously discussed in relation to revolver dentition, a great white can lose and replace teeth at such a rapid rate that they can go through some 20,000 teeth over the course of their lives!

Notable to the shark attacks discussed in this book, it is important to know that great whites can travel on average fifty miles per day, with some even recorded as traveling one hundred miles in a day. Also, particularly notable in reference to this book's topic, it is important to know that the great white 'is blamed for three and a half times the number of attacks than the tiger shark or the bull shark.'[37]

**The bull shark** (*Carcharhinus leucas*) is also a large sea animal that has oftentimes been mistaken for the great white. Unlike a great white whose grey top starkly contrasts with its white underbelly, the grey top of a bull shark gradually fades into their white bellies. Bull sharks are also smaller than great whites with the average size about seven feet long and between 2-300 pounds (though larger specimens have been spotted up to ten feet and nearly 700 pounds). Most notably, the bull shark represents one of the few exceptions to the typical saltwater environment of sharks; bull sharks can tolerate swimming in freshwater regions such as rivers and creeks. This is an important and unique distinction that will become very relevant over the course of our analysis of the 1916 shark attacks.

Bull Shark. (*Subphoto | Adobe Stock Photo*)

**The tiger shark (*Galeocerdo cuvier*)** is unique in appearance. The tiger shark has a blunt-shaped head, stripes (like a tiger) along its sides, and notched teeth.[38] The average tiger shark is between ten and thirteen feet in length and 850 to 1,400 pounds in weight (though

Tiger Shark. (*Michael Geyer | Adobe Stock Photo*)

there are documented cases of tiger sharks reaching fourteen feet in length and more than 1,700 pounds in weight). Tiger sharks have been referred to as the 'swimming trash can' as they will eat virtually anything, including, quite literally, trash.[39]

Finally, the **sand bar shark** (*Carcharhinus plumbeus*), also known as the **brown shark**, has a white underbelly that contrasts with the brown hue of the upper portion of its body. The average sand bar shark can be anywhere from six to eight feet in length and between 1-200 pounds (with the largest recorded sand bar shark reaching over eight feet in length and almost 300 pounds). Sand bars generally feed on fish and invertebrates but are not considered to be dangerous to humans.

Sand Bar Shark. (*Vladimir Wrangler | Adobe Stock Photo*)

In the one month before the shark attacks of July 1916, there were several human encounters with sharks along the American East Coast. On June 22, 1916, a group of fishermen fishing in Little Egg Harbor, New

Jersey, told stories of a shark attacking their boat.[40] Only days later, on June 27th, two more fishermen off of Staten Island, New York, reported being followed back to the port by a shark.[41] And even on June 30th (just one day before the fatal 1916 shark attacks began), an unnamed man experienced a nearly fatal encounter with a shark in North Atlantic City. While swimming in the ocean, he was ambushed by a shark that appeared to make a beeline directly for him. The shark latched onto his foot, tearing the heel away from the rest of his body.[42] He successfully fought off the shark, and bystanders helped him to shore and safety. There is little else known about this encounter. We do not know the extent of the man's injuries. We do not know if his injuries were fatal. We do not even know the man's name! What we do know though is that this event would mark the start of a series of shark attacks along the Jersey coast unlike anything the world had ever seen before, or since.

But again, these stories were not well known at the time and have therefore not been well-documented for future generations to analyze. These events that took place only days before the events of the 1916 shark attacks are often not even discussed in the context of that summer of horror.

And although there is historical evidence that dates back thousands upon thousands of years that reflects a fear of sharks, most people did not have much of an awareness of sharks prior to 1916. Before the terrifying string of attacks in the Summer of 1916, humans had a fear of something that they believed to be mythological. Up to this point, the lack of research surrounding sharks had led the public to believe that real-life sharks were actually rather unintelligent creatures and that they had little to no interest in coming close to humans. Dr Frederic Lucas, the Director of the American Museum of Natural History and a world-leading shark expert, promoted these theories when he was quoted as saying in April of 1916 that a shark's jaw was not even powerful enough to go through a human bone and 'that there is practically no danger of an attack from a shark about our coasts.'[43]

That was until three, short months later…

Chapter Two

# Beach Haven: The Beginning of the Horror

*'All along the 127-mile Atlantic coast of New Jersey that Sunday, the first documented case in American history of a man taken as shark prey was attended by silence. From Cape May north to Atlantic Highlands, thousands of swimmers blissfully took to the beaches, unaware they shared the water with a rogue shark that had taken human flesh.'*

*Michael Capuzzo*

Beach Haven, New Jersey is an obvious location for a summer vacation. This eighteen-mile-long borough situated on Long Beach Island was initially established in 1873 as a summer location

An Ad for Beach Haven Dated 1912. (*New Jersey Maritime Museum*)

for upper-class Philadelphians. But by the 1870s, with the completion of the Tuckerton Railroad (and its later expansion that connected Philadelphia all the way to New York), people from various walks of life – and even different parts of the country – now had greater accessibility to the beautiful beachfront resort towns. This railroad system was revolutionary with four scheduled round trips a day between Philadelphia and Beach Haven alone, making the beachfront resort town that much easier of a quick getaway locale.[1]

1916 was a unique time to take a vacation. It may be surprising to learn that it wasn't until just the year before, in 1915, that the American tourism industry really took off. Prior to 1915, taking a vacation was a luxury relegated only to the wealthiest of Americans. Only the wealthy could afford to take extended time off from work as well as pay the expensive fees associated with travel. By 1910, a significant percentage of white-collar employees were granted paid time off by their employers, something that was not afforded to the majority of blue-collar employees at this time.[2]

This wasn't for lack of trying. In 1910, Twenty-Seventh US President William Howard Taft made a proposal that every American employee should be granted two to three months of vacation on an annual basis. He asserted that the current state of American employees was detrimental to their 'health and constitution' and that having extended periods of time off from work was necessary for the American man 'in order to continue his work next year with the energy and effectiveness that it ought to have.'[3] US legislators were quick to reject the proposal and thus, here we are, more than one hundred years later, still feeling guilty for taking an hour off of work every six months for our routine dental appointments.

But even with this harsh reality, the tides were slowly shifting. And by 1915, taking a vacation was becoming more accessible to the average American.

This was true for several reasons. For one, this time period saw a significant increase in personal ownership of motor vehicles. In 1908, American businessman and founder of Ford Motor Company, Henry

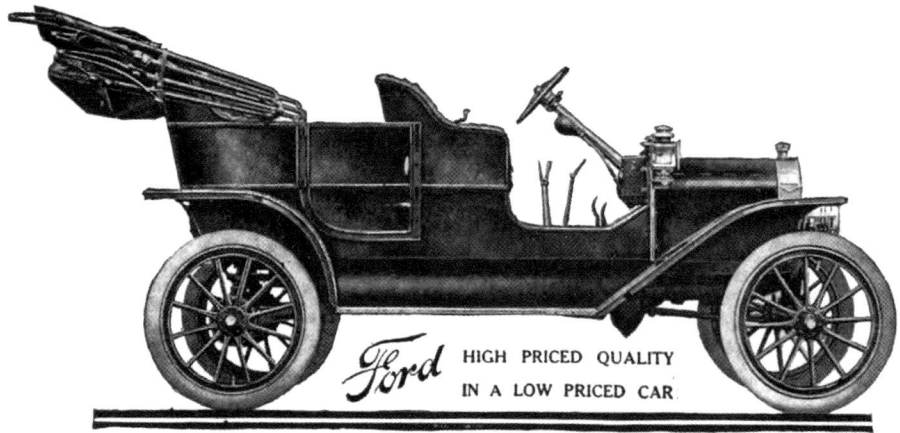

1908 Ford Model T. (*Public Domain*)

Ford, released the Model T, a gas-powered motor vehicle with a price tag of $850.[4] Considering inflation, this is the equivalent of roughly $30,000 today. This was considered to be a highly affordable vehicle for many Americans at the time as the only alternatives were generally thousands of dollars in comparison. The Model T came in various styles which included a two-seat runabout, a five-seat touring car, and a seven-seat town car.[5] This meant that Americans from practically any walk of life – a single, childfree businessman or a family man with multiple children – could find an available style of the Model T to fit their lifestyle.

Then, in 1913, Ford did something that not only changed the lives of Americans all across the country but would also change the way businesses operate even to this day. In 1913, he introduced the first moving assembly line, allowing for the mass production of motor vehicles. The assembly line was revolutionary. It decreased the amount of time it took to build a car 'from more than 12 hours to one hour and 33 minutes.'[6] The mass production of motor vehicles also helped to decrease the overall costs. Year by year, the price of the Model T reduced, reaching $306 by 1916, the equivalent of about $10,000 today. The Model T became the first mass-produced, affordable American motor vehicle, allowing personal ownership of an automobile to be accessible to more Americans than ever before. For context: In 1900, there were approximately 8,000 cars registered in the United States. Just one decade later, the number of registered motor vehicles increased to 619,000.[7] The personal ownership of a motor vehicle allowed Americans to travel more freely. For many, this opened up the idea of leisure and vacation stays for the very first time.

Additionally, as mentioned previously, public transportation via railways was increasing with new rail expansions being created around the clock. In fact, 1916 was the peak year in American history for railroad travel with a total of 254,251 miles traveled that year.[8] The majority of these rail lines were located in the East, often weaving through popular vacation towns.

Finally, another reason for the increased ability of Americans to vacation was the rise of tour agencies and travel writers in 1915.[9] Less than one decade prior, in 1906, both the *New York Times* and the *New York Tribune* became the first newspapers to publish travel sections in their Sunday editions.[10] Other newspaper outlets were not far behind and it became a favorite pastime to pull out the newspaper and admire the latest and greatest in travel intel. It also helped that the early 1900s saw the development of the first middle-class hotel chains.[11]

1916 truly was a unique time to take a vacation. This was not only because of the greater accessibility and affordability of travel that was broadening at the turn of the century, but also because of the increasing need for Americans to escape everyday life.

A polio epidemic was sweeping the East Coast and, along with it, causing terror and panic amongst American citizens. Poliomyelitis, more commonly referred to as 'polio,' is an infectious disease that once plagued human civilization, beginning in prehistoric times. It continued to plague human civilization until the polio vaccine was created in 1955 (Interestingly, Jonas Salk, the American physicist who developed the first successful polio vaccine, was only 1 year old when the 1916 polio epidemic began.[12]).

Polio is an incredibly infectious disease with the potential to spread for up to six weeks. The vast majority of those infected with polio, roughly seventy-five percent, are either asymptomatic or exhibit only mild symptoms (things like coughs, fevers, and sore throats). Unfortunately,

## Beach Haven: The Beginning of the Horror 25

however, there are more severe cases of polio which can result in permanent paralysis, or even death.

Children are particularly susceptible to the worst cases of polio, and this is what the American population – particularly the East Coast – was seeing in 1916. Because of the way the disease affected children so destructively, as well as the general lack of knowledge that existed about polio at the time, the disease was originally referred to as 'infant paralysis' or 'infantile paralysis.'

During my research specific to the shark attacks of 1916, I was reviewing newspaper headlines from this period. One from July 8, 1916, published by the *New York Times*, caught my attention:

It read, in part, 'PARALYSIS KILLS 22 MORE BABIES IN NEW YORK CITY: Death Total Now 187, and 87 New Cases Bring Number in City to 797.'[13]

A *New York Times* Article Dated July 8, 1916, and Titled 'PARALYSIS KILLS 22 MORE BABIES IN NEW YORK CITY'. (*The New York Times*)

And even though I came across this headline while searching for articles about the shark attacks and it may seem as though these two separate events have nothing to do with one another, it is quite the contrary. The 1916 New York City polio epidemic, which led to mass quarantining and the closure of many public spaces, quite literally forced residents out of the city and onto the New Jersey beaches.

We are going to take a brief dive into the 1916 polio epidemic, so please bear with me; this is not the moment where you need to refer to the cover of this book to confirm that you did indeed pick up a book about the 1916 shark attacks. I promise that I will make a clear correlation between the 1916 polio epidemic and the 1916 shark attacks shortly. You will soon see that the importance of the correlation between these two life-altering events cannot be understated.

In an archived copy of the State of New Jersey Department of Health's annual report for the year 1916, they detailed how prevalent the infection was in New Jersey due to the state's proximity to New York City. The report read:

> 'It is quite natural that the disease should have exacted a heavy toll in New Jersey, as approximately one-third of the permanent population of the state reside in municipalities within 25 miles of New York City, and a large number of the persons residing in these municipalities commute daily to that city. It is also true that a large number of persons residing in towns in New Jersey as far distant as fifty miles are daily commuters to New York City.'[14]

The annual report stated that, between July 1st and October 31st of 1916, 3,973 cases of infantile paralysis were reported to the State Department of Health.[15] This means that, by the end of the epidemic, New Jersey was 'the highest case incidence that [had] thus far occurred in any state involved in the epidemic.'[16]

In efforts that may sound familiar to many of us that experienced the 2020 coronavirus pandemic, the response to the 1916 polio epidemic resulted in several social distancing measures.

Fortunately, protective measures have evolved since 1916 and those of us that experienced the 2020 pandemic did not have to suffer the particular public embarrassment that officials inflicted upon infected individuals in 1916. For example, it was customary during the 1916 epidemic to publish the names and addresses of polio-positive citizens in the daily newspaper as a means of reducing the public's contact with them.[17] Police officers were quite literally stationed outside of the homes of those known to be infected to enforce quarantine measures and ensure no one escaped. There was also a heavy presence by the United States

Public Health Service along state borders and high traffic areas. This was because some of the neighboring states had what was later deemed to be 'sometimes ill-advised' rules against allowing anyone, particularly children, from leaving New York and entering their territory.[18] In fact, many children under the age of sixteen were required to carry specific identification on their person in order to travel from state to state. Below is an example of a table provided by the New Jersey Health Department

TABLE 7—NUMBER OF CHILDREN INTERCEPTED AT INTERSTATE POINTS.
August 15, 1916, to October 3, 1916, inclusive.

| INTERSTATE POINT. | Number children accompanied by certificates substantially complying with regulations. | Number children accompanied by certificates not acceptable under regulations. | Number children having no certificates. | Number children accompanied by unsatisfactory certificates or having no certificates who were *turned back*. | Number children accompanied by unsatisfactory certificates or having no certificates who *proceeded*. |
|---|---|---|---|---|---|
| *Highways.* | | | | | |
| *Mahwah | 7,576 | 157 | 636 | 282 | 511 |
| †Montvale | 1,148 | 28 | 390 | 352 | 66 |
| §Norwood | 2,113 | 145 | 676 | 439 | 382 |
| *Ferries.* | | | | | |
| Albertson's | 36 | 0 | 7 | 7 | 0 |
| Burlington | 623 | 2 | 23 | 25 | 0 |
| Camden (Federal) | 16,956 | 79 | 594 | 372 | 301 |
| Camden (Kaighn) | 5,344 | 131 | 77 | 94 | 114 |
| Camden (Cooper) | 118 | 0 | 1 | 1 | 0 |
| Chrome | 29 | 3 | 30 | 30 | 3 |
| Englewood Cliffs | 349 | 3 | 32 | 34 | 1 |
| Gloucester | 1,498 | 0 | 162 | 162 | 0 |
| Penns Grove | 529 | 20 | 7 | 11 | 16 |
| *Bridges.* | | | | | |
| Belvidere | 0 | 0 | 0 | 0 | 0 |
| Byram | 54 | 0 | 4 | 4 | 0 |
| Delaware | 550 | 17 | 18 | 20 | 15 |
| Dingman's | 71 | 0 | 12 | 12 | 0 |
| Lambertville | 219 | 0 | 21 | 18 | 3 |
| Milford, Pa. | 23 | 0 | 5 | 5 | 0 |
| Phillipsburg | 5,519 | 27 | 438 | 357 | 108 |
| Washington's Crossing | 17 | 0 | 2 | 2 | 0 |
| | 42,772 | 612 | 3,135 | 2,227 | 1,520 |

\* At Mahwah, one highway was guarded during the week; two on Sundays.
† At Montvale, two highways were guarded during the week up to Sept. 11th, and three on Sundays.
§ At Norwood, two highways were guarded during the week, and four on Sundays, up to Sept. 10th.

The Number of Children Intercepted at Interstate Points During the 1916 Polio Epidemic. (*The New Jersey State Library*)

depicting how many children were intercepted at interstate points during the height of the epidemic.

These certificates of identification were in no way a guarantee that children under sixteen years of age were, in fact, not infected by the disease. As the Department of Health's report stated, 'In some instances, children traveling with certificates were found to be actually paralyzed upon reaching their destinations.'[19] This is because, as many of us who experienced the 2020 coronavirus pandemic will recall, one may actually have the illness days before they exhibit symptoms, if they ever do exhibit symptoms (which is the case in people that are asymptomatic). Therefore, it was nearly impossible to place limits on the dissemination of the required identification cards. So long as you were not actively exhibiting symptoms of polio and could confirm that you had not recently been directly exposed to the infection, there wasn't much standing in the way of obtaining a certificate of identification for travel.[20] Families used this opportunity to travel in droves, taking their children out of the infected city and into more open-air environments, such as the New Jersey beaches.

This was certainly a very frightening reality. But beyond the frightening reality occurring on their own soil, Americans had reason to want a vacation to get away from a stark reality overseas as well. In Europe, the First World War was waging. After more than a year of conflict, Twenty-Eighth US President Woodrow Wilson continued to insist that he would keep Americans from becoming involved in the bloodshed.

Wilson himself was a major proponent of vacations, specifically along the Jersey coast. Having served as the governor of New Jersey from 1911 to 1913, Wilson actually stayed in a 52-room mansion in New Jersey called Shadow Lawn as he campaigned for re-election in the Spring of 1916.

Sharing a coastline with Shadow Lawn is the town of Beach Haven. As 1915 had been the most successful summer for tourism in Beach Haven history, employees of the tourism industry were eager for another booming summer the following year.[21] The Summer of 1916 was also shaping up to be a hot one. A sudden heat wave had hit the entire Eastern Region of the United States. But for the tourism industry, this was encouraging news. A heat wave was a guaranteed way to draw in even more visitors that hoped to escape to the cooler, coastal breeze that the Beach Haven resort town could provide. Given that air conditioning would not become widely available to Americans until the 1950s, the idea of spending your time along the beach was exceptionally appealing.

So many visitors were expected at Beach Haven in the Summer of 1916 that the resort town already had plans in place to extend the length of the town boardwalk. They did this in an effort to best accommodate the expectedly larger crowd.[22]

The Engleside Hotel, in particular, was preparing for a busy 1916 summer season. The Engleside Hotel, founded by Robert Engle, was known later as the 'first large hotel in the borough to popularize' Long Beach Island.[23] With its three gorgeous balconies that allowed guests to lounge in chairs and look out over the ocean to its unique activities such as tennis, baseball, and organized dances, the Engleside Hotel quickly became one of the most popular and most beautiful hotels on the island.[24] An ad from 1910 that was placed in the newspaper for the Engleside Hotel read:

The Engleside Hotel Ad (1910). (*Public Domain*)

'The best combination of seashore features on the coast. Matchless bay for sailing and fishing, perfect beach and bathing. The Engleside has all the modern conveniences, private baths with sea and fresh water.'

Given what could be called the 'prestigious' nature of the Engleside Hotel, it is no surprise that many of its guests came from affluent and prestigious families as well.

Enter the Vansant family. The patriarch of the family, Dr Eugene Vansant, was a highly reputable laryngologist who operated his successful practice out of 1299 Chestnut Street, Philadelphia. Vansant and his wife, Louisa, had six children; two of whom had passed as infants.[25] Like many facing the polio epidemic of 1916, Vansant decided to take his family on a summer vacation away from the city environment which was believed to be riddled with the disease. It was many of those people, escaping the polio epidemic that was killing their babies, that found their way to the beaches of New Jersey that fateful summer. As the 1916 New Jersey Department of Health annual report stated:

> '...the outbreak occurred in the summer, when the resorts in New Jersey normally receive their greatest influx from New York and other cities, and that as the disease became more prevalent in New York, parents became alarmed and hastened from the city with their children, taking up temporary residence in the resorts and in the rural districts of New Jersey.'[26]

Dr Vansant was no different than so many other parents in the Summer of 1916 when he proposed that he, his wife, and their remaining children – eldest son Charles, and his daughters Mary Eugenia, Louise, and Eleanor – get out of the city and away from the deadly epidemic. Traveling to the beach for a vacation had only recently developed as a recreational activity for Americans, and Dr Vansant was eager to enjoy the new trend, especially with the way the summer temperatures were rising upward.

On July 1, 1916, the Vansant family hopped on the 3:35 PM Tuckerton Railroad/Beach Haven Express route with a destination time in Beach Haven shortly after 5:00 PM.

The eldest Vansant, Charles, was a particularly impressive figure. A graduate of the University of Pennsylvania and a broker at the Folwell Brothers brokerage firm, the 23-year-old was upholding the family name well. While in school, 'Charlie' or 'Van,' as his friends called him, had been a business manager for his school's newspaper and a member of the various campus clubs, including the varsity golf club.[27] By all accounts,

## Beach Haven: The Beginning of the Horror    31

he had a wonderful life ahead of him. But, of course, no one expected the horror that was to come.

When the Vansant family arrived at Beach Haven, they checked in at the Engleside Hotel where they were advised of the hotel's two dinner serving times: 6:30 PM and 8:00 PM. While the rest of the family settled into their hotel room and prepared for the early dinner, Charles decided to stroll along the beach and take a quick pre-dinner swim. According to Dr Richard G Fernicola, the leading expert on the 1916 shark attacks and author of *Twelve Days of Terror: Inside the Shocking 1916 New Jersey Shark Attacks*, 'it was the custom at this time…for all young men to take a pre-dinner dip.'[28] Author Michael Capuzzo agreed with this sentiment, stating in his book about the 1916 shark attacks, titled *Close to Shore*: 'It was the custom…for young men, upon checking into their hotel, to take an immediate dip in the ocean – morning, afternoon, or evening, no matter how cold the water or how rough the weather.'[29] And so that is exactly what Charles did. As he walked along the shore, preparing for his brief swim, he made contact with a Chesapeake Bay retriever that was also strolling the beach. Together, the two entered the water with Charles swimming far enough into the ocean that he was chest deep. Charles even captured the attention of onlookers on the beach who cheered him on as he dashed through the water, impressed by his strong and quick stride.

Charles had no idea what danger lurked just below the ocean's surface. Likewise, he had no idea that bringing the retriever along with him into the water may have heightened his chances as a target. Ichthyologist George Burgess, the former Director of the International Shark Attack File and the author of several books about sharks, has said:

> 'The irregular swimming actions of animals are extremely attractive to sharks. The front paws doggy-paddling, creating a maximum splash, the rear legs bicycle-pedaling, four rapidly moving legs making a blending motion at the surface couldn't be a whole lot more attractive.'[30]

Perhaps after drawing unwanted attention from an unknown threat, the retriever seemed to abandon course partway through and returned to the shore. Charles called out after him, but the dog ignored his pleas. Witnesses stated that it was at roughly this time that they noticed a fin gliding just above the ocean's surface, heading straight for Charles. It was initially presumed to be a porpoise; something that would not have been an uncommon sight. But when it was realized that it was a solo fin (porpoises travel in groups), witnesses began to grow concerned. Some even hollered out warning cries to Charles, but he didn't seem to hear them. Given that Charles had been playfully yelling after the dog, it is no surprise that when Charles began to holler out for another reason entirely, he too was initially ignored. For not long after the retriever's departure, Charles began to emit a spine-chilling scream. One witness on the beach that day, a fellow Philadelphia man that had traveled to the Jersey Shore for respite, recalled mistaking Charles' cries for joking. But Charles' screams could not go ignored for long as witnesses along the beach noticed a red liquid pooling around him: It was blood. His blood.

Onlookers – which now included Charles' own family who had made their way to the beach after settling into their lodging – watched in horror as Charles struggled to fight off what appeared to be a giant beast in the water. We now know that the creature spotted to have a dorsal fin and hundreds of teeth was, indeed, a shark. But at this time, most people had never seen a shark before. It was not immediately obvious to the Beach Haven beachgoers what this creature was that was invoking tragedy just outside their beachfront resort.

Charles struggled to safety until he reached just forty feet from the shore. At this point, the local lifeguard, Alexander Ott – a man with an impressive background, having once been on the American Olympic swim team – raced out to rescue Charles. This was a courageous act that cannot be understated; the fact that anyone would enter 'shark-infested' waters to save another provides me with much-needed encouragement about humanity. But to Ott's horrifying surprise – as well as the surprise of all the other traumatized witnesses – the shark followed Charles to the shore, its jaw affixed tightly to his thigh. Witnesses reported that the shark did not loosen its grasp until 'its belly scraped the bottom of the sand.'[31] Even when the shark did release its hold on Charles' leg, it continued to linger nearby. In hindsight, experts believe the shark was waiting for Charles to bleed out before it made its return for its prey. This is called 'bite and wait' behavior in which a shark viciously bites its prey, releases it, and then watches it from a safe distance. This allows the shark to ensure that the prey will not fight back and cause injury before it has a chance to finish the kill. This 'bite and wait' tactic is common behavior for sharks, but not in the scenario in which it is presumed that the shark mistook a human for a marine animal. Surely, this shark knew that the flesh it had pierced had not belonged to a seal. So why did it attack repeatedly? And why did it wait for its prey to slowly bleed to death?

Two other men along the beach, John Everton and Sheridan Taylor, jumped in to assist Ott, and the three of them created a human chain. As they dragged Charles to the shore, the giant beast scurried back into the ocean water and disappeared. But before the shark could make its dash, Ott observed it closely and later reported that he believed the monster to be nearly 500 pounds! Charles' sister, who had watched the terrifying ordeal, was quoted as saying,

> 'Everyone was horrified to see my brother thrashing about in the water as if he were struggling with some monster under the surface. He fought desperately, and as we rushed toward him, we could see great quantities of blood.'[32]

When Charles finally reached the shore, the realities of the gruesome attack were revealed. The shark had nearly ripped his left leg off his body, tearing the flesh from his bones. The nature of his injuries was unlike anything anyone had ever seen before; the extent of his gushing blood was unreal. For many of that summer's beachgoers, they had found their way to the beachfront resort in an attempt to escape the horrors occurring on both their own soil and overseas. They hadn't gone on vacation to witness more horror firsthand.

Ott hastily constructed a tourniquet from fabric torn from a nearby woman's dress and wrapped it around Charles' thigh to slow the bleeding. Fearing that Charles would not survive the trip to the nearest hospital, which was approximately thirty miles away, the men – which now included Charles' own father, Dr Vansant – carried Charles' weakening body into the Engleside Hotel. Here, the men placed Charles on the manager's desk. At this point, Charles was already unconscious, never to speak again. And it was there, little more than one hour after he had first entered the water, that he passed away at 6:45 PM.

Charles Vansant's Death Certificate. (*New Jersey State Archives, Department of State*)

If it is of any relief to the reader, research has shown that most victims of shark attacks do not actually feel substantial pain. Rather, it is theorized that the initial bite from the shark causes so much nerve damage that it limits the amount of pain the victim feels. (Later, a doctor involved in treating some of the 1916 shark attack victims would suggest that the initial inability to feel pain from a shark bite wound is because the shark's bite contains venom. Similar to that of a snake, it was once believed that a shark's bite contained venom that served as numbing agent to the victim before the poison eventually overtook the body and killed them. Certainly, we know today that this is not true. But with the severely limited knowledge that existed in relation to sharks in the early-1900s, this meant that even the experts were grasping at straws to make sense of the horrifying situation.[33]) And while the information that a shark attack victim does not often feel intense, initial pain may be relieving in hindsight, the amount of terror and pain felt by all on July 1, 1916, was very real and raw and palpable.

Dr Herbert Willis, a medical doctor who later served as mayor for New Jersey, prepared Charles' death certificate, writing that the cause of death was 'hemorrhage from femoral artery, left side' and that he had been 'bitten by a shark while bathing.' This was the first time in American history that the cause of death noted on an official death certificate was that of a shark bite.[34]

And here, the rumor mill began. Beach Haven residents and tourists alike – whether they had personally witnessed the incident or not – began spreading tales like wildfire about the horrific event that had taken place that pivotal July evening. One witness, a Mr WK Barklie,

**DIES AFTER ATTACK BY FISH**

C. E. Vansant Had Been Bitten While Swimming at Beach H..ven.

*Special to The New York Times.*

BEACH HAVEN, N. J., July 2.— Charles Epting Vansant of Philadelphia, who was badly bitten in the surf here on Saturday afternoon by a fish, presumably a shark, died late last night.

He was less than fifty feet from the beach and was swimming in when those on the shore saw the fin of a fish coming rapidly toward him. They called to him to hurry and yelled warning at him but before he swam many feet the fish closed with him. Vansant shouted for help and then went under. Alexander Ott, an expert swimmer and a member of the American Olympic swimming team, dashed to his assistance, but arrived too late to prevent his being bitten. After a struggle, Ott brought him ashore.

Mr. Vansant was the son of Mr. and Mrs. Eugene L. Vansant of 4.038 Spruce Street, Philadelphia, and was in his twenty-fifth year. He was a graduate of the Department of Fine Arts of the University of Pennsylvania and was connected with the firm of Nathan Folwell & Co., of Philadelphia.

It is said that large sharks have been seen recently a few miles out.

A Zoomed-In View of the Article Titled 'DIES AFTER ATTACK BY FISH'. (*The New York Times*)

A Full Page View of Page Eighteen of the *New York Times* on July 3, 1916. (*The New York Times*)

stated in an interview with a reporter that Charles Vansant's death was 'the most horrible I ever saw.'[35] But over time, rumors twisted and turned until it was alleged that perhaps the monster in the water had not been a shark after all. Perhaps instead, it had been a giant sea turtle or even a large tuna.

This is what the *New York Times* reported two days later in the minor article they wrote about the incident, tucked away on page eighteen of the July 3, 1916, edition. The title of the article read: 'DIES AFTER ATTACK BY FISH.'

The article did acknowledge that the big fish was 'presumably a shark' and that 'large sharks' had been spotted recently in the general vicinity.[36]

But despite this, Charles' shocking and horrifying death received minimal coverage. In hindsight, we might understand this minimal coverage to be intentional. After all, it was summertime in Beach Haven, New Jersey. More specifically, it was the first week of July in Beach Haven, New Jersey, which coincides with the Fourth of July holiday, the most popular vacation time for Americans. An upset in the fabric of the American tourism industry may very well have caused a significant loss in money; something that the New Jersey economy simply could not accept. It has been reported that Beach Haven officials did not send out an alarm about the attack beyond the immediate hotel.[37] This is a shocking fact. Capuzzo captured the weight of the decision to not broadly disseminate this information when he wrote in his book:

> 'All along the 127-mile Atlantic coast of New Jersey that Sunday, the first documented case in American history of a man taken as shark prey was attended by silence. From Cape May north to Atlantic Highlands, thousands of swimmers blissfully took to the beaches, unaware they shared the water with a rogue shark that had taken human flesh.'[38]

In response to the tragedy, Robert Engle of the Engleside Hotel gathered funding to place wire netting 300 feet from the shore to keep visitors at a safe distance from any potential threats. But beyond that, officials did little to warn citizens of the possible risks at hand.

In fact, one could argue that they did quite the opposite. State Fish Commissioner of Pennsylvania and Former Director of the Philadelphia

Aquarium, James Meehan, spoke to the *Philadelphia Public Ledger* and stated:

> 'Despite the death of Charles Vansant and the report [of] two sharks having been caught in that vicinity recently, I do not believe there is any reason why people should hesitate to go in swimming at the beaches for fear of man-eaters. The information in regard to the sharks is indefinite and I hardly believe that Vansant was bitten by a man-eater. Vansant was in the surf playing with a dog and it may be that a small shark had drifted in at high water, and was marooned by the tide. Being unable to move quickly and without food, he had come in to bite the dog and snapped at the man in passing.'[39]

Charles' horrific death continued to be downplayed in the media and by city officials in order to keep raking in money during what was one of the most popular Beach Haven summers of all time. After all, every Beach Haven hotel had been booked for the holiday weekend. By all accounts, apart from a 'minor' mishap (i.e. the traumatizing mutilation and subsequent death of a young Beach Haven visitor), the Summer of 1916 was expected to be a success for the New Jersey tourism industry.

The Vansant family, on the other hand, would continue to be plagued with grief over the loss of Charles whose brutal death would replay in their minds like a horror movie on repeat for the rest of their lives.

Chapter Three

# Spring Lake: 'The Most Likeable Employee'

*'...a shark, popular belief to the contrary notwithstanding, is not particularly strong in the jaws.'*
           Frederic Lucas, John Nichols, and Robert Murphy

Beach Haven is certainly not the only resort town along the New Jersey coastline. In a 2024 article written for *Leisure + Travel* magazine, local experts ranked the ten best beach towns in Jersey Shore. Beach Haven ranked number three out of ten, followed shortly thereafter in the number four slot by a stunning beach town called Spring Lake.[1]

A Postcard of the Essex & Sussex Hotel in the Early-1900s. (*The Monmouth County Historical Association*)

Just forty-five miles north of Beach Haven, the beach town of Spring Lake was also experiencing a busy summer of tourists, sunshine, and money, money, money. Known to primarily host folks from 'high society,' it was not uncommon to spot high-ranking government officials in Spring Lake, particularly at one of its most spectacular hotels, the Essex & Sussex Hotel (or the 'E & S,' as some refer to it). The beautiful hotel, which had only been built two years prior to the Summer of 1916, stood out amongst the other hotels as a dominant force in size and proximity to the gorgeous Atlantic Ocean.

To operate a hotel of such magnitude required staff whose commitment to excellence was of a parallel caliber. Bell captain Charles Bruder was exactly that. As bell captain, the 28-year-old Swiss with nearly two decades of hospitality experience (yes, you read that correctly; two decades of hospitality experience at only 28-years-old), would have been responsible for managing the bell staff, assigning tasks, supervising work, and overall, keeping a tight ship. Bruder was widely known as 'the most likeable employee by hotel guests' not only for his professionalism and the way in which he executed his work, but also for his kind and playful demeanor.[2] Bruder worked hard so he could play hard. It was common knowledge that Bruder took his lunch break at roughly 1:45 PM every day and, during the hot summers (especially in the sweltering heat of the Summer of 1916), Bruder used this lunch break to take a quick swim in the ocean.

On July 6th of that year, Bruder and one of his colleagues, Henry Nolan, used their lunch break to hop into the ocean water and swim out to the area designated for hotel employees. After some time, Nolan retired, but Bruder seized the opportunity to take a solo swim further out into the ocean. Bruder was known to be a strong swimmer who enjoyed exercising his strength and boldness when possible. In fact, Bruder had shared inspiring stories with colleagues about his time in Catalina Island just the year before when he swam in the ocean alongside the local blue sharks. Bruder was aware of the gossip about a possible shark attack that had taken place days before – roughly fifty miles south of Spring Lake, in Beach Haven – but he, like many others, did not believe that Vansant's fate had been decided by a shark. As far as Bruder was concerned, sharks were harmless. With this sentiment in mind, he swam approximately 130 yards from shore…

And that was when the nightmare began.

Hotel guests and sunbathers alike recalled seeing the ocean water explode as if a torpedo had erupted through the surface, followed immediately thereafter by screams. But then, for just a moment, they saw nothing. Nothing other than what one female witness described as what she believed to be a capsized canoe. A red canoe, to be more specific. Because surely, that was the only explanation for why there was a glob of red amid the otherwise blue sea water…right?

The lifeguards onsite, Chris Anderson and George White, knew immediately that the red mass they were witnessing was not a canoe. What they were witnessing was a pool of blood. Charles Bruder's blood.

The two men grabbed their lifeguard boat and raced out to the bleeding victim as quickly as their arms could row. When they reached him, they could see him inching closer and closer to unconsciousness, though he was able to utter the words, 'A shark bit me!'. The men pulled Bruder up onto the boat, which they reported took far less effort than they had expected—Bruder had weighed significantly less than they had anticipated. It was as they pulled his body onto the boat that they realized why he had been so light: The shark had removed his legs from his body.

In the boat, the men hastily tied tourniquets on Bruder's maimed limbs as the bottom of the vessel filled with his blood. Just before slipping away to unconsciousness, Bruder told his rescuers that the shark that had bitten him was 'as rough as sandpaper' and that it had attacked him over and over again.[3]

Within just minutes of being in the boat, Bruder underwent hemorrhagic shock from the severe loss of blood. Shortly thereafter, he died. As his body was rowed to the shore, it was reported by the *New York Times* that at least one witness fainted at the sight of his mutilated body and that many others 'were so overcome by the horror of Bruder's death that they had to be assisted to their rooms.'[4] Still, others swarmed around his lifeless body with the *Asbury Park Evening Press* reporting that the 'morbid crowd…[was] intent on seeing the remains.'[5]

With Bruder's body on the shore, a medical doctor staying at the Essex & Sussex, Dr William Schauffler, was able to more thoroughly examine the extent of Bruder's injuries. It was here that he found that Bruder's right leg below the knee had been shredded. The left leg, in far worse condition, had been eviscerated so completely that the left foot was missing entirely. The left leg also bore a deep gash that stretched from the femur up to the abdomen. Schauffler later stated in the official medical report, 'There is not the slightest doubt that a man-eating shark inflicted the injuries.'[6]

The Spring Lake doctors that later conducted an examination on Bruder's lifeless body, William Trout and John Cornell, likewise concluded:

> 'On examination, we found that both legs were missing; bitten or broken off about 4 inches above the ankles and a large cut above the knee. The flesh [was] torn off the right leg from just below the knee to where the bone was bitten or broken off, leaving the bones protruding without any flesh. A piece of flesh bitten out of the right side below the ribs, also showing tooth marks. We are of the opinion that these injuries were caused by a shark. In our judgement, we do not think there is any doubt.'[7]

Soon thereafter, rumors spread about what had occurred as witnesses attempted to come to grips with the horror they had seen. Some later reported that they witnessed Bruder's body flung up into the air between bites. Others said that they witnessed the shark lunge at Bruder multiple times with the *Philadelphia Inquirer* reporting that Bruder had been attacked 'like an aeroplane attacking a Zeppelin.'[8] And others even reported that they had seen Bruder himself climb out of the water on one leg before collapsing on the beach and succumbing to his fatal wounds. While the whispers and the gossip may have twisted and turned the facts, one thing was clear: His injuries, examined and documented by medical professionals, confirmed that the shark had brutally attacked him repeatedly. This is outside the standard behavior when a shark mistakenly bites a human. Why did the shark repeatedly bite Bruder when surely it must have known that its victim was indeed a human being?

Locals raised funds to help support Bruder's mother, who lived in Lucerne, Switzerland, and who depended on the money Bruder regularly sent to her for financial assistance. Due to the ongoing war in Europe, it was decided that Bruder's body would not be shipped back home to his mother but rather, that it would remain in the US. So loved by the guests of the Essex & Sussex, it was these people that covered the expenses of his funeral. Due to the horrific state of his body, his service was a closed casket.[9]

Whatever the exact circumstances of Bruder's attack may be, one thing was for certain: This incident, unlike the one that had occurred in Beach Haven less than one week prior, could not and would not be ignored. Bruder's horrendous death had had several more witnesses and the actual attack had been so much more brutal that it was impossible to keep this one under wraps. It is also worth noting that President Woodrow Wilson's Secretary of the Treasury, William McAdoo, happened to be staying at the Essex & Sussex at the exact same time as the horrific murder. This fact alone made the media swarm to the site and cover the matter extensively.

Unlike Charles Vansant's death, which had been tucked away on the eighteenth page of the *New York Times* two days after the attack, Bruder's

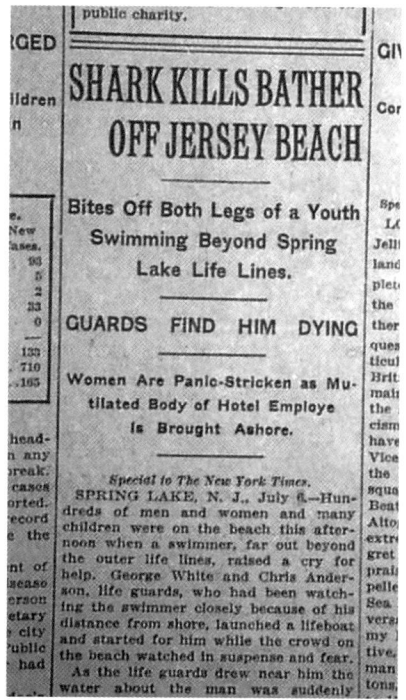

The *New York Times* Article Titled 'SHARK KILLS BATHER OFF NEW JERSEY BEACH' Dated July 7, 1916. (*The New York Times*)

death reached the front page of the newspaper the very next day with the headline: 'SHARK KILLS BATHER OFF NEW JERSEY BEACH: Bites Off Both Legs of a Youth Swimming Beyond Spring Lake Life Lines. GUARDS FIND HIM DYING. Women Are Panic-Stricken as Mutilated Body of Hotel Employee is Brought Ashore.'

The media across the country picked up the story with newspapers in Boston, San Francisco, Chicago, and more, covering the event in big, bold headlines.[10] In New York City where the infectious polio epidemic was running rampant, twenty-four people died on this single day.[11] This meant that, at this point in the epidemic, they were averaging one death per hour. But this is not what the headlines read on July 7, 1916. Rather, the headlines read in big and bold print all about Bruder's fatal attack.

Residents of Spring Lake became fearful of the sea monster within their midst with author Michael Capuzzo writing:

> '…for the first time in American history, people en masse were afraid to enter the water. The four hundred to five hundred bathers who swam in the waters…on Thursday dwindled on Friday to half a dozen brave souls drifting in and out of the surf. Finally, the surf emptied for good.'[12]

The hotel manager for the Essex & Sussex, David B Plumer, called the central telephone operator and demanded that every other central operator in the area disseminate a message to all the hotels along the coast that there were deadly sharks in the New Jersey waters. This call marked 'the first coastwide shark alarm in U.S. history.'[13] This alarm appeared to do the trick with thousands of beachgoers along the coast vacating the waters within a matter of just twelve minutes![14] According to Dr Fernicola, this mass exodus of the waters extended all the way from Spring Lake to Cape May (a more than 100 mile stretch of coastline)![15] According to Dr Google Maps, it would take more than eight times as long to drive the distance between the two locations than it did for word of the latest shark attack to spread.

The tourism industry had no choice but to concede that there was danger afoot. But how much they were willing to concede was yet to be determined. On July 8, 1916, the day after Bruder's attack, a press conference was called at the American Museum of Natural History in Manhattan, New York, in which experts were brought together to discuss the situation at hand and to put the public at ease. Those present on the panel were Dr Frederic Lucas, the museum director, Dr John Nichols, an ichthyologist and curator at the museum, and Robert Murphy, the director of the Brooklyn Museum. Together, the three men spoke to the pressing media and assured them that the possibility of a third shark attack was extremely unlikely.

Whether they genuinely believed this or were simply 'saving face' is unknown. For just three months prior, on April 24, 1916, Dr Nichols and Murphy published a piece in the *Brooklyn Museum Science Bulletin* specifically about sharks. Included in this piece was an entire section – of which, Dr Lucas also contributed – that was dedicated to the probability of shark attacks. Together, the three men expressed in the piece it to be their belief that, not only was it unlikely that a shark would attack a human but that, if one did, the jaws of a shark were not even capable of severing a human bone. They wrote of great white sharks, specifically:

> 'One of the commonest statements is that "the shark bit off the man's leg as though it were a carrot," an assertion that shows that the maker or writer of it had little idea of the strength of the apparatus needed to perform such an amputation. Certainly, no shark recorded as having been taken in these waters could possibly perform such an act, though this might occur if a shark thirty feet or more in length happened to catch a man fairly on the knee joint where no severing of the bone was necessary…Moreover, a shark, popular belief to the contrary notwithstanding, is not particularly strong in the jaws.'[16]

Despite the three men being the country's leading shark experts at the time, it is worth noting one large fallacy in their publication: As you may recall from Chapter One when we discussed the anatomy of a great white shark, even the largest known great whites to date only measure up to twenty feet in length. There has never been a confirmed sighting of a great white shark that has reached thirty feet or more.

Not only did they refute the possibility of a great white shark having the ability to sever a human bone; they also expressed in this journal that the likelihood of a great white shark existing in the waters off the Jersey coast was next to impossible. To their knowledge, great whites only existed in small quantities in tropical waters. According to the experts, they were unaware of any great white-related encounters 'within one hundred miles of New York.'[17]

To further prove their point, they recalled for the raptured audience – just as they had in their scientific bulletin – the Oelrichs Reward.

In 1891, a multimillionaire from New York named Hermann Oelrichs advertised a reward of $500 in the *New York Sun* to anyone that could prove that a shark had attacked a human along the East Coast. Oelrichs was a man with many interests, including being credited as the first person to introduce the game of polo to the United States.[18] One of these many interests included hunting sharks, of which Oelrichs had boldly proclaimed were 'cowardly' in nature.[19] Oelrichs was convinced that the ancient legends that told of the terrifying, 'man-eating' creatures lurking in the ocean were exactly that: mythological legends. It was this belief that led Oelrichs to advertise the $500 reward in the *New York Sun*, demanding for 'such proof as a court would accept that in temperate waters even one man, woman, or child, while alive, was ever attacked by a shark.'[20]

Although there had been rumors of shark attacks along the East Coast, none had been verified (There is evidence to suggest that the first known shark attack in North America occurred in Maryland in 1640. Amazingly, this discovery was not made until just recently, in 2023![21]). The 1916 panel of experts used the lack of evidence of known shark attacks to their advantage and reminded the concerned audience that still, twenty-five years after the Oelrichs Reward had first been proposed, it had yet to be claimed. They stated in their publication: 'That this reward was never claimed shows that there is practically no danger of an attack from a shark about our coasts.'[22]

According to the panel of experts, sharks do not bite humans. Or, at least, they didn't think so…

Interestingly, while the experts were steadfast in their belief that a third attack would not occur, they did acknowledge that 'there is something peculiarly sinister in the shark's make-up,' noting its 'chinless face, his great mouth with its rows of knifelike teeth' and the way that its fin 'zigzags' through the water in silence until it suddenly appears in time to snap at its prey.[23]

Out of an abundance of caution, Dr Nichols urged New Jersey residents and tourists to stay within the netted bathing areas that several public beaches and resorts had installed at this point.

Not only did the supposed experts make every effort to ease the public and assure them that a subsequent shark attack was impossible; the tourism industry did so as well. At several resorts along the Jersey coast, hotel management assured their worried guests that they had motorboats patrolling the open waters, scanning for sharks, with guns in tow. The *Asbury Park Press* seemed to reiterate the efforts made by the coastal resorts with a headline dated July 7th that read: 'NETS AND ARMED MOTORBOATS TO PROTECT BATHERS: BELIEVED PRECAUTION TAKEN WILL ASSURE ABSOLUTE SAFETY TO BATHERS ALONG NORTH SHORE…'[24] Not long after, the *Press* assured their readers further by stating rather bluntly that the Asbury Park waters were 'free from sharks for the very simple reason that no sharks can enter them.'[25]

Whether to reduce the level of fear or simply guided by misinformation and the severe lack of knowledge about sharks that existed at the time, many continued to argue that Bruder's horrific death had not been the result of a shark at all. The commissioner for the United States Fisheries, Hugh Smith, shared that he was of the belief that perhaps the attacks on both Vansant and Bruder had been conducted by swordfish.[26] He added to this theory by stating that sharks could not possibly be responsible for the attacks because 'sharks are not vicious.'[27] He concluded by saying:

> 'When we consider that there are hundreds of thousands of bathers on our eastern coasts every year and that for as long as anyone can remember no one has been bitten until these two recent cases, I think it is a word in favor of the sharks.'[28]

Even Dr Nichols, who was considered to be one of the world's leading shark experts, declared that he too did not believe it was a shark that had killed Bruder. He stated that the marks on Bruder's body were too jagged to belong to a shark and rather, it must have been a killer whale that had decided the fate of the young swimmer. Much like the lack of knowledge surrounding sharks that existed at this time, there was also severely limited knowledge related to orca. Fishermen and scientists alike were aware of the orca's behaviors when it came to killing other whales, so it was not a far stretch for Dr Nichols to propose that an orca might also kill a human.[29] In hindsight with today's knowledge, we of course know that there have been no documented cases of killer whales killing humans in the wild (the only documented cases of killer whales attacking or killing humans have occurred in captivity). But as the *New York Times* concluded of Dr Nichols' evaluation, 'It is not settled that the killer whale attacks humans, but Mr Nichols thought there was as much reason to suppose it was a killer whale as to suppose it was a shark.'[30]

Local newspapers interviewed avid fishermen as well, citing these men as experts who were 'familiar with the habits of sharks.' With this familiarity as the extent of their credentials, the fishermen declared that sharks would never come near a human – or any commotion, for that matter – so Jersey beachgoers had nothing to fear. The District Superintendent for the US Coast Guard, John Cole, agreed, stating that sharks are 'timid as rabbits.'

And so, slowly but surely, locals and vacationers alike began returning to the beaches, clinging to a false sense of security. Even 19-year-old

## Spring Lake: 'The Most Likeable Employee'   49

lifeguard Russell Cable expressed to Dr Fernicola in an exclusive interview that the safety nets placed along the beaches were simply put there to 'soothe the feelings and the thinking of the people' and that the nets were intended to make people *think* 'they had a safe place to go swimming,' whether this was true or not.[31]

To be fair, there cannot be much judgement passed on those that felt comfortable returning to the waters. It was not just local fishermen and Average Joes that claimed to know a thing or two about sharks. It was the nationwide experts – people like Dr Nichols, Dr Lucas, and Murphy – who advised beachgoers that they had nothing to fear; that the idea of a shark approaching a human and attacking them was not only preposterous – it was impossible.

By July 10th, only three days after Bruder's attack, newspapers moved on, foregoing any further coverage of the two shark attacks that had occurred along the Jersey Shore.[32]

Chapter Four

# Matawan Creek: A Highly Unusual Location

*'What pain he bore we will never know
We did not see him die*

*We only know that he is gone
And never said good-bye'*

*Agusta Fisher Nichols*

In the days following the Bruder attack, there were reports of an increase in shark sightings along the coast. One distinct incident in Asbury Park drew a significant amount of media attention.

Asbury Park, another beachfront city along the Jersey Shore, was a particularly popular spot for summer vacationers. An article in the *New York Times* titled 'ASBURY PARK: POPULAR JERSEY SHORE RESORT RAPIDLY FILLING WITH VISITORS,' published in 1912, read:

> 'Asbury Park is undergoing its annual transformation from a quiet Winter community of 10,000 inhabitants into a lively metropolitan Summer city with a changing population that sometimes exceeds 200,000 persons.'[1]

Asbury Park was so popular that, during the summer months when President Wilson was staying at Shadow Lawn (his New Jersey mansion that was affectionately referred to as the 'summer White House'), the rest of his staff resided nearby in a five-story building in Asbury Park.

Asbury Park was known to host the rich and famous. While all resort beach towns along the Jersey coastline are of course beautiful, Asbury

Park stands out amongst the rest, securely holding a position in *Travel + Leisure*'s top ten best New Jersey beach towns to this day.² Due to its notoriety, you could rest assured that, if something happened in Asbury Park, the country would soon know all about it.

And so, it was here in Asbury Park at the Asbury Avenue Beach that the lifeguard captain, a man named Benjamin Everingham, claimed to have not only spotted a twelve-foot-long shark, but to have also beaten that shark repeatedly with an oar. Everingham, who had been patrolling the waters in a small boat, was surprised when he spotted a dorsal fin peaking just above the ocean's surface and heading straight toward him. Everingham had been told by his employer to carry an ax and a rifle while on lifeguard duty to better protect the beachgoers in his care from the lurking, 'man-eating' sharks.³ Everingham, like many others, did not take the shark attacks particularly seriously though, believing the likelihood of a subsequent attack to be nearly impossible. And so, it was to his unarmed surprise when the shark headed straight toward him, forcing Everingham to stand up in his boat and beat it with an oar (the only weapon he had on hand) until the shark eventually took off. Everingham then raced to land and warned the locals to stay out of the water, causing hundreds of beachgoers to race up the shore. This incident resulted in beach closures, the construction of steel netting at Asbury Park, and a growing level of concern from locals about the potential of a return attack. This incident was so alarming, in fact, that it made the front page of the *Asbury Park Evening Press* on July 8, 1916, as well as other national newspapers.

This wasn't the only shark-related sighting to occur in Asbury Park. Chicago's *The Day Book* publication reported 'four large sharks, believed to be of the man-eating variety' seen off Asbury Park just a few days later.⁴

On the very same day as the Everingham incident, about fifty miles up shore in Bayonne, New Jersey (nearly adjacent to Brooklyn, New York), a group of kids were playing in the water near the Robbins Reef Yacht Club when they spotted a shark. The kids screamed, 'It's a shark!', calling attention to nearby police lieutenant Dennis Colohan. Colohan, along with the superintendent of the city water department, Amos Harker, climbed into a motorboat and took off after the creature. Colohan brought the boat within several feet of the shark and, after noting how large the animal was (he reported it being eight feet in length and its dorsal fin standing three feet above the water), he pulled out his revolver and started to shoot.[5] Colohan later reported that the shark 'seemed stunned for a moment' before eventually swimming off.[6]

Not long after this incident, a fisherman named John Ketcham reported a school of sharks that attempted to turn over his boat near Long Beach.[7] Later, Esterbrook Carter, the nephew of Charles Evan Hughes (the Republican candidate running in opposition to Woodrow Wilson for the presidency in 1916) also reported a shark swimming underneath his boat while he was out to sea.[8]

Two men that lived in Spring Lake ignored the warnings about the 'shark-infested' waters and chose to take a long swim in the ocean on July 6th. Though neither officially encountered a shark, eyewitnesses told them later that they had spotted sharks following the men for the duration of their swim and that the two men were lucky to have escaped with their lives. Following this experience, it is reported that both men swore off swimming in the New Jersey waters ever again.[9]

Yet another man, this one named Thomas Richard, narrowly survived an encounter with a shark while swimming in Coney Island. Apparently, some fifty people that were eating at a nearby beach hotel noticed what appeared to be a shark swimming in close proximity to Richard. They shouted out after him, 'Shark!'. Richard whipped around to see a dorsal fin cutting across the water's surface, heading straight toward him. Miraculously, he was able to climb aboard a nearby motorboat before he could become yet another unfortunate victim of a shark.[10]

Reports of sharks spotted in the ocean reached nearly every mile of the Jersey coastline with some sharks allegedly spotted as far out as Connecticut, Florida, and Alabama. There were so many sharks in the waters, in fact, that the US Coast Guard even stated that 'a patrol of cutters would be useless' against them.[11]

Now it's worth mentioning here that, while – yes, the New Jersey beaches were certainly experiencing an unprecedented increase in the number of sharks spotted in their waters that summer – it is entirely possible that several of these 'encounters' were, at best, gross exaggerations and, at worst, downright fabrications. It became popular at this time to share personal stories of near-death experiences or, at a minimum, personal sightings of sharks. Therefore, many of these tales from over 100 years ago could be just that: tales.

These sightings and 'near-death' experiences took an abrupt turn on July 12th, just under a week after Bruder's horrific death. For just thirty miles north of Spring Lake, tragedy struck once again. And this time, the shark did not settle for just one victim.

This time, tragedy found itself at Matawan Creek, a highly unusual location for a shark attack; much less, for the presence of a shark at all. Unlike the Atlantic Ocean, Matawan Creek is much smaller, muddier, and more inland. These eleven miles of creek are marshy and twisty before they spill out into the Raritan Bay, a body of water in the Atlantic Ocean that sits just between the states of New York and New Jersey. Given all these factors, the Matawan Creek was not known to contain sharks. Even to the layman with minimal knowledge of sharks, it can be argued that it is fairly common knowledge that sharks do not often frequent small, shallow bodies of water such as murky creeks. With few exceptions, most sharks require the saltwater of the ocean to survive. There are only a few species that have adapted to survive – or tolerate – freshwater environments such as rivers, lakes, and creeks.

The Matawan Creek, in particular, is no more than forty feet across at its widest parts and is still known to this day to be a rather quiet and peaceful place (though, since it was dammed in the late-1920s, what used to be somewhat of a tidal river has since turned into more of a stream). So, when a local sea captain and resident of Matawan, Thomas Cottrell, reported that he had seen what he believed to be an eight-foot-long shark swimming in the town's otherwise tranquil creek, no one believed him.[12] Cottrell was adamant that he had spotted the shark in the water as he went about his daily walk across the trolley bridge that hovered over Matawan Creek. But despite his insistence, he continued to be met with resistance. One local even remarked of Cottrell's alleged discovery: 'I didn't realize Captain Cottrell had such a splendid sense of humor.'[13] When Cottrell specifically sought out John Mulsoff, the town's chief of police and barber (very small town vibes), Mulsoff met him with laughter and assumed the combination of the sweltering heat and the stories downstream of shark attacks along the Jersey coast had caused Cottrell to hallucinate.[14]

Cottrell's warning was not the only one. Just one day prior, 14-year-old Rensselaer 'Renny' Cartan was swimming in the creek when something sharp scratched across his chest. He could not see what had hurt him, but he could feel the strength of a massive animal rush by. He jumped out of the creek and looked down at his chest which was covered in bloody scrapes. He called back at his friends that were still swimming in the creek, 'Don't dive in anymore! There's a shark or something in there!'[15] These cries fell on deaf ears, however, much like Captain Cottrell's warnings the following day.

Matawan is a small town, not like the fancy beach towns of Beach Haven, Spring Lake,

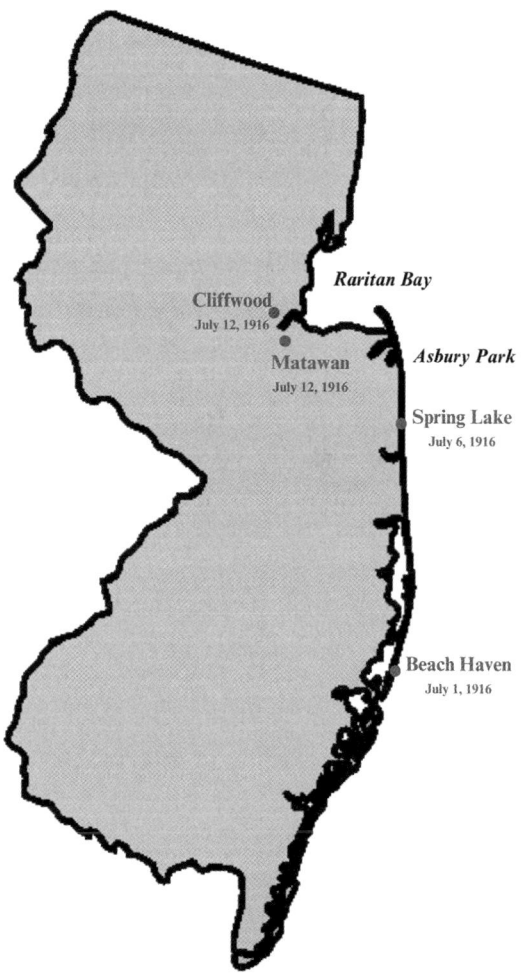

A Map of the New Jersey Shark Attacks. (*Rachel Lee Perez*)

and Asbury Park. In the early-1900s, it was a blue-collar community with several businesses – such as a tile company, a basket-making factory, a hardware store, a barber shop, a bakery, a tailoring shop, and more – lining its Main Street.[16] Despite sharing a close proximity to the gorgeous beach towns that hosted the rich and famous, Matawan was a far humbler community of working-class people with many in town wearing multiple hats. We already mentioned that the town's chief of police was also the town barber. This duality was true across the town with the Assistant Marshall, Bart Tice, also serving as a baker, and the chief of the volunteer Fire Department, Levi Emmons, Jr, also serving as a blacksmith.[17]

Matawan was small, too. In 1916, the town boasted roughly 1,200 people.[18] The town remains small with the 2020 United States Census reporting its population as less than 10,000.[19] It is a tight-knit community where everyone there knows everyone, and everyone there knows that the likelihood of a shark lurking in their small creek was highly improbable. The *New York Times* even reported later:

> 'How could a shark get ten miles away from the ocean, swim through Raritan Bay, and enter the shallow creek with only seventeen feet at its deepest spot and nowhere more than thirty-five feet wide?'[20]

July 12, 1916, sadly proved them all wrong.

That afternoon, a group of boys from the neighborhood walked down Main Street and to the Matawan Creek for a swim; something they did nearly every day. Amongst these boys was 11-year-old Lester Stillwell. Now known to most likely be epilepsy, Stillwell suffered from seizures and was therefore treated with extra care by family and friends.[21] These afflictions, however, made him no different than the other town boys whose favorite pastime was splashing around in the muddy creek just off the Wyckoff dock. The dock, which had not been used commercially since 1903, now stood abandoned, making it the perfect spot for the local boys to jump off and hang out.[22]

Taking a quick afternoon swim was customary for many of these young boys who used the excursion as a break from a long day of work. It was not outside of the ordinary for Matawan town boys to work alongside adults in the community's thriving businesses, and Stillwell was no exception. That summer, Stillwell worked as an apprentice to his father at the Anderson Basket Factory where the young Stillwell helped by nailing fruit baskets together.[23] In those days, the young apprentice received fifty cents for every 100 baskets he made. This meant that, at the end of a day in which he really hustled, he could expect to take home roughly three dollars (the equivalent of just under $90 in today's money). After hours of work and seeing what an excellent job his son had done at assembling the fruit baskets, the senior Stillwell sent his son off to the 'crick' (as local residents referred to it) to enjoy the hot summer afternoon with his friends. Mr Stillwell reminded his son to be careful and mindful in case he felt his 'shakes' coming on.[24] As Mr Stillwell watched his son dash out of the factory to catch up with his friends, he had no idea that that was the last he would see his son alive…and in one piece.

The group of town boys raced down Main Street and headed to the creek; some sources say they were joined by a dog (and, if you will recall from Chapter Two, this detail may be important as the paddling motion that dogs make in the water can be exceptionally attractive to sharks lurking just beneath the water's surface). The boys undressed completely and swam in the nude; the creek water was too murky for anyone to worry about being exposed. Once in the water, they began playing, showing off different tricks. Stillwell joined in on the fun, pushing himself out into the water and floating across it. He hollered back to his friends, 'Watch me float, fellas!'[25] In a sobering conversation I had with Matawan town historian Kurtis Roinestad, I learned that Stillwell's particular pride in being able to float along the top of the water was because he had only just recently learned how to swim not long before that fateful day. This detail alone really hit me in the heart and brought this historical event into a much more real and personal light.

One of Stillwell's friends, a boy named Albert 'Ally' O'Hara, reported that he sensed something that felt like sandpaper scrape across his leg. As he looked down to detect what had grazed by him, he spotted what he believed to be a large marine animal.

Not long after this, when it was shortly after 2:00 PM (roughly ten to fifteen minutes after the boys had first arrived at the creek), Stillwell let out a small scream, followed by a splash. The local children watched in horror as an unknown object seemed to rush toward Stillwell, pulling him under the water. Johnson Cartan, one of the young boys that had been at the creek with Stillwell that day (and the cousin of 'Renny' Cartan who had been scratched by the mysterious creature in the water the day before the Matawan attacks), later shared in 1985 in an exclusive interview with 1916 shark attack expert and author Dr Fernicola, 'We didn't think it was a shark. We thought it was an old, weather-beaten board.'[26] But the creature made itself known shortly thereafter, confirming for the young boys that what they were witnessing was indeed an attack by a ferocious shark. The massive creature with hundreds of teeth lunged at Stillwell once more, taking him under the surface, not to be seen alive again.

The boys ran from the creek – still naked and now covered in mud – and into the town where they screamed various iterations of the phrases: 'Lester is gone! A shark got Lester! There's a shark in the creek!' The boys' cries for help caught the attention of a 24-year-old man named Stanley Fisher. Fisher was a beloved member of the town – particularly beloved by the children for the hours he spent playing baseball with them between working his job as the local dry cleaner and tailor. Fisher immediately made his way down to the creek with significant concern for the missing boy with epileptic seizures. Fisher, like most other townspeople, did not think the story of a shark in the Matawan Creek carried much credibility. Rather, he worried that the young boys had mistaken an epileptic seizure for a shark attack. Along the way to the creek, Fisher enlisted the help of two other local men, George 'Red' Burlew and Arthur Smith. The three of them climbed into a small rowboat and took to the water in search of Stillwell. As the boat floated into the water, they couldn't help but notice that the creek's typical muddy brown hue had taken on a red tint. A blood-like red tint. Even still, the men initially refused to believe that a shark had been responsible for this mess. Surely, Stillwell had merely bumped his head – maybe the result of an epileptic seizure – and the injury had caused his blood to pool in the water. The alternative – a shark in the Matawan Creek – was simply impossible. Though the longer they were in the water, the more they were forced to face the reality that the amount of blood they were immersed in was more than one would expect from a head bump. Rather, the quantity of blood better aligned with someone who was bleeding out entirely…

The men used long poles to probe at the water from where they sat in their boat, hoping to locate what they now expected to be the little boy's corpse. With the amount of blood and the rising belief that the stories of a shark in Matawan Creek must certainly be true, there was no expectation that they would find Lester Stillwell alive. But it was important to the men that they retrieved his body.

When their probing attempts came up futile, the men began taking turns diving off the boat and into the creek. At some point in these recovery attempts, Burlew reported being hit by something that felt to him like sandpaper. The injury stung so furiously that Burlew abandoned the mission momentarily to examine the wound. When he reached the shore, he realized that he was gushing blood from his leg. The extent of his injury was severe enough that it would later require more than a dozen stitches.[27]

Sources provide varying accounts about whether Stillwell's body was indeed found by Fisher. Some state that Fisher *did* locate Stillwell's body at the bottom of the creek and that witnesses watched him bring what was left of the poor boy's body up to the surface. Other sources indicate that this did not happen and that they never saw Stillwell (alive or dead) again. As for Fisher, he later reported that he had indeed found Stillwell's body deep in the water and that, when he found it, he saw what he interpreted as a wooden log violently thrashing over the little boy's body. Little did he know that that harmless, wooden log was actually a sea creature with hundreds of sharp, serrated teeth.

Amid this commotion, a crowd of townspeople had gathered along the shore, including Stillwell's mother and father. The *Keyport Weekly* reported anywhere between 200 and 300 people eventually crowded by the creek, many of which called out after the men to get out of the water; no one in Matawan wanted to see another one of their loved ones lost.[28] But motivated by what he felt was his duty, especially after seeing the grief-stricken looks on Mr and Mrs Stillwell's faces, Fisher decided to dive back into the water one last time.

And so, it was there, in full view of the attentive audience, that Fisher – just as he was certain he had found Stillwell's body – let out a loud scream. In full view of the large audience, a shark came straight for Fisher, catching him in the right thigh. Given the number of people standing alongside the creek when this happened, it can be argued that the attack on Fisher may very well be the most eye-witnessed shark attack in history. Locals reported witnessing Fisher fight with the monster through violent attacks – with one eyewitness stating that Fisher 'fought the shark like a madman' – before he was finally able to break free and rescue himself.[29] Burlew reported on the incident:

> 'Stanley was a big man, and he fought back at the shark, striking it with his fists. He was fighting desperately to break away, striking and kicking at it with all his might. Three or four times during the struggle the shark pulled him under, but each time he managed to get back to the surface. He seemed to be holding his own, but at best it was an uneven battle. The shark was at home in the water—and Stanley wasn't.'[30]

Realizing he could be of no help to his friend, Burlew himself raced to shore with 'the awful fear that the shark was right behind me and had slated me for his next victim.'[31]

Having rescued himself, Fisher quickly raced to land. It wasn't until Fisher had managed this feat that the extent of his injuries was realized: Ten pounds of flesh had been removed from his right thigh, exposing his bone to the horrified audience![32] His femoral artery had been severed completely with his blood spurting out violently from the source. According to the *Matawan Journal*, '…the sight of Mr. Fisher being brought ashore was sickening, to state it mildly.'[33] Several of the townswomen fainted at the sight. It is reported that when Fisher himself saw his mangled leg, he exclaimed, 'Oh, my God!'[34]

A medical doctor onsite, Dr George Reynolds, later described Fisher's injuries as 'a wide, jagged laceration, measuring approximately eighteen inches, spanning from below the hip to just above the knee.'[35] Dr Reynolds tied a tourniquet around Fisher's thigh in an attempt to stop the bleeding. Fisher, very conscious at this point, pleaded with the attending physician to be honest with him and reveal the extent of the damage. Dr Reynolds, ever the professional, assured Fisher that the damage wasn't too bad, although he knew in his heart that this was not true.[36] Despite being in significant pain, Fisher was insistent upon telling those that would listen that he had found Stillwell's body at the bottom of the creek where he had seen the shark viciously feasting on it.

In hindsight, it is interesting to note that – even though Fisher, Burlew, and Smith had been in the water, making a commotion as they searched for Stillwell for a good hour or so – the shark did not attempt to strike them during this time. It was only when Fisher went to retrieve Stillwell from the feasting shark that it must have felt threatened and lashed out in response. This is interesting behavior on behalf of the shark. If what we know about sharks not being man-eating monsters is true, why was this shark devouring Stillwell's body for an extended length of time? Why did it not take one bite, realize its mistake, and retreat? Why also did the shark only engage with the other humans in the water when it feared its current meal of human flesh may be taken away?

Dr Reynolds, and other men from the town, created a makeshift stretcher out of planks and carried Fisher on it through the town and to the train station. It was Dr Reynolds' belief that, due to the severity of Fisher's wounds, he would not survive a trip to Saint Peter's Hospital via automobile. In those days, the road was not paved, and the bumpy commute was sure to lead to Fisher bleeding to death along the way. It was decided that a train to Monmouth Memorial Hospital was the only option. However, the train posed its own set of problems: The next train was not expected to arrive for another two hours! The acting Mayor of Matawan, Arris Henderson, arranged for the next train to skip as many stops as possible in order to reach Matawan more quickly and to transport Fisher to the nearest hospital immediately.[37] The train arrived at 5:06 PM, meaning that Fisher did not reach the Monmouth Memorial Hospital in Long Branch until around 5:30 PM that evening (a roughly twenty-mile distance and, had the train been on its regularly-scheduled route, a nearly three-hour train ride away). The physician at the hospital, a Dr Edwin Field, later stated that, even amongst the series of injuries he had personally treated during the Spanish-American War nearly twenty years prior, Fisher's shark bites were worse than anything he had ever seen before.[38] At 6:35 PM, about an hour after Fisher arrived at the hospital, he bled to death. But just before he passed, Fisher whispered to Dr Field, 'Doc, I found the boy in the bottom; I got Lester away from the shark. Anyhow, I did my duty.' These were reportedly his final words. Up until the moment he died, he was resolute in his mission and carried no regrets.[39]

Fisher's family knew nothing of the attack or his condition. In fact, they were not even in Matawan at the time, but were instead in Minneapolis, Minnesota, visiting Fisher's sister.[40] Hours after Fisher passed away, acting Mayor Henderson sent a telegraph to them, simply stating: 'I regret to inform you that Stanley has died as a result of his injuries…'[41] Even still, the family did not know what his injuries were nor how they had occurred. They only learned that Fisher had been killed by a shark when they spotted the story in the newspaper as they were on the train the next day, rushing back to Matawan.

As for Stillwell, his body surfaced on July 14th, two days after the horrifying incident, roughly 150 feet from where the attack occurred. In the two days between his disappearance and recovery, his family was wracked with both grief and disbelief. Without knowing where Stillwell's body was, they allowed their minds to wander: Had the shark consumed him whole? Or was the poor boy's body sunken to the bottom of the creek? Or, even still, was there the smallest possibility that little Stillwell could still be alive? Studies of grief show us that one of the first stages we experience when faced with the death of a loved one is denial. This denial can become particularly strong when you do not physically see the lifeless body of your loved one. It is the brain's way of protecting you from the worst possible truth: That your loved one is indeed gone. And that worst possible truth was revealed for the Stillwell family when, on July 14th, Lester Stillwell's body was discovered. The body was left absolutely mangled by the ferocious monster, his left ankle missing, his left thigh destroyed, and his abdomen torn apart so badly that it exposed his internal organs.[42] Nearly the only part of his body that remained intact was his face, which the shark seemed to have avoided entirely. The local townsman that had discovered Stillwell's body while on his routine morning walk, Harry Van Cleaf (also seen written as 'VanClief'), was apparently so disturbed by the sight that he never spoke of it, even to his own family. In fact, his family did not know that it was Van Cleaf that had discovered the body until this news was reported later in the newspaper.[43]

The media flocked to the tiny town of Matawan with the *Matawan Tribune* covering the story on the first page with the headline: 'MAN EATING SHARK CAUSES DEATH OF MAN AND BOY.' Another news source, the *Newark Star-Eagle*, falsely and disgustingly reported: 'SHARK KILLED AT KEYPORT; HUMAN BODY INSIDE. SHARK TERROR SLAIN NEAR SCENE OF TRAGEDY.' The article alleged that a shark captured near the mouth of Matawan Creek had been sliced open, his stomach contents revealing the body of Stillwell. This false reporting was sensational, however, and journalists at the time were not above fabricating headlines to make a bite (no pun intended).

The media sensation that descended upon the small town of Matawan did nothing but further trigger the town's grief as they mourned the lives of the heroic Stanley Fisher, and of the frail Lester Stillwell. In an interview with Stanley Fisher biographer and Matawan historian

A Modern-Day Mural of a Shark Mouth Painted Over the Mouth of the Matawan Creek. (*Tyler Cole*)

Allan Savolaine, I learned that Fisher had been loved by all in town. In fact, when Savolaine wrote his book about Fisher, titled *STANLEY FISHER: Shark Attack Hero of a Bygone Age*, he shared that he struggled to find anything negative to say about the man. Every story he read and every interview he held revealed that Fisher really was a stand-up guy with a heart of gold. He was one of the town's most beloved residents, and his passing was a true and aching loss that was felt by all.

That following weekend, on Saturday, July 15th, Matawan laid both Fisher's and Stillwell's bodies to rest at the Rose Hill Cemetery. Fisher's body was placed in the Fisher family plot which, coincidentally, 'is located almost directly above Lester's grave,' according to Savolaine. The funeral and burial proceedings did nothing to provide closure to the community that was completely shattered by the sudden loss, disbelief, and confusion of it all.[44] It took them several years to come to grips with the tragedy that had struck along their unexpected shores.

The community honored their lost loved ones in small but beautiful ways as the years carried on. With a life insurance policy that Fisher had ironically acquired not long before the tragic events of July 12th, his family paid to have a stained-glass window placed in the family Methodist Church on Main Street where Fisher – with his beautiful tenor voice – used to sing.[45] Along with the window, the memorial included the Bible verse, John 15:13, which reads: 'Greater love hath no man than this, that a man lay down his life for his friends.' Sadly, according to the Matawan Historical Society, when the church was demolished in the 1970s, the stained-glass window was auctioned off and its current whereabouts are unknown.[46]

The Fisher family continued to grapple with the sudden and tragic loss for many years to come. In July of 1918 (nearly two years to the day of the tragedy), the *Matawan Journal* published a poem that had been written by Fisher's sister, Agusta Fisher Nichols, who had been pregnant at the time of his passing. The poem read:

> *'It was hard to part with him*
> *The one we loved so dear*
>
> *The heart no greater pain could feel*
> *No sorrow more severe*
>
> *What pain he bore we will never know*
> *We did not see him die*
>
> *We only know that he is gone*
> *And never said good-bye'*[47]

Having also been pregnant when I suddenly lost my own sister, this poem strikes a particular chord with me. I ache for the Fisher and Stillwell families as they attempted to come to terms with their respective losses and worked to navigate what life after loss looked like for them.

The town itself commemorated the 100th anniversary of the tragedies with a nine-day centennial event hosted from July 9th through the 17th in 2016. The Matawan Historical Society, along with the Chamber of Commerce and borough of Matawan, commemorated the event with a live shark viewing at the Center for Aquatic Sciences at Adventure Aquarium, a 'Hero Walk' to retrace the steps that Stanley Fisher took from the dry cleaner business to the creek, Matawan Creek kayak tours, a memorial service at the Rose Hill Cemetery, self-guided tours of the town, the display of various 1916-era artifacts, and more.[48] This event received international attention with more than 3,000 people in attendance, some coming from as far as Canada, Australia, and England, strictly for the

The Memorial Plaque for Lester Stillwell and Stanley Fisher, Dedicated by The Matawan Historical Society. (*Matthew H Ward*)

centennial commemoration event. Even the *New York Times* attended and reported on the event.

The organizers of the event took special care in how they structured the centennial event as to not upset townspeople that do not appreciate the perceived glorification of such a tragic marker in the small town's history. In an exclusive conversation I had with Kurtis Roinestad, Matawan town historian, he shared that, prior to 2016, he equated the 1916 shark attacks to the Salem Witch Trials in the way in which each respective community all but refused to discuss the sobering events.

What many people are unaware of is that most Salem Witch Trials museums and merchandising locations that exist in Salem, Massachusetts today (an industry that makes up approximately eighty percent of Salem's annual income) are not where the witch trials took place. Roughly sixty years after the Salem Witch Trials, Salem Village renamed their city to Danvers in an effort to dissociate themselves from the mistakes of their past. Nearly any Salem Witch Trials tour you take in the Salem that exists today won't even take you into Danvers where it all actually took place.

Now, I've gone down another historical rabbit hole, but with a purpose: Matawan historian Roinestad said that, similar to Danvers' avoidance

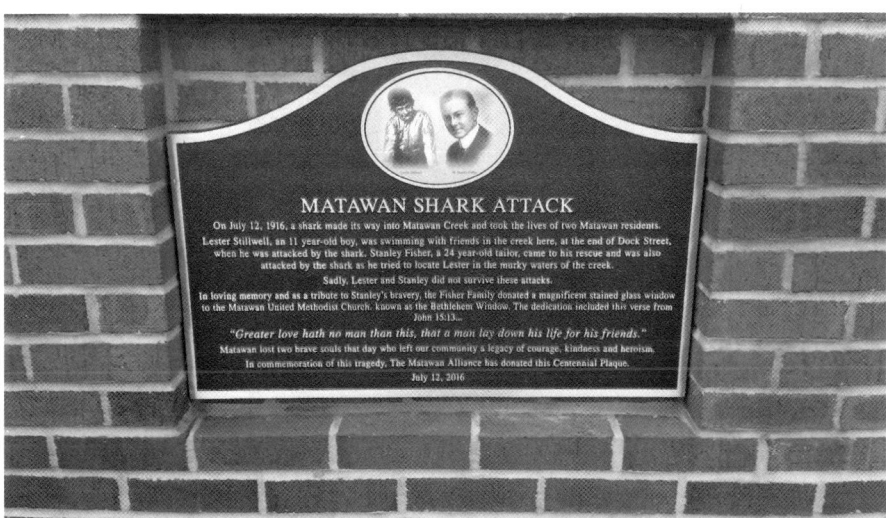

The Memorial Plaque for Lester Stillwell and Stanley Fisher, Dedicated by The Matawan Alliance. (*Matthew H Ward*)

of their own troubled history, Matawan too has long viewed the 1916 shark attacks as 'a bruise on our history.' As recently as 2016 when Roinestad, Savolaine, and the Matawan Historical Society organized the centennial shark event, there was a small faction of townspeople that refused to become involved, going so far as to have their own monument constructed, separate from the one the Historical Society commissioned. This group of people, known as The Matawan Alliance, constructed a monument around the time of the 100-year anniversary that they placed near the creek. Unfortunately, this area is now private property where it is inaccessible to the public. The Matawan Historical Society, on the other hand, dedicated a plaque on the exact 100-year anniversary which they revealed during their centennial memorial event. This monument is situated in a public park along Main Street (where Stillwell's friends would have run along, screaming for help) in honor of poor Lester Stillwell and brave Stanley Fisher, two innocent lives lost on that fateful July day.

The generational trauma of the shark attacks has slowly begun to fade as the generations go by. With the attacks more than 100 years in the past, fewer and fewer people alive today have a direct connection to the horrific events of that brutal day. Savolaine shared with me that there is now a sense of pride associated with the attention the shark attacks have brought to their humble town. This attention is far-reaching. Once, when checking into a hotel in London, England, Savolaine wrote on the check-in sheet that he was from Matawan. This caused the hotel attendant to exclaim, instantly, 'Oh, wow! That's where those shark attacks took place!'

Even though the passage of time has allowed the Matawan shark attacks to become more of a distant event (and, perhaps, even, a small point of pride), there are still Matawan locals that tell stories about how their moms demanded they never swim in the Matawan 'Crick.'

Chapter Five

# Cliffwood: The Forgotten Victim

*'Suddenly, I felt a tug, like a big pair of scissors pulling at my leg and bringing me under. I felt as if my leg had gone! I believe it would have swallowed me.'*

*Joseph Dunn*

Unbeknownst at the time to the residents of Matawan, only thirty minutes later and 400 feet up creek, the ferocious monster would strike again; this time, in the small town of Cliffwood. Much like the young boys of Matawan, 12-year-old Joseph Dunn, his brother, 14-year-old Michael Dunn, and their friend, 16-year-old Jerry Hourihan, played in the local creek that afternoon. The Dunn brothers, originally from New York, had just arrived in Cliffwood that morning for a planned trip to visit their aunt.

Cliffwood is an even smaller town than that of Matawan with the 2020 United States Census recording the population as just over 3,000.[1] But, like the residents of Matawan, those in Cliffwood regularly spent many summer afternoons cooling off in the Matawan Creek that ran through the town.

Given that the attacks on Stillwell and Fisher had only just occurred thirty minutes prior, it is almost hard to believe that the Dunn brothers and their friend did not pick up on all the commotion occurring downstream. The residents of Matawan were not quiet in their horrified screams nor were they quiet as they hopped in their boats and surveyed the waters in their efforts to capture the murderous beast. It wasn't until the boys had already begun swimming in the water that their attention was finally called to the matter at hand. A local townsman, aware of what had occurred in Matawan, ran towards the three boys and urgently advised them that there was a shark in the water.

The three boys scurried to get out of the water, with Joseph at the tail end. It was as Joseph was just about to reach the dock ladder that he felt something big and strong crash into his body. Almost as if it were a scene from a movie, Joseph pulled himself up to the dock just in time for the shark to attack the foot he left dangling behind.

The violent shark that had caught up to the young New Yorker fought viciously to take him underwater with it. The shark latched onto Joseph's left leg, tearing at the flesh. Joseph later explained to the *Asbury Press*:

> 'I was about ten feet from the dock ladder, when I looked down and saw something dark. Suddenly, I felt a tug, like a big pair of scissors pulling at my leg and bringing me under. I felt as if my leg had gone! I believe it would have swallowed me.'[2]

His brother Michael, and a local Matawan man named Jacob Lefferts, jumped into the water and attempted to retrieve Joseph from the shark's powerful jaws. Within moments, a man who had been circling the waters in his boat to issue warnings about the preying shark – none other than Captain Thomas Cottrell – arrived on the scene just in time to assist. Michael, Leffert, and Cottrell fought bravely against the giant animal until they were miraculously able to break Joseph free of its determined grasp.

The shark disappeared as Joseph was pulled onto Cottrell's motorboat. The sight of the young boy's mangled leg was alarming. Cottrell rushed Joseph and Michael back to the Wyckoff dock where the town of Matawan was still gathered around Stanley Fisher's slowly depleting body.

As for Joseph, he was treated by another onsite doctor, Dr Herbert Cooley, who noted that, while 'the front and side portion of the boy's lower left leg was cut into ribbons from knee to ankle,' no bones or major arteries had been severed.[3] Overall, this placed him in a much better condition than can be said of any other 1916 shark attack victim. This meant that it was decided that he could survive the sixteen-mile trek via curvy roads to Saint Peter's Hospital.[4] At the hospital, Joseph was initially reluctant to provide staff with his name or home address as he did not want word of his attack to travel back to his mother who he knew would be gravely concerned. Not long after his arrival, however, he received the incredible news that the doctors would be able to save his leg!

Joseph Dunn ultimately survived the attack, making him the shark's only victim with such a fortunate fate. He underwent several months of medical treatment and rehabilitation, however, forcing him to remain in the hospital until September of that year, more than two months after the shark attack in the creek. Joseph bore scars on his leg for the rest of his life but otherwise recovered remarkably. He eventually was able to walk normally once again without even so much as a limp. Both at the time of the traumatic attack and after, several people remarked on Joseph's bravery and optimism that was present at nearly all times, even as he was actively plagued with shark-fueled nightmares. When asked how he dealt with the nightmares, Joseph said that he reminded himself over and over again how much luckier he was than the other shark victims. When he considered his nightmares in relation to Stillwell's and Fisher's brutal deaths, he felt they paled in comparison and, therefore, did not warrant much attention or fuss.

Perhaps because Cliffwood is so much smaller than Matawan – or perhaps because Joseph survived the attack – Joseph's encounter with the deadly shark is often referred to as the 'forgotten attack.' Many that retell the stories of the 1916 shark attacks entirely gloss over his traumatic encounter with the ferocious beast.[5]

\* It is worth noting that the *New Jersey Shark Attack File* (NJSAF #58) has one additional shark encounter documented as occurring on July 13, 1916, one day after the Matawan attacks.[6] Three men went fishing at Sea Bright, a borough along the Jersey coastline. The men reported a large shark circling their boat and eventually ramming into it with such force that it threw the three men overboard. One by one, the men fought against the shark as they righted the boat and climbed back onboard. It was only after they reached land that they learned of the horrible attacks that had occurred along the Matawan Creek just the day before. This encounter is rarely mentioned in relation to the 1916 shark attacks.

Chapter Six

# 'The Largest Scale Animal Hunt in History'

*'Bathing has come almost to a stop along the Jersey coast, especially those areas where the man-eater has attacked, and a new sport, and public service, the hunting of sharks, has spring up.'*

*The New York Times*

In just twelve days, the New Jersey coast experienced four deaths and one severe injury by a mysterious monster (or monsters), dicing its way through their previously friendly waters. Fear settled in amongst beachgoers, particularly vacationers who began packing their bags for home. The once-booked hotels of the Jersey beachfront quickly vacated. In fact, hotels reported a seventy-five percent vacancy rate, resulting in a loss of $250,000 (the equivalent of more than $7 million in today's money). New Jersey's tourism industry which depended on vacationers – and, quite frankly, *expected* them, particularly during the historically most popular vacation month of the year for Americans – began to crumble. Some hotels, such as the Asbury Park Hotel, closed altogether.[1]

Legend has it that the fear of another shark attack was so intense that a woman ended up drowning in the ocean after she got a cramp while swimming. She cried out for help, but no one would come to her rescue as witnesses feared her screams were a response to being attacked by a shark. If this story is true, perhaps this innocent woman could also be considered a victim of the 1916 shark attacks, though not directly.

Along the entire coast, beachgoers avoided the ocean at all costs. The *New York World* reported: 'Terror of Sharks Keeps a Million Bathers on Shore.'[2] Due to the fear of entering the ocean, many of the vacationers that chose to finish out their stays at their beachfront resorts opted instead to swim in the hotels' pools. This led to severe overcrowding in the hotel pools, requiring one hotel, in particular, to empty and refill their pool multiple times a day on account of sanitation.[3]

On or about July 14th, just two days after the double murder along the Matawan Creek, actress Gertrude Hoffman had her own terrifying encounter with a shark. Later known for her roles in Alfred Hitchcock's *Foreign Correspondent* and H.G. Wells' *The War of the Worlds*, the actress was swimming at the Coney Island beach off the Brooklyn coast when she claimed to have encountered a shark. She 'beat up the water furiously' in her attempt to scare the shark away, a technique she said she read about in the *New York Times*. With some time and hindsight, however, Hoffman later told the *Times* that she was not sure if she had perhaps overexaggerated the encounter or if she had, indeed, 'barely escaped her death.'[4]

Whatever the circumstances of Hoffman's encounter with the shark, it was clear that it helped stoke the fear that had already begun to permeate even beyond the State of New Jersey. Panic about the shark attacks affected beachgoers 'from New England to Florida,' with people avoiding the entire Eastern coastline at all costs.[5]

The stories of the 1916 shark attacks reached so far that even the *London Times* reported on them with a headline that read: 'DANGEROUS SCHOOLS OF SHARKS TERRORIZING THE COAST OF THE U.S.'[6] The fact that the *London Times* reported on the shark attacks at all is rather remarkable when you consider the timeframe. Britain and France were actively engaged in the Battle of the Somme, a major First World War conflict that began the very same day as the first shark attack on Vansant. In fact, this day, July 1, 1916, marked the bloodiest day in British military history with over 57,000 casualties. And yet, the shark attacks along the Jersey Shore were groundbreaking enough that they penetrated through stories of monumental war coverage.

New Jersey could no longer downplay the shark attacks. The government needed to act, and it needed to act now. New Jersey citizens wrote to government officials – from the local level all the way up to the White

House – pleading with them to help. Thousands upon thousands of letters, telegraphs, postcards, and telephone calls were directed at the government, begging for them to get involved and provide assistance to the frightened American people.[7]

Washington, D.C.'s *The Sunday Star*, culminated the sentiment of the moment when they wrote:

> 'For the first time in history a fish has become such a menace to the safety of the citizens of the United States that the federal government finds it is necessary to turn its attention to plans for a campaign against it. Surely some odd battles have been fought by this government, but never before has it turned its cannons upon a regiment of fish.'[8]

Finally, New Jersey Governor James Fairman Fielder held a press conference to address the issue at hand. In the press conference, he expressed his belief that the Jersey coast had been invaded by more than one killer sea animal and admitted that he did not know what to do to fix the problem. Instead, he begged residents to be careful and for hotels to construct safety nets to keep ocean-bathers within a safe distance. It was decided by Coast Guard Captain Commandant GL Carden that these safety nets must be 'not less than No. 9 gauge steel.'[9] Of the costs incurred to place these safety nets at all public beaches, he said, 'This is a legitimate overhead expense and is part of a burden which will have to be borne if the public is to be safeguarded.'[10] US Coast Guard Keeper William Van Brunt was ordered to personally visit the various beaches along the Jersey coast to ensure that each and every location was following instructions and constructing the safety nets right away.

Government officials also received suggestions from concerned – and, apparently, 'expert' – citizens regarding how they should approach the shark crisis that had ruined their summer. Many of these armchair experts stated that the government should secure animal meat to boats or other floating devices in order to entice the sharks. Or, certainly more alarming,

Dynamite Explosion in Matawan Creek. (*The Matawan Historical Society*)

there were those that suggested that the meat be designed in a way to resemble little human boys, since that apparently was what most satiated the wild animal's uncontrollable appetite.[11] Yikes.

The people of Matawan were more impassioned and motivated to tackle the shark problem themselves. They took measures into their own hands and constructed a makeshift net – complete with pieces of meat adhered to it – which they placed at the mouth of the creek, hoping to trap the shark. Then, they dumped tons of dynamite into the Matawan Creek, likely destroying any and all marine life that existed there. It was believed by the townspeople that the bursts of explosions would kill the man-eating monster. But these efforts were two-fold, as townspeople also hoped that the explosions would bring Stillwell's body to the surface, allowing his family the opportunity to bury him properly (though, at this point, many in the town were of the belief that the shark must have swallowed the boy whole).

For Matawan residents, their sadness and grief were replaced with anger and sheer determination to kill the monster that had destroyed the tranquility of their small town. The angry mob that had stationed itself at the creek continued there for hours on end with guns, clubs, axes, harpoons, and more, in hand. The Matawan townspeople continued to patrol the creek until the late, dark hours of the evening until delirium and paranoia set in and caused them to shoot aimlessly at invisible threats. As the *New York Times* reported of their efforts, 'The one purpose in which everybody shares is to get the shark, to kill it, and to see its body drawn up on the shore, where all may look and be assured it will destroy no more.'[12]

Matawan acting Mayor Arris Henderson printed WANTED posters and offered a reward of $100 (the equivalent of nearly $3,000 in today's money) to anyone who could capture and kill the shark that had entered the creek and killed the two, beloved Matawan citizens. The poster read:

$100 REWARD! THE ABOVE REWARD WILL BE PAID TO THE PERSONS KILLING THE SHARK BELIEVED TO BE IN MATAWAN CREEK.

IN THE EVENT THERE IS MORE THAN ONE SHARK KILLED, A PRO RATA SUM WILL BE PAID FOR KILLING EACH SHARK.

ARRIS B. HENDERSON
ACTING MAYOR OF MATAWAN

To the town's dismay, on July 16th, roughly four days after the attacks in the creek and two days after Stillwell's lifeless body surfaced, they noticed that the net they had placed at the mouth of the creek was destroyed and the meat was gone. Whether this was the handywork of a shark or it was merely due to the way the net had been constructed so haphazardly is unknown.

The overall commotion at Matawan was enough to draw the skeptical, but intrigued, Dr Nichols, to the site. Initially still in disbelief that a shark could have caused the damage at hand, he was bombarded by eyewitness accounts that described a roughly 250-pound grey creature with a white underbelly, stretching approximately nine or ten feet in length, and displaying hundreds of sharp teeth. For the first time since the horrific string of attacks began, Dr Nichols' mind was finally shifting to the dark reality that there may indeed by a rogue, man-eating shark in their midst. The *New York Times* reported on this sudden change of heart, stating, '… the foremost authority on sharks in this country has doubted that any type of shark ever attacked a human being, and has published his doubts, but the recent cases have changed his view.'[13]

Like the Matawan Mayor before them, the *New York Evening World* also posted their own bounty, offering $100 to anyone who could capture the shark that was terrorizing the East Coast beaches.[14]

The Patterson Chamber of Commerce also joined in on the offers of a bounty. Their reward money was relative to the weight of the shark captured[15]:

- $2 (equivalent of about $58 in today's money) for a 110-pound shark
- $5 (equivalent of about $145 in today's money) for a 200-pound shark
- $100 (equivalent of about $2,886 in today's money) for a 300-pound shark
- $25 (equivalent of about $722 in today's money) for a 400-pound shark
- $50 (equivalent of about $1,443 in today's money) for a 500-pound shark[16]

(According to Dr Fernicola, 'The $100 tag on the 300-pound shark was either a misprint – meant to be $10 – or those setting the bounty must have believed that the accurate witness testimony from the creek revealed a "300-pound shark".')[17]

For those hoping to score a bounty, many were severely disappointed when they learned that the captured shark's stomach contents had to contain human body parts in order to qualify.[18]

And finally, on or around July 13th, United States President Woodrow Wilson called for an all-day meeting with his Cabinet to address the terrifying shark attacks and what the government could do to bring them to a halt. Wilson promised to 'do anything in his power…to rid the Jersey coast of the shark menace.' Perhaps inspired by his connection to the State of New Jersey, having served as governor of the state from 1911 – 1913, or perhaps motivated by the fact that it was an election year and the perception of public opinion matters, Wilson put the force of his executive power behind ending the killing spree on New Jersey beachgoers. As the *Philadelphia Inquirer* reported on July 14th, the federal government was committed to do all it could to 'drive away all the ferocious man-eating sharks which have been making prey of bathers.' New Jersey Congressman Isaac Bacharach introduced a bill to the US House of Representatives to appropriate $5,000 to the Federal Bureau of Fisheries to assist with 'the extermination of man-eating sharks.'[19] President Wilson's Treasury Secretary William McAdoo (whom you may recall was staying at the Essex & Sussex at the same time of Bruder's terrible murder) announced that the US Coast Guard and the Bureau of Fisheries would join together to complete this mission, though perhaps not in the way the American people had hoped. As the *New York Times* reported in an article dated July 18, 1916, 'the suggested campaign of extermination against sharks along the Atlantic' was ultimately determined to be 'impractical' and abandoned in place of simply extending the steel nets at the beaches where they were already in use.[20]

Perhaps partially emboldened by what they perceived as a lackluster response from the government, rogue citizens performed acts of vigilante justice to rid the waters of the killer sea creature on their own, essentially establishing a terrifying and unprecedented open season on sharks. And thus, according to Dr Fernicola, 'the largest scale animal hunt in history' ensued.[21] Even the *New York Times* stated in a deeply troubling report:

> 'Bathing has come almost to a stop along the Jersey coast, especially those areas where the man-eater has attacked, and a new sport, and public service, the hunting of sharks, has spring up.'

In response to this 'call to arms,' people loaded up their boats with guns, axes, and dynamites, and took to the sea to destroy what they were not sure was a singular, rogue monster or a swarm of man-eating killers.

The purchase and use of guns during this period was unlike anything Americans had ever seen before. It became customary to equip lifeguards with shotguns to be used if necessary.

Both motivated by a sense of duty and by a desire to collect some bounty, citizens across the Jersey coast hopped into motorboats and roamed the ocean, rifles at the ready. In Matawan, townspeople continued their station at the creek, shooting bullets and dumping dynamites into the water aimlessly.

And with that, a killing spree on sharks that had never been seen before began. Every day, fishermen, servicemen, and average citizens alike killed sharks in the hundreds and – when possible – carried that prize ashore to boast. Citizens of all kinds took to the waters to kill the beasts that had

Female Matawan Residents Holding a Gun and Pointing it at the Creek. (*The Matawan Historical Society*)

wreaked havoc on their summer, their economy, and their families. One of the most striking images from this period in history is that of three women standing in a boat in the Matawan Creek with a rifle pointed at the water, a devious smile on the lips of the gun-wielder.

EF Warner, a columnist for *Field and Stream* magazine, shot a sandbar shark in the head three times with his .38 firearm. The Bayonne Police Department also fired shots at a shark that they spotted, swimming toward a group of children (Yes, they shot their firearms in the vicinity of children).[22] Others used their oars or axes to violently beat to death the sharks they encountered. One group of men pulled two sharks ashore and sliced them open to view the contents of their stomachs, an engaged audience there and ready to cheer them on.[23] Even Captain Thomas Cottrell – the Matawan resident that assisted 12-year-old Joseph Dunn to safety – claimed to have caught a shark near the mouth of the creek which he later displayed for public viewing with a sign that read: 'TERROR OF MATAWAN CREEK, 10 CENTS A LOOK.'[24] (There is much speculation as to whether Cottrell actually captured and killed the 230-pound, seven-foot-long shark that he later placed on display. There were rumors that Cottrell actually orchestrated for this large shark, that was reported to have been found roughly a mile and half away from the creek, to be bought by his nephew, John Cottrell, and brought to him. There is substantial speculation that this is the shark that he claimed to have killed himself.)

For animal rights activists, or anyone with common decency and a moral compass, this horrific 'open season' behavior was deplorable. This mass killing of sharks was something the world had never seen before and would not see again until 1975, nearly sixty years later (but more on this in Chapter Twelve).

On July 14, 1916, the horrors of the Summer of 1916 took an interesting turn, at the hands of none other than a Barnum & Bailey Circus animal trainer named Michael Schleisser. Schleisser, at the time 45-years-old, was a taxidermist, lion tamer, and overall animal trainer for the world-renowned traveling circus group, Barnum & Bailey. Schleisser, like many

Americans, was closely following the news of the shark attacks along the Jersey coast from where he resided in Harlem, New York. He and a friend, John Murphy (no relation to expert Robert Murphy of the Brooklyn Museum), decided to travel to New Jersey to join in on the hunt for the man-eating monsters. The two were able to gain access to a large motorboat, set off from South Amboy, and made their way for the Raritan Bay.

The Raritan Bay is situated perfectly between New York and New Jersey. If the shark that had killed Stillwell and Fisher and injured Dunn had continued north, it would make sense that it would find its way into the Raritan Bay.

When Schleisser and Murphy were approximately four miles from where the Matawan Creek spills out into the Raritan Bay, they decided to drop a dragnet. They were not there long before something caught in the net; something large enough that it jerked the entire boat! In fact, the boat was jerked so violently that the engine died immediately. When Schleisser *was* able to see what was pulling at the boat – and also notice that the creature was nearly the *size* of the boat – it is reported that he exclaimed, 'My God, we've got a shark!'[25] Thinking quickly, Schleisser grabbed a broken oar that he had kept in the boat and began taking whacks at the ferocious beast. Schleisser beat the shark to death as the shark fought against him, attempting to capsize the boat. Schleisser later stated that his battle with the shark was 'the hardest fight for life I've ever had'; an amazing statement coming from someone that quite literally had experience in the circus ring with lions and tigers and bears (oh, my!).[26] When Schleisser had accomplished his task of killing the shark, he signaled for a larger boat that was passing by to assist in bringing the animal to shore. Once there, Schleisser – who, as you will recall, was a trained taxidermist – decided to slice open the stomach of the shark and inspect it for anything significant. And inside the shark's stomach were significant findings, indeed. With a crowd watching, including two medical doctors, Schleisser pulled from the shark's insides what an article in the *Bronx Home News* later said was 'fifteen pounds of human remains,

'The Largest Scale Animal Hunt in History' 83

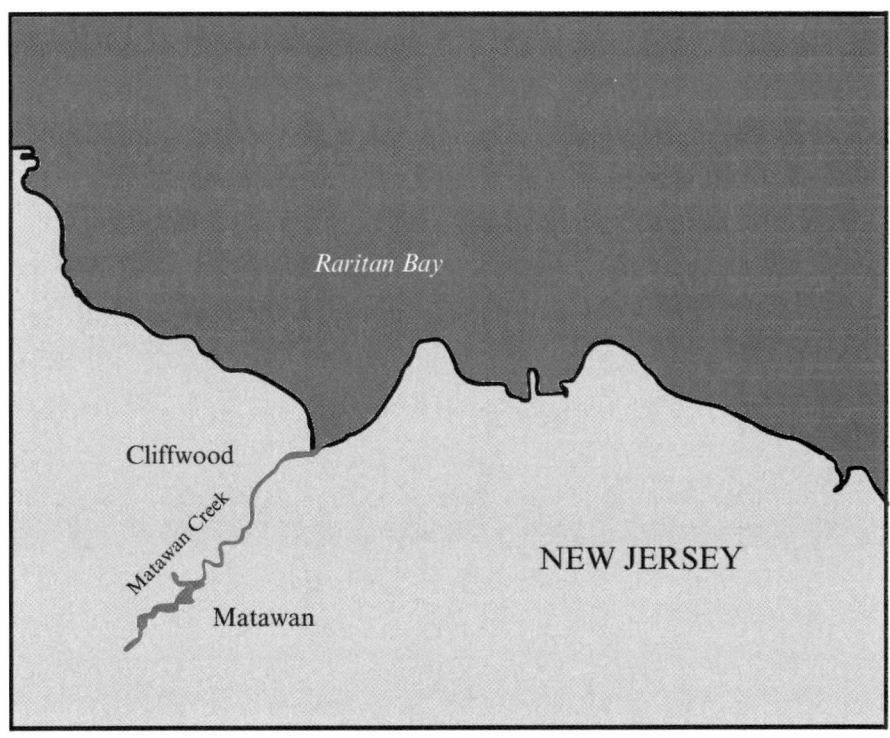

A Map to Show the Distance of the Raritan Bay from Matawan and Cliffwood. (*Rachel Lee Perez*)

including a boy's shinbone and a rib section.'[27] The taxidermist, familiar with gutting animals, completed the job of cleaning out the shark and then loaded it up into his car. Although the thought of carrying a dead and gutted shark in one's vehicle might seem odd and even squeamish to some, this was not entirely out of the ordinary for the well-known taxidermy expert. In addition to the gutted shark, Schleisser also brought along with him the pieces of bone he had discovered and the human flesh (although, in reference to the latter, he unfortunately got rid of it on account of the fact that its 'smell became quite offensive.' From a historic and forensic standpoint, it is disappointing that this flesh has been lost to history and can therefore never be tested to assist in providing answers to the many questions we still have today about the 1916 shark attacks).[28]

Schleisser worked feverishly over the next few days to prepare and preserve the shark's body which measured seven and a half feet long and weighed 350 pounds. And on July 19th and 20th, less than a week from when he had caught the 'man-eater' in the Raritan Bay, Schleisser placed the shark on display at the office of the *Bronx Home News*, located at 155 W 125th Street, New York.

The news article that ran concurrent to Schleisser's public display, titled 'Harlem Man In Tiny Boat Kills A 7 ½ Foot Man-Eating Shark,' stated of the display: 'The Shark can be seen in The Home News Window to-day and to-morrow until 12.30 p. m.'[29]

Some 30,000 people came to view the monster that they believed had murdered four people and destroyed the summer innocence of the New Jersey coastline. There were so many people in attendance that a police presence was requested to help maintain the crowd.[30] It is important to note that, for many of these onlookers, this was the first time they had ever seen a shark in person. The misconceptions about sharks and what they looked like were pervasive; so pervasive that many of the fascinated onlookers still refused to believe that what they were observing before them was indeed a shark.

Michael Schleisser Displaying His Shark Outside the Bronx Home News. (*Courtesy of The Bronx County Historical Society's Research Library Microfilm Collection*)

Among the observants were none other than the three men that had made up the experts panel at the American Museum of Natural History roughly ten days prior: Dr Frederic Lucas, Dr John Nichols, and Robert Murphy. The men knew about Schleisser and his great capture because Schleisser had actually mailed them the bones found in the shark's stomach for further examination. Upon analyzing the bone fragments, Dr Lucas wrote back to the taxidermist:

> 'Dear Mr. Schleisser: I am very much obliged to you for your courtesy in letting me see the bones taken from the shark. They are parts of the left radius and ulna and one of the anterior ribs, all human. There is no doubt about this. They have been badly shattered. Can you tell me the exact species of shark from which these bones were taken, or if you are in doubt, I am sure that Mr. Nichols would be very glad to call and determine the species exactly? Again thankful for your kindness, I am.'[31]

Having had the opportunity to determine that the shark's stomach contents were indeed human, the three men were resolved to see the responsible beast in person. The experts inspected Schleisser's shark in great detail and, after careful consideration, were able to provide the attentive crowd with the answer to one of their most burning questions: What species of shark was it? Dr Nichols stated with absolute certainty that what they were looking at was a great white shark. Not a porpoise. Not a sea turtle. Not a swordfish. A great white shark. Dr Lucas and Murphy both agreed that this very creature before them – the one Schleisser had caught in the Raritan Bay – was indeed *the* 'Jersey man-eater.'

Unfortunately, Schleisser's shark ended up going missing, lost to history as no one has ever been able to determine where it eventually landed.

Following the capture of this shark, there was not a single shark attack along the Jersey Shore for the rest of the Summer of 1916. For the first time in two weeks, the residents of New Jersey released a collective sigh of relief.

Chapter Seven

# This Vicinity Will Be Alive with Sharks

*'It must be admitted that deaths from shark bite within a short radius of New York City would seem to be one of those unaccountable happenings that take place from time to time to the confounding of savants and justification of the wildest tradition.'*

*John Nichols*

So, what happened? What happened to make a shark (or multiple sharks) attack the Jersey Shore in a way that had never been seen before nor has ever been seen since?

One of the most widely speculated beliefs of the time was that the shark infestation had been the result of German U-boats. Remember that

German U-Boat in Roughly 1918. (*DeGolyer Library, Southern Methodist University*)

larger conflicts overseas were taking place simultaneous to this terrifying streak of shark attacks. In 1916, Europe was engaged in the middle of the First World War. Germany, in particular, utilized marine machinery unlike any other country involved in the conflict. In fact, they were the first to use submarines during the Great War, commonly referred to as German U-boats (the 'U' stands for *Unterseeboot* which is the German word for 'undersea boat').

These U-boats were a marine force unlike anything else the world had seen up to this point. They were so powerful that they could successfully take down boats '20 times their size from both above and below the surface with their deck guns and torpedoes.'[1] By the end of the war, Germany had built 334 U-boats and was in production to make another 226.[2] In February of 1915, and again in January of 1917, Germany announced that it would sink any and all ships that crossed its U-boats without warning and without cause.[3] This included merchant ships, even those belonging to countries not involved in the war. Germany certainly became a formidable force in the seas and even made its presence known in the waters of the – at the time, neutral – United States.

One particular German submarine, the *Deutschland*, made its maiden voyage in late-June of 1916, just a handful of days before the first shark attack at Beach Haven. The *Deutschland*, which was labeled by the Germans as a merchant ship, caused pause for many Americans who suspected the vessel to be a warship. The submarine made its way to Baltimore with the front page of Baltimore's *The Sun* stating on July 10, 1916: 'UNARMED GERMAN SUBMARINE WITH MERCHANDISE CARGO NOW LIES NEAR BALTIMORE.'[4] Whether this submarine was indeed a weapon of war or simply a cargo ship was of little importance to Americans with strong anti-German mindsets.

It cannot be forgotten that on May 7, 1915 (just one year prior to the shark attacks along the Jersey coast), a German U-boat launched a torpedo into the *Lusitania*, a passenger ship carrying 1,959 passengers and crew members. This attack caused the ocean liner to sink within just twenty minutes, leading to the drowning deaths of 1,198 people, 128 of which

An Example of the Three Largest News Stories on July 13, 1916. (*The New York Times*)

were innocent American citizens. Following this tragedy, the United States continued to maintain its stance of neutrality in the Great War, but this event certainly led many Americans to have ill thoughts – and, in some cases, ill intentions – towards Germans.

For the nearly six million Germans that had immigrated to the United States between 1820 and the start of the First World War, the US became a very hostile place for them. For Americans that already had anti-German sentiments, this prejudice and hatred was spurred on and given permission to be openly expressed when even the highest executive power in the country, President Woodrow Wilson, spewed the same harmful rhetoric. In an awful speech he gave in 1919, he condemned all immigrants, but particularly 'German-Americans,' for hyphenating their nationality. He said, 'Any man who carries a hyphen about with him carries a dagger that he is ready to plunge into the vitals of this Republic whenever he gets ready.'[5] With this speech, he essentially told the American public that German immigrants could not be trusted, if only on the basis that many chose to hold onto their heritage – while also acknowledging their American citizenship – by hyphenating their nationality.

For Germans that did not want to be thrown into the catch-all bucket of supposedly disloyal and dishonest traitors, they changed the names of their German businesses, they cast away their native language, and some even changed their own names (names like 'Braun' and 'Schmidt' would be changed to 'Brown' and 'Smith,' forever altering their ancestral lineage). Schools and libraries removed German books from their shelves, with some libraries banning German texts altogether.

Cities and streets that had once been named Berlin were changed to more English-sounding names (e.g. Berlin Street in Cincinnati, Ohio, was renamed to Woodrow Street, in honor of President Woodrow Wilson[6]). Popular German foods like sauerkraut and frankfurters took on more Americanized-patriotic names like 'liberty cabbage' and 'liberty sausages,' respectively.

Some places throughout the country even made it illegal to speak any language other than English in public spaces.

The Justice Department went so far as to create a list of German immigrants that had not yet been naturalized and used this list to imprison thousands of Germans between the years of 1917 and 1918. The number of Germans interned varies drastically across historians though most agree the total number is somewhere between 4,000 and more than 11,000![7]

The internment of German Americans during the First World War is an often-untold story and one that many Americans are not familiar with. Americans are more familiar with the internment of Japanese Americans during the Second World War, but similar treatment inflicted upon German Americans during the First World War is oftentimes overlooked or entirely undisclosed.

In 1917, many German Americans were required to carry registration cards on their person at all times and were forced to report to the government if there were ever any changes made to their place of work or residence.[8] In worst case scenarios, these 'aliens' were interned at camps overseen by the United States Justice Department's Enemy Alien Control Program.

This horrific prejudice and racism culminated in the lynching of Robert Prager. Prager was a German-born man who emigrated to the United States in 1905 when he was only 17 years old. Prager quickly adopted American patriotism, even attempting to enlist in the US Navy when the United States joined the Great War. Due to medical reasons, he was not allowed to join the service and instead ended up in Collinsville, Illinois, where anti-German sentiment was at a particular high. In fact, in late 1917, the local paper, the *Collinsville Advertiser*, wrote in an article: 'Every German or Austrian in the United States, unless known by years of association to be absolutely loyal, should be treated as a potential spy.'[9]

It was here that Prager took a job as a laborer at the Dunk Brothers Coal and Coke Company, though his ultimate goal was to become a miner. Naturally, he attempted to join the United Mine Workers of America Local 1802, but was rejected, likely on account of his German origins. Upset by this rejection, Prager wrote a letter expressing his disagreement with the decision; he then publicly posted this letter near the local mines and saloons. In this letter, he declared his American loyalty and patriotism, stating: 'I am heart and soul for the good old USA. I am of German birth, of which accident I cannot help.'[10]

When the local miners left work that day – April 5, 1918 – and saw the letter, they became incensed. Later that evening, these miners – along with other local men that were intoxicated after spending the day in the saloons – showed up at Prager's place around 9:45 PM and forced him out of his house. They demanded he take off his shoes and forced him to walk along Collinsville's Main Street, barefoot, and with an American flag draped around his shoulders. An angry mob surrounded Prager until there were nearly 300 men present. Eventually, police officers apprehended Prager and placed him in the jail as a means of protection.[11] The angry mob pressured Mayor John H Siegel to allow them to search the jail for Prager and, once Siegel was under the impression that local law enforcement had removed Prager from the jail, he complied. What Siegel did not realize was that the police had not entirely removed Prager from the jail; rather, they had haphazardly hidden him in the building's drainage system. It didn't take long for a couple of the townsmen to locate Prager and drag him back out onto Main Street where the angry mob was waiting for him. Here, he was beaten, forced to sing patriotic songs, and made to walk barefoot on shattered beer bottles. Eventually, men in the crowd found rope and decided Prager should be lynched. And in front of a crowd of a couple hundred people, that is exactly what they did.[12] Later, when twelve men were placed on trial for Prager's murder, every last one of them was acquitted.

Now I'm sure you as the reader did not pick up a book about shark attacks and anticipate learning about German internment during the First World War, am I correct? I am certain you have just finished reading this section and are wondering what the relevance is to the 1916 shark attacks. The answer to that question is that the relevance is, in fact, quite stark.

Given the intense anti-German sentiment that not only existed amongst American citizens but was also expressed, allowed, and encouraged by American politicians at the highest levels of government, it is no surprise that an explanation for the 1916 shark attacks – which occurred at one of the most hostile times in the United States for German immigrants – would find a way to tie itself back to this hatred. German U-boats as a weapon of warfare became synonymous with the anti-German sentiment that was at an all-time high in America in 1916. Therefore, it is not a surprise that the German U-boat was used as a possible explanation for why sharks had swept in and murdered bathers along the Jersey coast.

Although written off as a ridiculous theory, the *New York Times* even published an article that reported that some people speculated that Charles Bruder had never encountered a shark after all; rather, it was alleged that he had been injured by the propellers of the *Deutschland* submarine.

Beyond the theory that the *Deutschland*'s propellers had caused injury to Bruder, the more widely spread allegation was that the carnage that German U-boats had left in their wake (i.e. the bodies of humans in the waters of the German war zones) had been eaten by sharks and that these sharks had then followed the German U-boats through the Eastern Atlantic, in search of their next meal. It was theorized by many that the excess of human bodies in the Atlantic because of sunken warships had created within sharks a thirst for human blood. As one anonymous citizen wrote to the *New York Times* in an article dated July 15, 1916:

> 'These sharks may have devoured human bodies in the waters of the German war zone and followed liners to this coast, or even followed the *Deutschland* herself, expecting the usual toll of drowning men, women and children. This would account for their boldness and their craving for human flesh.'[13]

Newspaper cartoonists even depicted images of German U-boats that resembled sharks, eating away at an image of the popular American government figure, Uncle Sam.

There was also a theory that the vibrations that the German U-boat engines and propellers emitted in the water had done something to the ocean's inhabitants. Was it possible that these electromagnetic currents coursing through the Atlantic Ocean had somehow caused one shark – or many sharks – to lose their minds and forego standard shark behavior?

While there is no scientific evidence to support any of the theories related to German U-boats and their role in the 1916 shark attacks, these were some of the most widely circulated theories of the time. Given the context and the spread of anti-German sentiment in the United States in the lead-up to American involvement in

A Political Cartoon Representing a German U-Boat as a Shark. (*The Day Book*)

the First World War, it is not surprising that theories like this took significant root.

A more reasonable theory behind the shark attacks, proposed by scientists, was that a temporary change in the gulf stream in the Summer of 1916 might have brought sharks closer to shore. There was documentation from sailors in 1916 in which they reported that they had seen more sharks that year than in years past, and in areas where they had never seen them before.

In a *New York Times* article dated July 18, 1916, the newspaper reported:

> 'GULF STREAM CURVE BLAMED FOR SHARKS. Incoming skippers report warm water nearer coast than ever before.
>
> Skippers of incoming vessels reported yesterday having sighted sharks in these waters and every seaman is either evolving or hoarding to an opinion as to why the man-eaters have made their appearance in force along the coast. Captain William Jensen of the United Fruit Liner Calamaries, that got in yesterday from Southern ports, voiced the opinion of many mariners when he said that the gulf stream had curved toward the coast. This opinion was corroborated by Captain Charles Satterlee of the Coast Guard Cutter Tampa…
>
> Captain Jensen reported that on Sunday night, when about two hundred miles from New York, he tested the temperature of the water and found it 74 degrees, an unusual one for the climate. He is certain that the gulf stream is flowing nearer the coast, and that from now until autumn, the Atlantic in this vicinity will be alive with sharks.'[14]

This article also mentioned the sighting of several schools of sharks; far more than the local and experienced fishermen had ever spotted in the ocean waters off the Jersey coast before.

We do know that the migration pattern of sharks is influenced by weather conditions, environmental changes, temperature, reproductive cycles, food supplies, and more. Dr Fernicola alleged that a possible change in the wind and water currents could explain the heavy presence of sharks along the Jersey coast that particular summer. He wrote in *Twelve Days of Terror* that the winds that summer were unusually, primarily northwest and that northern winds tend to carry Gulf Steam waters close to land.[15] This potential shift in the Gulf Stream would have shifted other marine life – life that sharks feed on – and this could have attracted or even forced the sharks to change course in a direction that brought them closer to the shore, closer to land, and therefore, closer to humans.

Another theory that may explain why sharks appeared to be so much closer to the shore in the Summer of 1916 than was typical was New York's sanitation and waste disposal practices, or lack thereof, during this period in history.

Prior to the 1930s, New York did not have any form of organized or consistent waste management system. In fact, New York City was rather synonymous with retched odors caused by the piles of trash that collected along the sides of the streets daily. There is an infamous photograph from the early 1900s in which a dead horse is laying in the street right next to a handful of children playing.

Unfortunately, this was not an uncommon sight. Robin Nagle, the author of *Picking Up: On the Streets and Behind the Trucks with Sanitation Workers of New York*, shared in an interview with *Collectors Weekly* that, in New York in the late 1800s, 'people were literally shin-high or knee-high in this muck that was a combination of street gunk, horse urine and manure, dead animals, food waste, and furniture crap.'[16]

It is no wonder that New York was plagued by so many diseases throughout much of its history (such as the 1916 polio epidemic). While other states established safe sanitation practices, New York continued to be 'infamously, disgustingly dirty,' according to this interview for *Collectors Weekly*.[17]

In an attempt to combat the tons a waste that New York citizens accumulated on a daily basis, people began utilizing the practice of ocean dumping in which they tossed their garbage – anything from milk bottles

Photograph of a Dead Horse in the New York City Streets Alongside Playing Children (Circa 1900–1903). (*Public Domain*)

to medical waste – into the water. In the 1880s, more than seventy-five percent of New York City's waste was discarded into the Atlantic Ocean. This is a staggering number![18] In the late 1800s, routine street cleaning was implemented, and ocean dumping waned, but the practice did not end completely. Believe it or not, but ocean dumping did not officially end in New York City until 1992 with the Ocean Dumping Ban Act of 1988. As recently as 1987 and 1988, so much medical waste (which included used syringes) washed up onto the beaches of New York and New Jersey that it forced the closure of several beaches as a matter of public safety. This 'syringe tide' incident cost the New Jersey tourism industry more than $1 billion (roughly $2.7 billion in today's money).[19]

Given the excessive amount of waste thrown into the Atlantic Ocean, particularly in the late-1800s and early-1900s, is it possible that this could account for why there were so many more sharks spotted along the Jersey Shore in the Summer of 1916? Author Michael Capuzzo theorized that this could be true. Matawan historian Kurtis Roinestad theorized further that, perhaps the medical waste thrown into the ocean – which could have included bloody bandages, test samples, and even body parts – gave the sharks a taste for human flesh; that one shark – or many – grew to love the taste of humans and would do anything to seek them out and eat them for dinner.

The theory that sharks acquired a taste for human flesh due to the possibility that they had consumed medical waste dumped into the ocean might be considered a bit of a stretch. But I certainly believe the very fact that there was excessive human waste and garbage dumped into the ocean in 1916 could have brought more sharks closer to the shore than had ever been seen before. Like we discussed in Chapter One, some sharks – specifically, tiger sharks – are quite literally referred to as the 'swimming trash can' of the ocean as they will eat virtually anything, including…well, trash.

Another theory that is supported by several modern-day marine biologists is that 1916 was, simply put, a 'shark year.' A 'shark year' is the concept that, for whatever reason (or even, a multitude of reasons), the presence of sharks fluctuates year by year due largely to a change in migration patterns. The result of this is that for some years, there are simply more sharks in the ocean. We see a similar phenomenon with several other types of animals and insects. For instance, the year 2023 saw its highest number of western monarch butterflies since the year 2000, with more than 335,000 western monarch butterflies spotted in California and Arizona alone.[20]

The 'shark year' theory was one that even experts, like Dr Frederic Lucas, Dr John Nichols, and Robert Murphy, suggested in the aftermath of the attacks. As the dust settled and experts and layman alike searched for theories to explain what had taken place that summer, Dr Lucas, Dr Nichols, and Murphy proposed that the closest solution they could come up with was that 1916 was indeed a 'shark year.'[21] Dr Nichols added though that, technically, 1915 had also been a 'shark year.' There had been several reports of an influx of sharks the prior year, but these stories had gone largely unnoticed as they were not accompanied by the horrific attacks that occurred in the Summer of 1916. Additionally, Dr Nichols – who may have been frustrated not by the influx of sharks but by the influx of the media in 1916 – made a quick quip that attention to the abundance of sharks in 1916 could be attributed to the mass media coverage of them. He said, 'Shark stories with a certain foundation and truth will always be forthcoming when reporters have been ordered to get them.'[22] (Dr Nichols was not immune to taking jabs at the media presence surrounding the 1916 shark attacks, once stating in the October 1916 issue of the *Brooklyn Museum Quarterly* that 'almost any shark more than five feet long must be a "man-eater," especially if it gets its photograph into the daily papers.').[23]

Finally, Dr Fernicola does make a brief mention in his book about the 1916 shark attacks that, for whatever reason, commercial fishermen were exceptionally guilty of dumping unused fish parts close to the shore in 1916.[24] Certainly, a plethora of fish carcasses could draw the attention of sharks on the hunt for easy prey. Unfortunately, there is not much documentation behind this theory other than some word-of-mouth accounts. But in the context of trying to determine how and why the 1916 shark attacks occurred, it is certainly food for thought (pun intended).

But perhaps the theory that carries the greatest amount of weight is also the simplest theory: More people equal more targets. And more targets equal more opportunity. In other words, the more people there are in the water, the more likely a shark attack is to occur. Between the polio epidemic pushing people out of the major cities and the heatwave that stretched across the entire Eastern region of the United States, there were more people at the beaches in the Summer of 1916 than ever before.

As mentioned in Chapter Two, sea bathing was still a relatively new recreational activity for Americans in 1916. While coastal resorts had been popular in Europe since the late-eighteenth century, this concept did not reach the United States until the late-nineteenth century. In fact, the first public beach – Revere Beach in Revere, Massachusetts – did not open until 1896 (1896 was apparently a big year for swimming as this year also marked the first time that swimming events were held at the Olympic Games in Athens). Swimming as a public leisure activity only began roughly two decades prior to the Summer of 1916 and its popularity grew in a slow trickle, culminating that fateful year.

Also, as we know from Chapter Two, public transportation, as well as the attainability of personal ownership of a motor vehicle, made travel easier for more Americans than ever before. 1916 saw a significant increase in tourism with the Beach Haven resort even planning to extend the length of the town boardwalk on account of the larger crowd of guests it was expecting that year.

Is it possible that the reason there were more shark attacks in the Summer of 1916 was simply because there were more people at the beach for said sharks to attack? As ichthyologist and former director of the International Shark Attack File, George Burgess, stated:

'As the worldwide human population continues to rise year after year, so does…interest in aquatic recreation. The number of shark attacks in any given year or region is highly influenced by the number of people entering the water.'[25]

Unfortunately, there is no simple or obvious answer to explain how and why the New Jersey beaches were hit with such a terrifying string of shark attacks in the Summer of 1916. Dr Nichols said it best when he was forced to retract previous statements he had made about the near-impossibility of a shark attack along the Jersey Shore. He conceded, 'It must be admitted that deaths from shark bite within a short radius of New York City would seem to be one of those unaccountable happenings that take place from time to time to the confounding of savants and justification of the wildest tradition.'[26]

# Chapter Eight

# The Rogue Shark Theory

*'It is quite within the realm of reasonable conjecture, indeed, that a single fish was at the bottom of the successive attacks at Beach Haven, Spring Lake, and Matawan.'*

*John Nichols and Robert Murphy*

*'…to try to make the facts as we know them conform to the 'rogue shark' theory is stretching sensationalism and credibility beyond reasonable limits.'*

*Richard Ellis*

How and why these attacks occurred is only one part of the mystery of the shark attacks of 1916. One of the other persistent conspiracies surrounding this series of attacks is whether they were conducted by one or multiple sharks. The fact that shark attacks along the Jersey coast ceased after Schleisser captured the great white shark in the Raritan Bay, referred to by experts as *the* 'Jersey man-eater,' lends credence to the theory that one, deranged animal perpetrated all four murders and the severe injury to another.

It *is* within the realm of possibility that a singular shark could have traveled the distance from where the first attack occurred at Beach Haven to where the last incident occurred in the Matawan Creek within the two-week time period in question. The total distance between Beach Haven and Matawan Creek is roughly eighty miles. From what we learned in Chapter One about great white sharks and their patterns, we know that a great white shark swims roughly fifty miles a day on average. Therefore, it is entirely possible that it was indeed a singular shark that swam the distance of more than eighty miles over the course of two weeks. Officials at the United States Bureau of Fisheries believed so at the time, stating that the lone shark 'probably had acquired a taste for human flesh as some four-footed beasts do…'[1]

Given this information, many people have theorized that this one shark may have been injured, had some sort of deformity, or was otherwise disoriented and that that is what caused it to go rogue. That, for whatever reason, this particular shark had a thirst for human blood and – in its sick and demented nature – would do anything and everything necessary to satiate that thirst. It is important to note that the term 'rogue' in relation to the 1916 shark attacks refers to a singular shark behaving in a way that was not common, but was instead, isolated in its aggression.

Experts, such as Dr Nichols and Murphy, were vocal in their belief that it had been one shark that had wreaked all that havoc on Jersey's peaceful shores. The two men stated in October 1916 in the *Brooklyn Museum Quarterly*, 'It is quite within the realm of reasonable conjecture, indeed, that a single fish was at the bottom of the successive attacks at Beach Haven, Spring Lake, and Matawan.'[2] In this article, they also continued to assert that the lone perpetrator had indeed been a great white shark, saying of the great white's abilities:

> 'The debated question as to whether a fish of this kind could actually bite through the bone of a man's leg is not particularly important, because it is evident that even a relatively small white shark, weighing two or three hundred pounds, might readily snap the largest human bones by a jerk of its body, after it had bitten through the flesh.'[3]

Quite a remarkable statement coming from the very men who, only a handful of months earlier, had agreed that a shark's jaw was not even strong enough to sever a singular human bone.

With the lack of knowledge that people had about sharks in 1916, I believe that it was simply easier to assume and accept that all this chaos had been perpetrated by a singular animal and that, once that singular animal had been captured and killed, the attack spree would end. In the years following the shark attacks, this theory of the lone shark was supported by various scientists and authors.

But while most modern scientists and experts of the 1916 shark attacks do agree that the 'rogue shark theory' is possible, they also agree that it is highly improbable. Marine biologist and shark expert Richard Ellis has said of this theory, '…to try to make the facts as we know them conform to the "rogue shark" theory is stretching sensationalism and credibility beyond reasonable limits.'[4]

One of the largest holes in the 'rogue shark theory' is the confusion regarding how a great white shark could end up in a creek. Again, as discussed in Chapter One, great white sharks are known to live in coastal, tropical ocean water. The idea that a great white shark would be swimming in a creek is not only unusual; it's highly unlikely. Tiger sharks (another aggressive species of shark that is second only to great whites in their propensity for attacking humans) also do not often venture into freshwater environments.

Bull sharks are one of the few exceptions to the typical saltwater environment of sharks. Bull sharks, which can often be mistaken in appearance for great white sharks, can tolerate swimming in freshwater regions such as rivers and creeks. Is it possible that it was actually a bull shark in the Matawan Creek that fateful day in July of 1916? Shark expert Richard Ellis certainly thinks so. Based on historical records that Ellis has reviewed, he has stated that it is his belief that the shark that Captain Cottrell supposedly caught at the mouth of Matawan Creek was indeed a bull shark and not a great white. Ellis has even gone so far as to allege that all the 1916 shark attacks – not just those that occurred in the Matawan Creek – were the doing of bull sharks. Further corroboration of the theory that the shark involved in at least the Matawan Creek attacks was not a great white shark comes from shark experts Ron and Valerie Taylor's book titled *Sharks: Silent Hunters of the Deep,* in which the details of Stanley Fisher's injuries were examined. This analysis revealed:

'When the wounds on Stanley Fisher's leg were examined and measured, it was found that the distance between teeth on opposite sides of the shark's jaw was about 12 inches. Comparisons seemed to indicate that a shark with jaws that size was probably longer than the shark witnesses reported seeing in the creek.'[5]

With this statement, the authors suggested that the labeling of the Matawan shark as a great white was incorrect and that the responsible shark was a different species entirely.

But we know that the shark that Schleisser captured with human bones and fifteen pounds of human flesh in its stomach was a great white shark (or, at least, we are to assume this information is accurate based on the findings of scientists in the early-1900s. It is, of course, worth noting and remembering that the identification of Schleisser's shark as a great white was made by the very same experts that once stated that sharks would not attack a human and, if they did, their jaws were not strong enough to cut through bone). If we are to assume that it was a bull shark that was in the Matawan Creek the day Lester Stillwell and Stanley Fisher were killed and Joseph Dunn was injured, the great white shark captured and killed in the Raritan Bay simply could not be the same creature.

This raises three possibilities: The first possibility is that the attacks in the Matawan Creek were perpetrated by a bull shark and the attacks in the Atlantic Ocean were perpetrated by one or more great white sharks.

The second possibility is that all the attacks were perpetrated by bull sharks and the human flesh and body parts found in the stomach of Schleisser's great white shark had nothing to do with the 1916 shark attacks at all. Based on the research we have analyzed related to the excessive amount of waste dumped into the Atlantic Ocean off New York (which included medical waste, like human flesh and body parts), is it possible that Schleisser's great white had simply consumed some of that? That the human remains found in the stomach of Schleisser's great white had not been the victim of a shark attack at all but, rather, the victim of an entirely unrelated medical issue?

The Rogue Shark Theory   105

The third possibility, of course, is that all the attacks – including those in the Matawan Creek – were perpetrated by great white sharks. In an exclusive conversation I had with Kurtis Roinestad, the town historian for Matawan, he shared on behalf of both him and the Matawan Historical Society that they are convinced without a shadow of a doubt that the shark involved in the Matawan incidents was, indeed, a great white shark. In data that is rarely examined in relation to the 1916 shark attacks, Roinestad and other local Matawan historians reviewed the tide charts for July 12, 1916 (the day of the Matawan attacks), and they found an anomaly: The tides in the Atlantic Ocean were so unusually high that day that the ocean water rushed through the mouth of the Matawan Creek and filled the creek up with water greater than was expected even at high tide. These tides pulled the water from the ocean into the creek and, along with it, changed the saline content of the creek to virtually mirror that of the Atlantic Ocean. When you consider this information, it is entirely possible that a great white shark could have entered and even tolerated the now saltwater environment that the Matawan Creek had to provide on this particular July day. Roinestad is of the mindset that the infamous quote by Nazi politician Joseph Goebbels holds true: 'A lie once told remains a lie, but a lie told a thousand times becomes the truth.' The more people that tell the 'lie' that the Matawan Creek was brackish, freshwater on that 1916 day and that a great white shark would never enter it on that account, the more this becomes the universally believed truth.

Further, Roinestad shared with me a conversation that he had with the son of Michael Dunn (the brother of Joseph Dunn, the only victim to survive the 1916 shark attacks), which shed some interesting perspective. Dunn's son said that when he and his father went together to see the 1975 film *Jaws* (which infamously depicts a ferocious great white shark), his dad turned to him and expressed that the shark in the movie – with its grey coloring on its backside and white coloring on its underbelly – looked exactly like the shark he had seen in the Matawan Creek that awful day.

Another valuable piece of evidence to suggest that the great white was the perpetrator for all the 1916 shark attacks is the very fact that

A Great White Shark Lifting Its Head Above Water. (*Uryadnikov Sergey | Adobe Stock*)

there were so many witnesses that observed the shark…because the shark's behavior allowed it to be seen. Great whites are one of only two species of sharks to regularly engage in a behavior called spyhopping (the other species is an oceanic whitetip shark which is not in the running of considerations for the 1916 perpetrator). Spyhopping is when a shark lifts its head above the water in order to take a look around. The purpose of this behavior is to assess their surroundings and hunt for prey. Most other sharks exclusively spot their prey from below the water, meaning that the killer may go undetected, if the attack is perpetrated by any shark other than a great white.

Numerous eyewitnesses involved in the 1916 attacks reported seeing the shark above water during the attack. This includes Michael Dunn who so vividly remembered the shark he had seen in the Matawan Creek that viewing the great white shark in *Jaws* so many years later brought back realistic and terrifying memories.

Not to confuse you further, but there has even been speculation that perhaps the Matawan attacks were perpetrated not by a bull shark, not by a great white shark, but by a sand bar shark. Though great whites and bull sharks can differ greatly in size, they have been confused with one another due to the similarity in their coloring. The sand bar shark, on the other hand, is smaller than both the great white and bull and has a brownish hue (this is where it gets its alternate name, the *brown shark*). But to the untrained eye, it is not outside of the realm of possibility that a bull shark and a sand bar shark could be confused with one another. The sand bar shark and the bull shark have more in common with one another insofar as coloring and size are concerned than the bull shark and great white do. Additional evidence to support the idea that the attacks may have been perpetrated by sand bar sharks is the fact that sand bar sharks are known to spend most of their time in shallow, coastal waters; shallow, coastal waters such as those mere feet from the shore. You will recall that horrified onlookers of Charles Vansant's killing witnessed his attacker follow him all the way to the shore; all the way until its belly touched the sand. This behavior would not necessarily be unusual for a sand bar shark that is comfortable swimming in such shallow conditions. Additionally, while not common, sand bar sharks have been found swimming in more inland, brackish environments, such as the Matawan Creek.

(Not to add more confusion to the argument but recent observations of great white sharks that have been tagged by marine biologists, such as Greg Skomal, have shown that they too will come 'within feet of the shoreline…almost touching the sand of the beach itself…there's no doubt…that they're moving within close proximity of humans, quite possibly routinely and they have been doing that for hundreds of years.'[6] Other studies, as recent as 2021, have shown that great white sharks spend nearly half of their time in water less than fifteen feet deep.[7] But I digress…)

It is confirmed that there were more sightings of sand bar sharks in the ocean in the Summer of 1916 than ever before. In fact, we know for certain that during the mass shark hunt that took place in the wake of the attacks, many of the sharks captured and killed were of the sand bar variety. We must remember though (as discussed in Chapter One) that sand bar sharks are not considered to be dangerous sea creatures. While there have been a few documented sand bar attacks on humans, they are incredibly rare. In fact, sand bar sharks are often considered to be one of the safest sharks for humans to swim with.[8] Nonetheless, even if the sand bar sharks did not directly inflict the damages on innocent people off the Jersey coast that historic summer, there is evidence to support the idea that simply the greater quantity of sand bar sharks in those waters could have led to a greater presence of great white sharks and bull sharks in the same waters. Great white sharks and bull sharks are known to feed on smaller sharks. Could simply the presence of more sand bar sharks have led to a greater presence of great whites and bulls which then led to the subsequent attacks on humans?[9]

Perhaps a more important question: Why did a string of attacks like the 1916 attacks not occur prior to 1916 nor have we seen one like it since? Does any one of the previous theories explain why it happened in 1916 (the U-boats; the change in the Gulf Stream; the greater presence of sharks in the Atlantic; or the heat wave, polio epidemic, and greater transportation ability that led more people to the beaches)? Or was it a combination of all the above? Those that tend to believe the theory of a deranged, rogue shark will hang their hats on the very fact that the world had and has never again seen another string of attacks such as the one in 1916. If these attacks had been conducted by multiple sharks (and even multiple different species of sharks), who's to say something like this could not occur again? Instead, if it was a singular shark that had a particularly devious thirst for human blood that exacted these murders, it makes far more sense why the 1916 shark attacks are a standalone case. But once again, the 'rogue shark theory' – while possible – is highly improbable and not accepted by many modern scientists today.

This is part of why the 1916 shark attacks are so perplexing. The events of 1916 are outside the realm of standard shark behavior. Extensive shark research has shown that sharks do not tend to prey on humans. Rather, if they do bite a human, it is most often a mistake. They engage in 'hit-and-run' behavior in which they take one bite, realize their mistake, and run. But the shark – or sharks – involved in the 1916 attacks did not do this. This shark – again, or sharks – returned to bite the victim over and over again. In the case of Charles Vansant, the shark was so insistent upon killing him that it followed him all the way to shore and then waited nearby momentarily as if it was hoping to watch Vansant bleed out. In Charles Bruder's attack, the shark attacked him so repeatedly that he removed both of Bruder's legs. For Lester Stillwell, the shark attacked him several times and then appeared to be feasting on his body at the bottom of the creek. The shark then appeared to be so territorial over Stillwell that, when Stanley Fisher attempted to retrieve the boy's body, the shark went after him. Eyewitnesses stated that they watched Fisher fight back against the sea monster that attacked him again and again. And finally, so intent on consuming human blood, the shark then took off 400 feet up the creek and caught Joseph Dunn's foot just before he escaped the water.

I fear there is no way to give a definitive conclusion about what exactly happened in 1916 because the reality of what occurred is so far outside our understanding of standard behavior. The world had never seen, and has continued to never see, another series of attacks quite like those along the Jersey Shore in the Summer of 1916.

The truth is that we will likely never know if it was a lone shark or multiple sharks responsible for the 1916 attacks. We will never know with absolute certainly which species – or multiple species – were involved in the attacks.

Beyond the fact that these incidents do not make any logical sense, we must also consider what sources we are analyzing in our attempts to apply logic. Consider all the factors at hand: these incidents occurred more than 100 years ago, and the documentation on these events is truly all over the place. Between initially being suppressed by the tourism industry that did not want the stories to get out to the eventual over sensationalism by media personnel jumping on the bandwagon and competing for who could put out the most salacious headline, it's hard to know where the line exists between fact and fiction. Consider how little coverage the initial attack received in the media; the horrific and witnessed killing of a vacationer was tucked away on the eighteenth page of the *New York Times*! Then, consider how just two weeks later, the *Newark Star-Eagle* falsely reported that Lester Stillwell's entire body had been found in the stomach of a captured shark. These two examples are polar opposites, and yet they demonstrate and represent a parallel in the media coverage at the time. Ethics in the media industry was not what it is today. This alone can make it incredibly difficult to find many of the primary sources of the time reliable.

Finally, we must remember the fact that human knowledge and understanding of sharks just simply was nowhere close to what it is now. For so many of those reporting on these incidents (as well as those witnessing the attacks and reporting what they had seen or heard to the media), this was the first time they had ever seen a shark. They simply did not know what they were talking about. Some had such a limited understanding of sharks that, even when looking at one face-to-face (such as the tens of thousands of people that showed up to view Schleisser's catch), they still did not believe that what they were looking at was indeed a shark. Instead, they spread stories that what they were viewing was a porpoise or even, perhaps, a sea turtle.

This is the unfortunate and overbearing flaw when researching history that occurred more than a century ago; and particularly, incidents in history in which the media had reason to either downplay or overplay the facts. We will always question and wonder what happened in 1916 to cause this unprecedented series of attacks…and if something like this could ever happen again…

# PART II

## Chapter Nine

## Shark Attacks 101

*'If you like to surf and you surf in this particular spot, the chances are high that you have been within 10 feet of a shark.'*

*Gavin Naylor*

When we analyze the 1916 shark attacks and the potential that something like this could happen again, I think it is most important to first examine what we know about shark behavior.

As discussed in Chapter One, there is research-backed evidence that supports the theory that, when a shark bites a human seemingly unprovoked, it is oftentimes a case of mistaken identity. Known as the Mistaken Identity Hypothesis (MIH), this theory alleges that, what was actually a human body, was initially perceived by a shark to be another large animal that they would more commonly consume (such as a seal). This behavior is called a 'hit-and-run' attack where the shark takes an initial bite but then, upon realizing its mistake, does not make any additional attacks and instead, 'runs' off. Further, because most sharks are generally color-blind or at least limited in their perception of colors, the color differences between a seal and a human in a wet suit is not obvious, leading to even more confusion for the shark as he seeks out his prey.

It is important to note though that, while this theory is widely accepted and does have evidence to suggest there may be factual basis to it, it is still an unproven theory. Critics of the MIH argue that this hypothesis exonerates the shark from malicious intent to harm or kill humans, and it is this sense of comfort that the hypothesis provides that makes it an easy one for humans to accept. Humans want to believe that sharks do not

A Comparison of What a Human on a Surfboard Versus a Seal Might Look Like to a Shark from Below. (*Jared James Lee*)

intend to harm them, and the MIH validates that for them. It is certainly worth noting in the context of the 1916 shark attacks that the shark (or sharks) involved in those events did not stop attacking after it was realized that their victim was not a marine animal. Rather, it attacked its human prey repeatedly, biting over and over again. In the case of Stanley Fisher, it would seem as though the shark only struck out when it appeared as though Fisher was taking the body of Lester Stillwell away from it. If this is true, the shark did not mistake Fisher for anything other than a human that was taking its meal away. The shark knew Fisher was a human and attacked him multiple times anyway.

Opposing research conducted by marine biologists suggests that sharks do not actually make a mistake when they bite humans; this is simply their way of exploring. Known as the Natural Exploration Hypothesis, marine biologists Eric Clua and Carl Meyer state that a shark's mouth is its only means of exploring and investigating its environment.[1] With its mouth at the forefront of its body, a shark does not have the choice like humans do to inspect things with its hands. It inspects them with the first thing that reaches the object: its mouth. If you have ever watched a nature documentary in which divers plunge into the ocean inside shark-proof cages as a means of better studying the surrounding sharks, you will have observed the sharks biting at the cage repeatedly. According to the Natural Exploration Hypothesis, this is how the shark explores and discovers this new and unusual contraption. It isn't necessarily that the shark is biting at the cage because it wants to break through the barrier and eat the human. Rather, the shark is biting at the cage as a way of investigating the unknown. Sharks have been spotted in the wild biting things like caves, boats, and even humans, as a means of exploration.

Human babies are very similar in this regard. Beginning as early as three to four months, human babies tend to gravitate towards bringing items to their mouths frequently. This technique – sometimes referred to as 'mouthing' – is a baby's way of examining an object and getting an idea of its size, shape, texture, and, of course, taste. As someone that has given birth to two babies in recent history, I can confirm that both of my twin daughters – though they are unique in so many ways – are similar in that they discover their world through their mouths. Everything they touch – whether it be a tasty cookie or a dirty rock – goes into their mouths immediately without a second thought. They're curious. They want to explore. And this is how they do it.

The significant difference between human babies and sharks using their mouths to explore is, of course, that a human baby's jaw strength is very unlikely to cause severe damage to the object it bites (though some breastfeeding mothers may disagree). Unfortunately for the objects which are being inspected by a shark, even the smallest of bites can be incredibly damaging and, in the worst-case scenario, fatal.

So how rare are shark attacks? As discussed in Chapter One, they are exceptionally rare. Statistically speaking, the chances of being attacked by a shark are one in 11.5 million and the chances of being killed by a shark are less than one in 264.1 million. The International Shark Attack

File (ISAF) was created to track exactly this information. The ISAF, which was founded in 1958, is 'the world's only scientifically documented, comprehensive database of all known shark attacks.'[2] Through their research, the ISAF has been able to document more than 6,800 known shark attacks that date all the way back to the 1500s. The oldest shark attack that they have investigated and documented comes from the year 1580 when a Portuguese sailor fell off his boat while traveling to India.[3] He was then seen being attacked and killed by a surprise shark.[4]

In an interview with former ISAF Director George Burgess, author William McKeever learned that the ISAF has a list of 200 different questions that they must ask and answer when investigating every shark attack that comes across their desks. This ensures that they capture all necessary details about the attack in order to make a proper assessment of how to categorize it. The following are the types of attack categories that the ISAF uses:

- **Unprovoked Bites:** This refers to an incident in which a live human is in a shark's natural habitat and does not provoke the shark in any way prior to an attack. These types of cases represent the majority of ISAF cases.
- **Provoked Bites:** This refers to an incident in which a human provokes the shark before it attacks. Examples include touching the shark, capturing the shark, attempting to feed the shark, and more.
- **Boat Bites:** This refers to an incident in which a shark bites a boat, whether provoked or unprovoked.
- **Scavenge:** This refers to an incident in which a shark feeds on a body that has already died for an unrelated reason.
- **Public Aquaria:** This refers to an incident in which a shark bites while not in its natural habitat.
- **Doubtful:** This refers to an incident in which the bites are determined to not be from a shark, but rather, another sea creature.
- **No Assignment Could Be Made:** This refers to an incident in which it is confirmed that a shark was involved, but, usually due to a lack of necessary details, they are unable to categorize the event.

- Finally, **Not Confirmed:** This refers to incidents in which they cannot determine if a shark was indeed involved or not.[5]

In a comprehensive worldwide shark attacks summary that the ISAF conducts on an annual basis, they found that of the 120 shark-human interactions they investigated for the year 2023, sixty-nine were unprovoked bites and twenty-two were provoked bites.[6] Fourteen of these 2023 incidents resulted in fatalities, ten of which were unprovoked.[7] This is an increase of fifty-five percent from the year prior. While this may feel staggering, the ISAF has assured that fluctuation and variation in these types of incidents is to be expected.

In the United States, there is an average of sixteen shark attacks per year with one fatality approximately every two years. In 2023, the United States continued to lead as the country with the most unprovoked bite incidents, representing fifty-two percent of all cases worldwide.[8] Florida, in particular, continued its trend in representing not only forty-four percent of the United States' total unprovoked bite incidents, but also twenty-three percent of unprovoked bites internationally.[9] More specifically, New Smyrna Beach, Florida, is the location of the most reported shark bites in the world, giving the county the nickname of 'the world's shark-bite capital.' In 2019 alone, there were three shark bite incidents at this beach within twenty-four hours of each other! Gavin Naylor, the director of the Florida Program for Shark Research at the Florida Museum of Natural History, was quoted as saying of this particular beach, 'If you like to surf and you surf in this particular spot, the chances are high that you have been within 10 feet of a shark.'[10]

Unprovoked bite incidents for 2023 were also reported in California (one of which was fatal), North and South Carolinas, New York, and New Jersey.

Australia had the highest number of fatal shark attacks in the world in 2023 with four of the fifteen shark incidents resulting in death.[11]

While all of this can sound scary (because it is), it is important to once again recognize how rare shark attacks are. Consider the fact that the odds of being struck by lightning are of a higher probability than being attacked by a shark. And of the more than 500 different species of sharks that inhabit the deep blue, only a small handful are dangerous.

Believe it or not, but the odds of being killed by a hippopotamus are more probable than being killed by a shark. While sharks kill, on average, one human every two years, hippos kill upwards of 500 people every single year in Africa![12] This makes them the deadliest large animal in the world. Hippos are more aggressive than most people realize, and they have more than one way they can easily kill humans: Not only do they bite people with teeth sharp enough to tear flesh and crush bones, but they also sit on top of people with their over 6,000-pound weight!

There are several other animals more likely to kill you than a shark. Insects like mosquitos and bees kill humans every year. Mosquitoes are responsible for more deaths than any other creature on the planet. This is because malaria, a disease caused by parasites (i.e. transmitted from an infected mosquito to a human), kills roughly 400,000 people every year. An additional 40,000 deaths each year are attributed to an infection called dengue, also transmitted by mosquitoes.[13] Bees (as well as hornets and wasps) are responsible for almost 500 deaths annually in the United States alone for those that are allergic to their sting.

Even man's best friend, dogs, account for somewhere between thirty and fifty deaths every year due to the rabies that they can pass along with their bite.

Snakes, spiders, cows, and even horses are all responsible for more annual human deaths than have ever been attributed to sharks.

Perhaps to put you at additional ease, you should know that there are several ways that one can help reduce the odds of being attacked by a shark. Because the exact cause of shark attacks cannot be consistently determined, it is difficult to also determine what exactly one must do to ensure they are not attacked by a shark. But experts have provided insight into the best ways to at least reduce the risk of falling prey to an unpredictable shark:

- It is suggested that you swim in groups as opposed to swimming in an isolated manner. Historically, sharks are more likely to attack an individual swimming alone than one in a group of other swimmers.
- Stay close to the shore. This suggestion is not made because swimming close to the shore makes it less likely that a shark will attack. In fact, most shark attacks occur within ten feet of the shore. Rather, this suggestion is made so that, if you are attacked by a shark, the closer you are to the shore, the closer you are to help and a hopeful escape.
- Do not go swimming at dawn or at dusk. Like many humans, sharks are most likely to eat at 'breakfast time' and at 'dinner time.' This is when they are most likely to be looking for a meal.
- Speaking of looking for a meal, do not swim in or around schools of fish. These are all prey for sharks and, if you happen to be amid a school of fish, you may become prey as well.
- Finally, do not wear shiny jewelry in the water. The reflection of the water on the jewelry can resemble the scales of a fish which may, once again, become prey to a hungry shark.

We also know of several activities that are particularly attractive to sharks. These can include the following:

- Irregular sounds (think of laughing along with friends or perhaps calling out after a dog).
- Producing blood. Sharks' sense of smell is incredibly strong. Contrary to popular belief, sharks are not particularly attracted to human blood. But they can sense it, and it is not outside the realm of possibility that they may be drawn to it. Many scientists and researchers have conducted experiments to prove that this is not true, but even the ISAF suggests on their website that people actively menstruating should avoid swimming in open water to reduce one's odds of being attacked by a shark.[14]

- Swimming with dogs. The very nature of the way in which dogs paddle and pedal in the water creates a particularly attractive motion for sharks.
- Strong movements, such as the strokes and strides of a strong swimmer.

In relation to the victims of the 1916 shark attacks, it is important to recognize potential vulnerabilities that may have placed those specific individuals at higher risk.

For one, as has been discussed previously, the New Jersey beaches were flooded with people in a way they had never been before. As the human population continues to grow, the odds of encountering a shark while visiting its habitat becomes greater. In fact, there has been research that has studied the proven parallels between a greater number of people on the beach coinciding with a greater number of reported shark attacks.[15] This significant increase in human activity in the water in 1916, which would have included irregular sounds and lots of strong movements, could have attracted the shark (or sharks) along the New Jersey coastline.

As we now know, isolation is also a big factor in many known shark attacks. Vansant and Bruder were both swimming alone at the time of their attacks. In a study conducted by George Burgess specific to great white sharks, he found that, in eighty-five percent of attacks, there were no other humans within ten feet of the victim.[16]

Further, Vansant had a dog with him, which could have created even more of an attraction for a shark. It is also possible that the group of boys accompanying Lester Stillwell to the creek had a dog with them. Could that dog have likewise been an extra attraction for a lurking sea monster?

It was known by many that Bruder was a strong swimmer. Could his strong and isolated movements have attracted a nearby shark? Vansant, too, received cheers from onlookers on the beach for his quick and powerful strides through the water.

Irregular sounds could have also attracted the 1916 shark (or sharks). Irregular sounds such as Vansant calling out after the dog that had left him, or the irregular sounds of Stillwell playing with his friends in the creek, and Dunn playing with his brother and friend in the water.

Finally, if it is true that blood attracts sharks, we must consider how bloodied and frenzied the creek water was when Fisher first entered it in his efforts to locate Stillwell. Witnesses reported seeing blood in the creek. They assumed that it belonged to Stillwell either having an epileptic seizure and bumping his head or, in the worst-case scenario, having been attacked and swallowed up by a preying shark. The presence of Stillwell's blood accompanied by the sudden and frantic movements Fisher – and others – made in their search for Stillwell could certainly have provided additional attraction for the shark.

| Higher Risk Activities | Vansant | Bruder | Stillwell | Fisher | Dunn |
|---|---|---|---|---|---|
| Isolation | Yes | Yes | | | |
| Irregular Sounds | Yes | | Yes | Yes | Yes |
| Producing Blood | | | | Yes | |
| Swimming with Dogs | Yes | | Possibly | | |
| Strong Movements | Yes | Yes | Possibly | Likely | Possibly |

Certainly, none of this is to blame the 1916 victims. The events of 1916 are horrific and tragic and something that, even if we had had more information at the time, may still have been unavoidable. The shark (or sharks) involved in the 1916 attacks was unpredictable and logic cannot necessarily be applied to make sense of it. But now that we have history and science and perspective on our side, it is worth looking at any factors that may have contributed to that summer's tragedies and, at a minimum, analyze what we can do to avoid a series of shark attacks like that occurring ever again.

Interestingly, something like the 1916 shark attack frenzy almost did happen again. In 2001, a series of shark attacks, so sensationalized that it became known as the 'Summer of the Shark,' occurred in various places throughout the United States. This series of attacks began shortly after the Fourth of July holiday; similar timing to that of the 1916 shark attacks.

The first attack occurred on July 6, 2001, when an 8-year-old boy named Jessie Arbogast was attacked by a seven-foot-long bull shark while standing in Langdon Beach in Pensacola, Florida. After Arbogast was rescued from the water, his uncle returned to the ocean to capture the attacking shark and kill it. They found Arbogast's arm inside the mouth of the shark which doctors were miraculously able to reattach to his body. The extent of his injuries was severe though. His arm was never the same, his right leg was destroyed, and the massive amount of blood loss he suffered resulted in brain damage. To this day, Arbogast remains in a home for special needs adults due to the injuries inflicted upon him by the shark that day.[17]

Not long after this incident, on July 15th, only six miles from where Arbogast had been attacked, someone else was attacked by a shark. In early-September, two more attacks (both fatal) occurred, one in North Carolina and the other in Virgina.

There was a hyper-fixation on the attacks by the media that summer with *Time Magazine* dubbing this period as the 'Summer of the Shark.'

News coverage followed the stories twenty-four hours a day. Helicopters hovered over oceans where swarms of sharks could be seen circling. The media warned the public to stay away from the beaches amid what they called a 'shark epidemic.' In an article written by Melanie Cooke for *The Guardian* dated September 4, 2001, she wrote:

> 'The mere sight of a dorsal fin has been enough to get a full airing on national network news and television crews have hired helicopters by the dozen in their hunt for big-fish footage. Aerial shots of sharks congregating off the Florida coast, in what look like huge super-predator conventions, have contributed to an atmosphere of near national emergency. Mothers have kept their children close by them, while full-grown men have decided that paddling is the better part of valor, and the US Coastguard has been running air patrols over the beaches in the look out for the enemy.'[18]

Minor encounters with sharks that would typically have gone unreported now filled the pages of newspapers and magazines as well as contributed to the constant barrage of shark attack coverage on the television. George Burgess, the then-Director of the ISAF, stated that, in a normal year, he handled about 300 inquiries (interviews, media statements, and so forth) related to sharks. But, in the months of July, August, and September of 2001, he was interviewed more than 900 times![19] Burgess said of this: 'I had more calls in those three months than I had in the previous three years combined.'[20]

And then, it all came to a screeching halt. On September 11, 2001, the United States experienced the deadliest terrorist attack in world history. Nearly 3,000 people were killed when the Islamist terrorist group al-Qaeda hijacked commercial airliners and crashed them into the Twin Towers of the World Trade Center in New York City, New York, and the Pentagon in Washington, DC.

These attacks, commonly referred to as 9/11, took over news stories for the foreseeable future, and the 'Summer of the Shark' was forgotten.

Although the media would have the public thinking otherwise, shark attacks had actually decreased in the year 2001. 2001 saw an annual total of seventy-six unprovoked attacks, a decline from the eighty-five that had been recorded the previous year. Additionally, while 2000 saw twelve fatalities, 2001 saw only five.[21]

Unfortunately, that is the nature of headlines when they are delivered by a source that we deem to be credible: Once you see a headline, you tend to trust it. As the American Psychological Association has found, the more emotionally driven misinformation is, the more likely we are to believe it. So, headlines and false information that evokes emotions such as fear are more likely to be believed and taken as fact.[22] This is precisely what happened with the 'Summer of the Shark.'

According to investigative journalist John Stossel, who extensively investigated this period, 2001 was a slow year for news (prior to 9/11, of course) and the media needed something to run with. According to Stossel, although there were about as many shark attacks in 2001 as there were in 1995 and 2000, 1995 was the year of the OJ Simpson trial and 2000 was an election year.[23] Therefore, news cycles were dedicated to other important events. Much like how the First World War took over headlines in late-1916 and into 1917 and caused any trace of the 1916 shark attacks to disappear from the papers.

The 2001 Summer of the Shark certainly was not an isolated series of events. The world has experienced several other freak shark attack sprees dating back to the 1950s, and yet, none of them quite replicate what America experienced in 1916.

Chapter Ten

# What Modern-Day Shark Attacks Can Tell Us About 1916

*'[The shark attacks of 1916] continues to stand out. Because of the sheer number of attacks in such ferocity and in such sequence that 100 years have passed and we haven't seen this type of behavior from a shark or sharks again, even on a worldwide basis.'*

*Richard G Fernicola*

No shark attacks have ever replicated those of the 1916 shark attacks. And yet, it is important for us to look at other documented attack sprees to truly understand just how unique and irreproducible the events of 1916 continue to be to this day.

### KwaZulu-Natal, South Africa
### (December 1957–April 1958)

Stretching a four-month span between December 18, 1957, and April 5, 1958, there were nine shark attacks – six of which were fatal – off the coast of KwaZulu-Natal, South Africa. This series of shark attacks were so dark and disquieting that they are often referred to as 'Black December.'

The first attack occurred in Karridene on December 18, 1957, and involved a 16-year-old boy named Robert Wherley. While surfing in the ocean, a shark attacked Wherley, leaving the young boy without a left leg below the knee and severe damage to the rest of the leg above. Fortunately, this attack was not fatal. Given the frequency of shark attacks in South Africa (the country experiences an average of six shark attacks per year), this incident did not cause significant alarm.[1]

The next attack occurred only two days later, on December 20th, in Uvongo, when 15-year-old Allan Green was standing in the ocean waters. From this position, a shark attacked him, inflicting multiple bites and enough damage that Green passed away as a result.[2]

And then, only three days later on December 23rd, this time in Margate, a shark killed another young man, 23-year-old Vernon James Barry, who had just arrived in the area for a five-day vacation.[3] While floating in the water, Barry was attacked so viciously by a surprise shark that his right arm was broken and stripped of its flesh, his left hand was removed completely, and other parts of his body (like his abdomen and thigh) were bitten severely.[4]

On December 26th in Port Edward, 20-year-old Donald Webster received non-fatal but serious injuries to his head and neck after a shark attacked him suddenly.

Then, on December 30th, again in Margate, a shark attacked its first female victim, 14-year-old Julia Painting. While standing in the water, Painting was attacked by a shark, severing her left arm, biting her torso, and causing injury to other parts of her body.[5] Painting survived.

The next attack is quite vague. The South Africa Shark Attack File does not have an exact date, age, or name for the next victim. Rather, it simply states that a 'young Zulu male' was killed by a shark while out fishing in the MaKakatana River.[6]

The year 1957 ended on this harrowing note with the brutal attack of six people, two of which were left dead. The following year would not be much kinder…

The new year picked up right away with its first shark attack occurring on January 4, 1958, when 42-year-old Derryck Garth Prinsloo was attacked by a shark while he was standing in the water in Scottburgh. The shark quite literally tore the lower half of his body off, severing the femoral artery, and causing him to bleed to death.[7]

It appeared as though the ravaged sharks took a momentary break; South Africa did not see another attack until almost exactly three months later. On April 3rd, 29-year-old Nicholaas Badenhorst was fatally attacked by a shark while swimming in Port Edward, receiving severe bites to his abdomen and legs.[8]

Just two days later, the series of horrifying shark attacks ended with one final death. On April 5th, 28-year-old Fay Jones Bester was killed by a shark while she was surfing in Uvongo.[9] No further details about the extent of her injuries are publicly available.

Of the three shark attacks to occur in the new year, every single one of them was fatal.

Much like the response by vacationers during the 1916 shark attacks, many fled the area, causing a devastating decline in the local tourism economy. Likewise similar to the 1916 shark attacks, officials had safety nets placed along the beaches in an attempt to keep the sharks out, but these nets were soon destroyed by the ocean's strong waves. And finally, similar once again to the response to the 1916 shark attacks, officials deployed explosives in the waters to kill the sharks. The explosives in this case were depth charges, a weapon of warfare that resembles a canister filled with explosives and meant to be used against enemy submarines. They dropped these depth charges into the water – much like those in Matawan dropped dynamites into the creek – but, for South Africa, this produced a counterproductive effect. Due to the number of fish that died because of the depth charge explosions, the area saw an influx in sharks who came to feast on the dead marine life.

When analyzing data from 1957 and 1958, there are several factors – referred to by experts as a 'perfect storm' – that may have contributed to this spree of shark attacks in South Africa. These factors included an increase in commercial whaling in the region which could have increased the number of sharks present. When a whale carcass is left in the water, it attracts sharks to the area to feed. It is reported that whaling ships were indeed operating in the KwaZulu-Natal area of South Africa in December of 1957.[10]

1957 also saw a significant increase in the number of people swimming in the KwaZulu-Natal providence oceans. Due to recent developments in the local resort town, a greater number of visitors traveled to the area and frequented its waters during this time. As we know, more people in the waters naturally leads to more shark attacks.

As a result of the 1957–1958 South Africa shark attack spree, the KwaZulu-Natal Sharks Board was established with their primary objective being the implementation of shark nets and drum lines along various beaches to keep ocean-goers safe.[11] To this day, KwaZulu-Natal ensures safety from sharks via these controversial and harmful methods, but more on this in Chapter Twelve.

## New Jersey
## (August 1960)

New Jersey experienced its own second wave of shark attacks in 1960. The first of these attacks occurred in Sea Girt, a beautiful beach town off the Jersey coast. Sea Girt is roughly two miles south of Spring Lake where Charles Bruder, the second of the 1916 shark attack victims, was killed.

On August 21, 1960, a 24-year-old man named John Brodeur was visiting his fiancée in the resort town when their afternoon took a dark turn. While swimming in the ocean only twenty-five feet from shore, Brodeur let out a cry, 'I'm bitten!'[12] His fiancée reported seeing the water turn red with blood and began slapping at the waves to distract the monster that had attacked her betrothed. Once Brodeur made it to the shore, he was assisted by his fiancée's parents (who had also made the day trip to visit their daughter), as well as an ex-Marine named Norman Porter, who immediately ripped off his belt and tied it around Brodeur's injured leg to stop the bleeding.

Upon applying the tourniquet, those onsite were able to better assess the damage. And the damage was bad. Brodeur's leg bone could be seen through his shredded flesh! When he reached Fitkin Hospital, the medical team there observed that:

'He had a huge jagged laceration extending through his thigh as well as his calf on his right leg. The tibia and fibular were both exposed, as were the major blood vessels, some of which were severed. Muscle tissue was shredded, and a wedge of bone was completely missing.'[13]

Brodeur's right leg would have to be amputated, and he lived the remainder of his life with a prosthetic leg.

Only one day later, on August 22nd, in Seaside Park (roughly fifteen miles south of Sea Girt), 14-year-old Thomas McDonald was playing with his friends in the water only a few yards away from shore.[14] Not long after 3:00 that afternoon, McDonald shouted out that he had been bitten by a shark. He made his way to land, and, upon examination, it was found that he had a laceration to his knee. Local doctors, however, were not convinced that the laceration was the result of a shark bite. Although McDonald's experience has been categorized officially in the New Jersey Shark Attack File, it still has not been definitively determined if he did indeed encounter a shark that day. The response to his injury was very similar to the response seen by the tourism industry in 1916. As beaches restricted access and hotels began worrying about their pocketbooks, McDonald's experience was downplayed. It was written off by officials as the fabrications of a teenager's mind that was already filled with concern about a news story he had read the day prior about the shark attack in Sea Girt.[15]

Then, on August 30th, the New Jersey coastline experienced the last in a small series of shark attacks in 1960. A 25-year-old man named Richard Chung was training to compete in a long-distance swimming competition. He swam about a half a mile off the coast of Ocean City and was in waters that were about thirty feet deep when he spotted what he perceived to be 'boiling waters.'[16] Before he could determine what exactly he was seeing, he was hit in the right calf. He looked down at his leg and saw a shark attached to it! As he beat at the shark, he reported seeing three more dorsal fins heading straight toward him.[17] All of the commotion captured the attention of local lifeguards who immediately set out in a rescue boat for Chung. The lifeguards tied a tourniquet around Chung's wounded leg once he was onboard, and they raced him to Shore Memorial Hospital. Amazingly, despite the fact that Chung's flesh and muscles had been torn with an injury down to the bone *and* despite the fact that Chung had visually seen his attacker, the onsite doctors did not believe his injuries were the result of a shark. Rather, they stated the massive wounds were 'an injury of some sort of fish.'[18] It is very interesting how the Jersey Shore appeared to replicate its initial response to the 1916 attacks a little more than forty years later.

## Sharm el-Sheikh, Egypt (December 2010)

The world would not see another series of shark attacks until 2010 when Sharm el-Sheikh, Egypt experienced what I would consider to be its own version of a 'Black December.' In a singular week in December of 2010, five people were attacked by sharks, one of which was fatal.

Sharm el-Sheikh is a beautiful resort town in Egypt, situated between Sinai Peninsula and the Red Sea. Sharm el-Sheikh is a very popular tourist location with millions of visitors every year.

The shark attacks began on December 1, 2010, in the Red Sea just outside of a beach resort in Sharm el-Sheikh. Four of the five people that eventually encountered a shark during this string of attacks would be injured on this singular day and within just minutes of one another. One victim was 48-year-old Olga Martsinko who was floating in the water when her left hand touched what she thought was a dolphin. She quickly learned, however, that that was not the case. What she had believed was a dolphin was actually a shark that attacked her so ferociously that she lost her hand and large chunks of her leg and buttocks to the beast.[19] I have seen the pictures of Martsinko's rescue and the state of her bloody body is truly upsetting.

Within minutes of the attack on Martsinko, 70-year-old Yludmila Stolyarova was also attacked. She reported that the shark had bitten off her arm but that she was able to push the shark off and swim to shore.

However, in her pursuit of safety, the shark followed her and bit off her leg.[20]

With witnesses alert to the horror taking place just before their eyes, the shark attacked again. This time, it attacked a 44-year-old man named Yevgeniy Trishkin whose severe leg injuries later required amputation.[21] Just moments later, the shark attacked 46-year-old Viktor Koliy who, while certainly injured, fortunately did not lose a limb to the ravenous monster.[22]

The Red Sea, which gets its name because of the way seasonal algae causes the color of the water to shift from blue-green to reddish-brown, was red for an entirely different reason that day. The Red Sea was full of blood. A bartender at a nearby al-Bahr beach restaurant named Mohamed Rashad reported that indeed, 'the sea went red.'[23]

Similar to the approach taken by officials during the 1916 shark attacks, Egyptian officials closed down the beaches and, as a result, the local tourism industry took a sharp decline. A large-scale hunt was engaged to capture the singular shark believed to be responsible for the numerous attacks. And not long after, a couple of sharks were indeed captured and identified as the likely culprits.

Given the successful captures, officials decided to reopen the beaches on December 4th, with the notion that things were once again safe for the many locals and tourists that had stopped funding the tourism economy in the interim.

Unfortunately, just one day later, on December 5th, a shark attacked once again. And this attack was fatal. A 71-year-old woman named Renate Seiffert, who was vacationing at the resort, was out snorkeling when a shark attacked her furiously. The extent of her injuries was so severe that the Global Shark Attack File later recorded them as simply 'not survivable.'[24] She was pronounced dead not long after she made it to the shore; it is believed that the ultimate cause of her death was either a heart attack or shock from the unfathomable pain and horror.

Following this incident, Egypt's Chamber of Diving and Watersports issued a mass warning across Sharm el-Sheikh to stop all snorkeling activities and to clear the waters right away.[25]

It appeared that, in their attempt to return to normalcy and to continue raking in money from tourists, officials had called for a return to the waters far too soon. Fortunately for all, Seiffert's horrific death marked the end of this spree of shark attacks along Sharm el-Sheikh.

But why did they occur in the first place? It is anyone's best guess. Even the leading shark experts that were called in to evaluate the cause, which included George Burgess, were rather dumbfounded by this string of attacks. Ultimately, officials determined that it could be a number of factors, saying in a statement on December 9th that it could have been:

'One or more incidents of illegal dumping of animal carcasses in nearby waters; depletion of natural prey in the area caused by overfishing; localized feeding of reef fish and/or sharks by swimmers, snorkelers and some divers; and unusually high water temperatures in Sharm El Sheikh.'[26]

## The Carolinas
## (May–July 2015)

The final string of shark attacks that we must examine are those that occurred in 2015 in the Carolinas. Over the span of just two months, eleven people were attacked by sharks in North and South Carolina. To this day, 2015 remains the year with the highest number of shark attacks recorded since the ISAF first began documenting such encounters. The Carolinas were the location with the second greatest number of shark attacks that year (Florida, as always, was in first place).

It all started on May 15, 2015, when a 30-year-old man was bitten by a shark in South Carolina off Sullivan's Island. The man was taken to a local hospital where he was treated with stitches for his non-life-threatening injuries. It was reported by eyewitnesses that the shark involved in the attack did not exhibit any aggressive behaviors following the singular attack.[27]

Less than a month later, on June 11th, a 13-year-old girl was bitten by a shark while riding on a boogie board at Ocean Isle Beach in North Carolina (which shares the same coastline as the location of the previous attack). The young girl stated that the shark bit both her foot and her boogie board but that she was able to kick off the shark who did not retaliate. She only sustained minor lacerations to her foot.[28]

On June 15th, only thirty miles up shore in Oak Island, North Carolina, a shark attacked a 12-year-old girl and a 16-year-old boy in less than ninety minutes of one another. These bites would cause significant injury. The young girl lost her left arm from the elbow down and sustained serious tissue injury to her leg. The young boy lost his left arm from the shoulder down.[29]

Despite the significant influx in serious shark attacks in the region, town officials did not issue widespread warnings nor mandate that the beaches be cleared of swimmers.[30]

Further down the coastline on Saint Helena Island, South Carolina, another shark attack occurred. On June 23rd, a 9-year-old boy was bitten by a shark while swimming in the ocean. The young boy was taken to the hospital to be treated for minor injuries.

The following day, on June 24th, an 8-year-old boy was swimming in knee-deep waters in Surf City, North Carolina, when he was bitten by a shark that caused minor injuries to his leg, heel, and ankle.[31] Once again, the town stated that it had no plans to warn beachgoers about the shark bites with the town manager, Larry Bergman, stating that he did not consider the attacks to be a 'big hazard' or an 'imminent danger.'[32]

Two days later, on June 26th, a 47-year-old man was bitten on his right leg and back while swimming at Avon Beach on Hatteras Island, North Carolina. Apparently, he was in the water with children when he spotted a shark. He yelled out a warning but, amid his attempts to save others, the man sustained non-threatening injuries from the sea creature.[33] Also on June 26th, on Hunting Island (which is in the same general vicinity as Saint Helena Island), a 43-year-old man was bitten by a small shark. The man reported seeing a shark swimming toward him and, while calling out a warning to others, was bitten by a different shark that he had not seen coming. He was taken to the hospital in stable condition.[34]

The very next day, on June 27th, in the town of Waves (which is on the same island as the prior day's first attack), an 18-year-old man was bitten by a shark in his right calf, buttocks, and hands. Despite swimming with friends, the young man was the only one injured. He was airlifted to the hospital in critical condition.[35]

On June 30th, a 12-year-old boy was bitten by a shark while standing in shallow waters off the Isle of Palms in South Carolina. The bite marks were not deep, and his injuries were non-life threatening.[36]

Days later, on July 1st, a 68-year-old man was swimming on Ocracoke Island, North Carolina, when he was taken under the water by a surprise shark. The shark bit him multiple times, injuring his ribcage, legs, and hands. This man, too, was airlifted to the hospital, but appeared to be in stable condition. One eyewitness reported seeing a trail of blood leading from the water to the shore but, in nearly the same breath, admitted that he intended to return to swimming in the ocean water himself.[37]

This would mark the end of the 2015 shark attacks in the Carolinas, none of which resulted in a fatality. And while the number of shark attacks that occurred that year may be shocking to the layman, for shark experts like George Burgess, the increase in attacks was expected. The Carolinas are certainly not immune to shark attacks (the region sees an average of six shark attacks per year[38]), but in order to nearly double this number in a two-month period, a sort of 'perfect storm' needed to exist. And this is exactly what Burgess claimed was the case.

The 2015–2016 El Niño was one of the strongest El Niño climate changes seen in over 100 years. This event alone led to significantly warmer waters, a factor that can shift sharks' migration patterns. El Niño can also be accompanied by drought, which was certainly seen in 2015. According to Burgess, 'drought conditions reduce the amount of freshwater making it to the sea, which creates an environment along the shore where higher salt levels attract more fish and sharks.'[39] Additionally, the increased human population at the beaches that summer (particularly those taking advantage of warmer water conditions) will always equal greater exposure to sharks and potential subsequent attacks.

To summarize the factors contributing to the 2015 Carolinas attacks, Burgess said, 'It's a perfect storm of environmental and biological variables as well as human activity.'[40]

It is important to study shark attacks in more modern history to properly evaluate how they both resemble and differ from those in 1916. When we speculate on what factors may have contributed to an increase of sharks in the New Jersey waters in 1916, we see many of the same factors in future shark attack strings.

Even still, nothing has quite replicated the 1916 shark attacks. No future shark attack sprees have garnered the same amount of attention and sensationalism as the Jersey shark attacks of 1916. I believe this is for a number of reasons.

For one, shark attacks in 1916 were novel. Up to this point, many people – including the nation's leading shark experts – did not believe sharks to be aggressive animals. Rather, they were believed to be timid, with no interest in approaching humans, and without the capability to even sever a human bone. This alone makes the 1916 shark attacks stand out amongst any other series of shark attacks. It was the first time that the world was forced to recognize the capabilities of sharks. It was also the first time in history that man was forced to recognize that an ancient fear of sharks that had existed since the days of Greek mythology had merit and was more than just myths and legends.

I also believe the reason why the 1916 shark attacks received unparalleled attention and sensationalism is because the 1916 shark attacks were, for lack of a better word, absurd. They do not make sense. When looking at the documented shark attacks of the last century, we can see how the shark (or sharks) in those events did not mirror those of the shark (or sharks) involved in the 1916 attacks. Having just looked at examples of shark attacks between the years 1957 and 2015, there were very few incidents in which a shark returned to take multiple bites of its human prey. In fact, in most of these cases, the human involved in the incident was not viewed as prey at all. Rather, these more modern encounters demonstrate an almost-inevitable truth that exists when a lot of humans are in the water with a lot of sharks: Bites are going to happen. But that is all they are: innocent bites, and then the shark moves on. The shark does not attack repeatedly and viciously, it does not linger nearby and wait for the human to bleed out, and it does not feast on the body of its human meal; all things that were present in the 1916 attacks.

Dr Fernicola said it best in an interview for the *Asbury Park Press* in 2017 when he reflected on the 1916 attacks: 'It continues to stand out. Because of the sheer number of attacks in such ferocity and in such sequence that 100 years have passed and we haven't seen this type of behavior from a shark or sharks again, even on a worldwide basis.'[41]

Much can be learned from the 1916 shark attacks, subsequent shark attack research, and statistics related to shark encounters. Considering all this information, and as we are just about to head into an in-depth look at the current state of sharks worldwide, I think it is important for each of us to reflect on small actions we can take every day.

What can we do as sea bathers to reduce our risk of being attacked by sharks? What can we do as leaders in the tourism industry to establish better ethics and ensure we are not putting the value of money over the value of human lives? What can we do as members of the government to make sure we are aiding to the best of our abilities those that we have sworn to represent and whose interests we have sworn to protect? And what can we do as vessels of the media to ethically report on events, provide factual information, and not sensationalize the horrific and sudden deaths of someone's loved ones?

# Chapter Eleven

# Sharks, Infantile Deaths, and the First World War

*'The New Jersey accidents of 1916, however, bring the whole shark question before us in a new phase. Here, in waters for a century considered safe, we are confronted with a situation, which, in addition to actual destruction of human life, has terrorized countless numbers of people who enjoy ocean bathing, caused a loss of perhaps tens of thousands of dollars to proprietors of beach establishments, has indeed been considered of such gravity as to be discussed in session by the Cabinet of the nation's President.'*
John Nichols and Robert Murphy

The impact and the legacy of the 1916 shark attacks is one that can still be felt and seen today.

In the immediate aftermath of the tragedies, there were several stories of accidents that occurred because of shark-driven fear. One such accident was reported in the *Asbury Park Evening Press* on July 25, 1916. It told the story of a 35-year-old man named Samuel Harding who died, not because of sharks, but rather, because of 'the fear of sharks.'[1] Harding was struggling while swimming in the ocean and called to onlookers for help. Before help could reach him, someone pre-emptively shouted out, 'Sharks! A shark's got him! Don't go in; there are sharks there!'

Fearful of an encounter with a shark themselves, no one came to his aid. It was not until twenty minutes later, when Harding's lifeless body was brought to the shore, that witnesses discovered that Harding had not been attacked by a shark after all. Upon examining his body, it was not immediately clear what his cause of death was. But one thing was for certain: His 'unmarked' body had not been touched by a shark. Rather, it

## SHARK-SCARED, CROWD LETS BATHER DROWN

Not sharks, but the fear of sharks, caused the death of a man yesterday in the Shrewsbury river, near Atlantic Highlands.

Samuel Harding, 35, of 10 Summit street, Newark, went swimming off Grevely Point and was not far from the shore when he threw up his hands and called for help. A number of persons, among them some strong swimmers, were on the beach, and two or three young men ran toward the water with the intention of going to the rescue.

But some one shouted: "Sharks! A shark's got him! Don't go in; there are sharks there!"

The neighborhood has been so worked up over the recent killings by sharks that this was the first thing some thought of. So the young men allowed themselves to be restrained, and the group on the beach saw Harding go down three times without offering him any aid.

About 20 minutse later his body was brought up by an oysterman's rake. It was not marked, so the shark scare had been mere hysteria.

Attempts to induce artificial respiration continued for more than an hour, but the body had been too long submerged.

An Article from the *Asbury Park Evening Press* Titled 'SHARK-SCARED, CROWD LETS BATHER DROWN' Dated July 12, 1916. (*The Asbury Park Evening Press*)

was quickly realized that 'the shark scare had been mere hysteria.'[2] Samuel Harding's death may very well have been prevented.

Shark experts of the time were forced to revise their previous stance on sharks. The same experts who had once suggested that a shark's jaw was not even powerful enough to break bone and that a shark would never intentionally attack a human now reverted the narrative. In the October 1916 issue of the *Brooklyn Museum Quarterly*, they stated:

> 'The New Jersey accidents of 1916, however, bring the whole shark question before us in a new phase. Here, in waters for a century considered safe, we are confronted with a situation, which, in addition to actual destruction of human life, has terrorized countless numbers of people who enjoy ocean bathing, caused a loss of perhaps tens of thousands of dollars to proprietors of beach establishments, has indeed been considered of such gravity as to be discussed in session by the Cabinet of the nation's President.'[3]

Of the great white shark's propensity for attacking humans, Dr John Nichols and Robert Murphy wrote for *Scientific American* magazine, saying:

> '…the white shark is perhaps the rarest of all noteworthy sharks… their habits are little known…judging from its physical make-up, it would not hesitate to attack a man in open water…because it is evident even a relatively small white shark, weighing two or three hundred pounds, might readily snap the largest human bones by a jerk of its body, after it has bitten through the flesh.'[4]

Finally, they once again perpetuated the same harmful narrative they had shared about sharks in a statement they had made months prior, saying now:

> '…there is something peculiarly sinister in the shark's make-up. The sight of his dark, lean fin lazily cutting zigzags in the surface of some quiet, sparkling summer sea, and then slipping out of sight not to appear again, suggests an evil spirit. His leering, chinless face, his great mouth with its rows of knifelike teeth, which he knows too well how to use on the fisherman's gear…'[5]

This harmful narrative continued to perpetuate for years – arguably, it lingers still to this day – and informed many modern-day perceptions of sharks as evil and sinister creatures. As author Michael Capuzzo so eloquently stated, from the very moment the *New York Times* first placed Charles Bruder's horrific death on the front page that historic day in July of 1916, 'the *Times* introduced the great white shark to American culture as a source for general fear, the twentieth-century sea monster.'[6]

Even though the experts – and the world, at large – had changed their previous opinion of sharks in the wake of the 1916 attacks, the tourism industry continued to report that the attacks were no cause for alarm. It is clear that they did so in a desperate attempt to regain profits that had been lost due to tourists frantically vacating their hotels and abruptly ending their stays. In fact, in a *New York Times* article dated July 18, 1916 (notably, this publication date is after four people had lost their lives and another had been severely injured), it read:

> 'BEACH MAYORS PROTEST: NO MORE SHARKS THAN ANY OTHER SUMMER, TEN DECLARE.
> Mayors of ten New Jersey coast resorts tonight issued a statement protesting against publication of stories which they declare "caused the public to believe the New Jersey sea coast is infected with sharks, whereas there are no more than any other summer."'[7]

The article closed out by stating that the 'shark scare' had resulted in 'hurt without cause' to the resort business.[8] Isn't it disappointing to see how little American culture has changed in the last century; that we still put the value of money over the value of human lives?

It is difficult to believe how fervently the tourism industry attempted to reverse the narrative when I have learned from local New Jersey historians that, even ten years after the 1916 shark attacks, these historians saw postcards from the beaches that clearly showed protective steel netting still in place. Evidently, in the decade following the events of 1916, the New Jersey beaches were still on alert to some degree.

But by and large, the world moved on and the 1916 shark attacks along the New Jersey coast were eventually forgotten. The world moved on so much so that when a shark attack occurred the following year, in Sea Bright, New Jersey (only ten miles north of Asbury Park), the incident received little attention.

On September 21, 1917, three lifeguards were patrolling the beaches at Sea Bright when they spotted what appeared to be a wooden barrel out in the water. It was a slow day on the beach (the summer season of vacationers had already come and gone) and, with visitors not needing their assistance otherwise, the small team of lifeguards made their way out into the ocean on their rescue boards with a mission of retrieving debris from the water.[9] The lifeguards took turns diving in and out of the water, cleaning it as they went. It was while the group was already far into the ocean that they spotted a dorsal fin gliding along the water's surface. Two of the lifeguards were able to catch an oncoming wave that safely returned them to the shore, but Daniel Thompson was not so lucky. A shark lunged at him, cutting his knee. Thinking quickly, Thompson caught the next wave and rode it to shore and safety. Other than the minor laceration to his knee, Thompson sustained no further injuries and was able to walk away from the New Jersey shark attack alive, something that the majority of the previous summer's victims were not fortunate enough to say.[10]

Could the same deranged shark from 1916 still be out in the ocean? Had it not been captured during the prior year's massive animal hunt? Could there still be a killer on the loose? And was New Jersey looking at a dangerous repeat of the bloody summer before? Whatever the case, the world didn't seem to care. Just a handful of months prior, in April 1917, the United States Congress declared war on Germany. More than two million American men would be drafted to join the conflict, giving Americans much bigger things to think about than if a 'man-eating' shark was on the loose. Hugh Smith, the commissioner for the United States Fisheries, was certainly motivated to not escalate the matter. Relieved to see the shark attacks of the year before slowly disappear in the rearview mirror, Smith wrote to Dr Frederic Lucas in August of 1916, saying: 'The excitement in this matter appears to have died down, much to the relief of this office, and I hope nothing will occur to resuscitate it.'[11]

As massive as the 1916 shark attacks were at the time, we may not know much about them today without the incredible investigative research conducted by people like Dr Richard G Fernicola, Michael Capuzzo, Allan Savolaine, and Kurtis Roinestad. But even as the world moved on and the news highlighted different stories (of which, there were plenty), there were certainly still impacts, effects, and legacies to come from that fateful summer.

One major effect of the 1916 shark attacks was the horrifically violent response towards sharks exacted by professionals and average citizens alike across the Jersey coast. Hundreds upon hundreds of sharks were killed every day during the two-week frenzy, either by genuinely concerned citizens or by money-hungry bandwagoners hoping to receive a bounty for their kill. It is reported that shark-watcher and Board of Managers of the New York Zoological Society member, Edwin Thorne, personally killed 102 of the 277 sharks he spotted that year.[12] The majority of the sharks he killed that year were brown sharks (also known as sand bar sharks). It is of great importance to note that brown sharks have never been connected with an attack on humans (there have been some possible brown shark-human encounters in Hawaii, but these have yet to be proven for certain).[13] In this case especially, the killing of these sharks was absolutely senseless and unnecessary. The 1916 shark attacks glamorized shark hunting and made it a sport that was not only romanticized but rewarded. This is a theme we will see once again in the 1970s, but more on that later.

Of particular interest when considering the impact of the 1916 shark attacks is the way in which they nearly changed the American political landscape; more specifically, how they may have significantly contributed to Woodrow Wilson's narrow re-election later that same year. In stark contrast to his landslide victory in 1912 in which he took home 435 electoral votes (the next closest opponent was Theodore Roosevelt who acquired eighty-eight electoral votes), Wilson only received 277 electoral votes in 1916. It is important to note that, in 1916, 266 electoral votes were required to win the presidency.[14] Compare this to his competition, New York Governor Charles Evan Hughes, who received 254 electoral votes that year. As Dylan Matthews reported for *Vox*, 'the end result was much closer than four years earlier, with a 3.1-point margin of victory for Wilson, and a narrow electoral college win with five states closer than 1 percentage point.'[15]

Of particular importance is the fact that Hughes beat Wilson in the State of New Jersey! If you will recall from Chapter Two, Wilson had most recently served as the governor of New Jersey, this was where he maintained his summer home that was referred to as the 'summer White

House,' and where his Washington staff relocated and worked towards his campaign. Is it possible that Wilson's response to the shark attacks terrorizing the shores of his home state had cost him a landslide victory there, particularly amongst voters in the beach communities? This is what political scientists Christopher Achen and Larry Bartels argued in a 2012 paper titled 'Blind Retrospection: Why Shark Attacks Are Bad For Democracy.'[16] In their research, they found that votes for Wilson in those communities most heavily hit by the shark attacks were down from 1912 by about ten percentage points come 1916.[17] This is pretty staggering. Wilson would, of course, ultimately win the election, on the slogan that 'He kept us out of war.' But even this statement would not be true much longer…

On April 4, 1917, the US Senate voted to declare war on Germany, officially marking the entrance of the United States in the First World War. America could no longer sit back and remain neutral amid what President Wilson considered to be a threat to democracy worldwide. Although the United States had initially turned a blind eye to the German U-boat attacks on passenger and merchant ships (and even let the *Deutschland* land in its waters without thorough inspection, as discussed in Chapter Six), the US could now no longer look away.

But an even more compelling reason for the US's sudden entrance into the conflict was, of course, the Zimmermann Telegram. On February 24, 1917 (a little over one month before the US announced its declaration of war on Germany), British intelligence agents provided the US government with a secret telegram that they had intercepted between Germany and Mexico. This telegram, named after the German Foreign Minister who sent it, Arthur Zimmermann, promised an alliance between the two countries if Mexico joined the Central Powers. Germany promised to help Mexico regain territories that America had acquisitioned (Arizona, New Mexico, and Texas) as well as provide financial aid to the country in exchange for Mexico's alliance. Finally, the telegram requested that Mexico, upon entering the war, engage in unrestricted submarine warfare against their common enemies.

It does not take a dedicated historian to recall the damage that the First World War caused. Over nine million soldiers and seven million civilians died as a result of the war, with many millions more injured. The war left cities and towns destroyed, and economies devastated. Empires would fall and, due to the circumstances of the Treaty of Versailles, the foundations for a Second World War began to take form.

Given all the attention the war required, the media (and therefore, the United States as a whole) took a greater focus on the conflict occurring overseas. By default, this allowed for the terror that had taken place on its shore the year prior to become a distant memory. Where headlines once read 'MAN EATING SHARK CAUSES DEATH OF MAN AND BOY,' they were quickly replaced with larger print stating 'U.S. OFFICIALLY AT WAR.'

It is worth mentioning that the war was certainly not the only monumental event plastering the covers of newspapers at this time. In 1918, an influenza pandemic – known as the 'Spanish flu' – hit the country, killing approximately fifty million people. This number of casualties is greater than the number of casualties killed during the war. And then, in 1920, the 19th Amendment to the United States Constitution was ratified, granting women the right to vote. Between a war, a pandemic, and the recognition that women are not second-class citizens, the 1916 shark attacks were virtually lost to history.

Despite the general overlook of the 1916 shark attacks, there are some authors and historians that wrote about them in the decades to follow. In 1963, Harold W McCormick and Tom Allen opened their book, titled *Shadows in the Sea*, with a chapter on the 1916 shark attacks. They briefly covered the attacks and the various theories as to why they occurred. In 1986, Ron and Valerie Taylor published their book, titled *Sharks: Silent Hunters of the Deep*, which also included a chapter on the attacks. Mary Batten's 1997 *Shark Attack Almanac* and Richard Ellis' and John McCosker's 1991 *Great White Shark* further discussed the attacks and even proposed some of their own theories about the factors that contributed to the attacks occurring in the first place. And of course, in

2001, Dr Richard G Fernicola and Michael Capuzzo published their works – respectively, *Twelve Days of Terror: Inside the Shocking 1916 New Jersey Shark Attacks* and *Close to Shore: A True Story of Terror in an Age of Innocence* – which provide the most in-depth investigative analysis in existence related to the 1916 shark attacks.

But nothing brought attention to the 1916 shark attacks quite like a book published in 1974 titled *Jaws*…

## Chapter Twelve

# The Jaws Effect

*'Considering the knowledge accumulated about sharks in the last 25 years, I couldn't possibly write Jaws today... not in good conscience anyway. Back then, it was generally accepted that great whites were anthropophagus (they ate people) by choice. Now we know that almost every shark attack on a human is an accident: A shark mistakes a human for its normal prey.'*
*Peter Benchley*

In 1974, New Jersey resident and freelance writer Peter Benchley published his breakthrough novel titled *Jaws* about a great white shark that wreaked havoc in the fictional seaside resort town of Amity, which was placed along the real-life Long Island shore (which is only a hop, skip, and a jump away from the Jersey coast). This series of shark attacks begins with the death of a young bather whose remains are found on the beach, showing obvious markings of a shark attack. The Amity police chief orders for the beaches to be shut down but the mayor refuses, fearful that drastic action like this could result in a decline in the local economy that is primarily funded by the beach resorts. This first attack is kept under wraps by the local government and media officials. But as the shark attacks continue, the town is forced to face the monster in its midst. The police chief, along with an ichthyologist and a renowned shark hunter, go on a mission to kill the gigantic sea monster. They succeed in killing the beast, but only the chief survives.

Sound familiar? Benchley, who passed away in 2006, always maintained that he was not inspired by the 1916 shark attacks to write his book. A *New York Times* article published on September 5, 2001, started this rumor, stating that they believed that the 1916 shark attacks had to be what had inspired Benchley in the first place.[1] But just days later, the *Times* issued a correction on the Corrections page (notably, buried deep within the newspaper where people rarely check) that Benchley had reached out to them and corrected the record that his novel had not been inspired by the 1916 attacks.[2] Rather, he wrote on his website that the true inspiration for his novel came in 1964 when he 'read a newspaper item about a fisherman who caught a 4,550-lb. Great White Shark not far offshore from Montauk, Long Island, and I wondered what would happen if such a huge shark were to appear in a seaside resort community.'[3] Benchley took this idea several years later and proposed to his agent the story of a man-eating shark attacking an otherwise peaceful beachfront town. The publishing company Doubleday picked up the pitch, offering Benchley an advance of $1,000 (the equivalent of roughly $10,000 in today's money) for the first 100 pages. Amazingly, the vast majority of these first 100 pages were rejected by the publisher, and Benchley was forced to rework and rewrite much of the book if he hoped to hold onto the advance money. Benchley admitted to procrastinating on the novel that would ultimately take him a total of a year and a half to complete. Even the infamous title was the product of procrastination. The iconic, one-word title was not chosen until just moments before the book went to print. In fact, Benchley reported that there were approximately 125 other potential titles to be chosen from. Even when the title *Jaws* was selected, it was done in haste and without much confidence.

But what a brilliant marketing decision it was. The book became an immediate bestseller; it

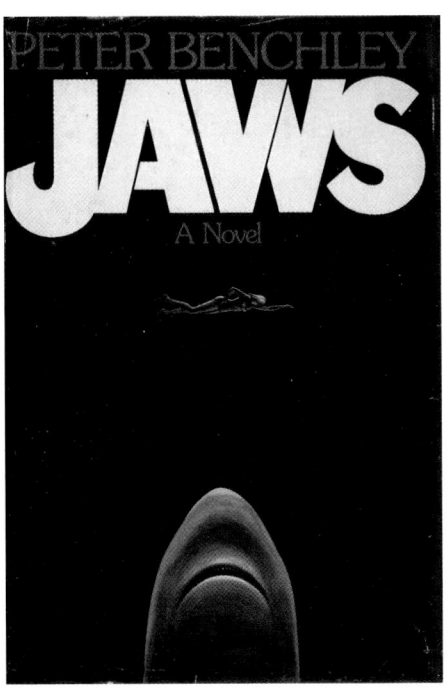

The Original *Jaws* novel cover. (*Public Domain*)

remained on the *New York Times* bestseller list for forty-four weeks! Personally responsible for the sale of hundreds of copies of the novel was the up-and-coming film director Steven Spielberg (along with producers David Brown and Richard D Zanuck) who were already in production to make a movie based on the book. In fact, by the time the movie hit the box office roughly one year later, the book had been sold more than five million times! Today, that number is estimated to be approximately twenty million.

But even if Benchley never acknowledged attribution to the 1916 shark attacks, Spielberg never denied it. In fact, a line was worked into the movie in which a character begs the mayor to shut down the beaches for fear that history will repeat itself. The concerned citizen tells the mayor, '…it's gonna happen again. It happened before! The Jersey beach! 1916! Five people chewed up on the surf!'. This isn't the only reference that *Jaws* has to the 1916 attacks.

In Benchley's book, the shark kills four people, exactly as it was in 1916 (five people are killed in the movie)[4]. In Benchley's book, the mayor initially disregards the attacks for fear that negative press and attention may discourage tourists from vacationing along their beaches, exactly as it was in Beach Haven in 1916. In Benchley's book, the shark attacks take place in a small, beachfront resort town, exactly as it was along the Jersey coast in 1916. And, in Benchley's book, the townspeople decided to initiate a mass shark hunt following the attacks, exactly as it was in 1916.

It is difficult to accept that Benchley was not, even minimally, inspired by the 1916 shark attacks. The number of attacks, the location of the attacks, the nature of the attacks, and the way in which city officials responded to the attacks appear to coincide almost directly with the 1916 New Jersey shark attacks. In conversations I had with New Jersey historians while researching this book, I was told of first-hand accounts in which Benchley confessed to friends that the 1916 New Jersey attacks had indeed been key inspiration for his novel. I guess the true answer will forever be up for interpretation.

An unfortunate parallel between the 1916 shark attacks and *Jaws* is the response that average citizens exhibited in the face of shark-driven fear. Regrettably, 1916 would not be the last time average citizens would engage in a mass shark hunt. Following the release of *Jaws* the movie in 1975, the world engaged once more in a grotesque and horrifying killing spree of sharks – inspired by the movie to capture the so-called man-eating predators – and then hung their kills up as trophies. The fearmongering of the movie has made a lasting and devastating impact on sharks. Since the release of *Jaws*, shark populations have declined by seventy-one percent with an estimated 100 million sharks killed every year.[5]

But before we can discuss this mass shark hunt, we must first dive (no pun intended) into the global impact that *Jaws* the movie had on the world, its cultural influence, and the way that it contributed to the perception many people have of sharks – even to this day – because of the false narratives portrayed in the film.

When the *Jaws* film was released, it was an immediate success at the box office, breaking the record of over $100 million in just two months! *Jaws* eventually earned over $470 million worldwide, making it the highest-grossing film of all time up to this point.[6] To this day, it continues to rank in the top ten best films ever made. *Jaws* became the first 'summer blockbuster' and really set the standard for the way summer movie releases are marketed and distributed to this day (prior to *Jaws*, summer releases were typically relegated to less exciting films. After *Jaws*, this all changed).[7] *Jaws* went on to be nominated for four Academy Awards and would win three of them, including Best Music (Score).

*Dun-dun-dun-dun. Dun-dun-dun-dun.* Just those simple words alone are recognizable even to people that have never watched the movie. Two notes (an E and an F note), repeated over and over and increasing in speed as the shark looms closer, are enough to make your skin crawl and the hair on the back of your neck stand up straight. Just two notes, forcing you to sit still on the edge of your seat in anticipation of what is bound to happen next. This score is considered to be the sixth greatest score of all time, according to the American Film Institute. That is how iconic the music for the movie is. But that is hardly the most iconic nor most memorable or long-lasting effect from the film.

The legacy of the film and the long-lasting effect that it has had is so monumental that it actually has a name. Proposed in 2015 by University of Sydney professor Chrisopher Neff, the term for the way in which the movie has changed and influenced the perception that people have about sharks is quite literally known as the 'Jaws effect.' As Jansen Baier of *Mongabay News* wrote:

'The three basic tenets of the "Jaws effect" are:

1) The belief that sharks intentionally bite humans;
2) That human-shark encounters are always fatal; and
3) That sharks should be killed to prevent future attacks.'[8]

These tenets run deep. Despite the fact that there are more than 500 species of sharks in the world, the great white shark – in all of its ferocity – has come to represent them all. When you think about sharks, you think about the great white. And when you think about the great white, you think about its massive jaw, lined with hundreds of teeth. You think about its hundreds of teeth, and you think about just how easily one bite from this beast could take your leg clean off. To simplify that anecdote, when you think of sharks, you think of the shark from *Jaws*, and you think about how easily it can (and would very much like to) kill you.

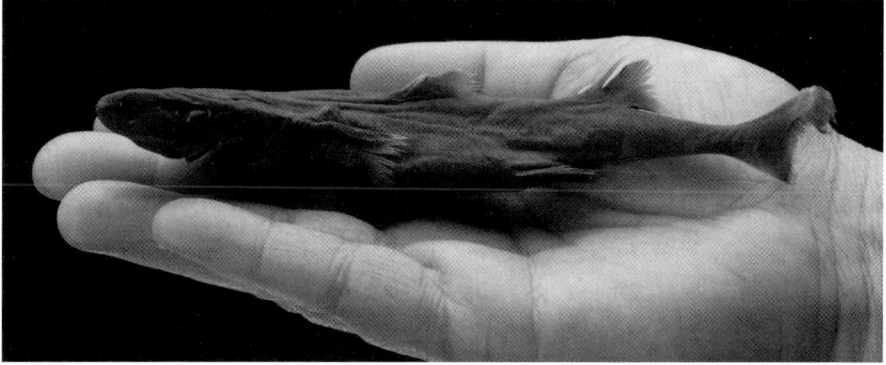

Dwarf Lanternshark. (*Public Domain*)

*Jaws* did this. *Jaws* removed all the beautiful attributes of the hundreds of harmless species of sharks known to mankind and replaced them with the scariest and most life-threatening version of this magnificent creature. Because of the overwhelming oversaturation of the great white, few people are even familiar with the hundreds of other species of sharks that exist. For example, many people have never heard of the harmless dwarf lanternshark, a shark small enough that it can fit in the palm of your hand (yes, it is adorable).

In Dr Neff's groundbreaking scientific article in which he first proposed the theory of the 'Jaws effect,' he analyzed the way in which the negative perception of sharks has influenced policymakers and how this perception has made a detrimental – and, quite frankly, deadly – impact on sharks today. According to Dr Neff, the effect that the movie had in Australia, in particular, allowed for the government there to implement shark culling programs.[9]

Shark culling, referred to as 'shark control' or 'shark meshing' by governments attempting to downplay the brutality and reality of what they are doing, is essentially the capture and murder of hundreds (sometimes, thousands) of sharks every year.

Shark culling is a horrifying and unethical practice justified by governments as a means of keeping the public safe. Across New South Wales, the beaches from Newcastle to Wollongong are littered with these shark nets for the duration of the September through April months.[10] At eighty-six beaches across Queensland, the nets remain all year round.[11]

But what inevitably happens when you cast a large net in a body full of marine life is you capture and kill hundreds of other species that are not on the set 'target list'. These other species become 'bycatch', a term that refers to species unintentionally caught, entangled, hooked, or trapped in gear intended for other species.[12] According to The Humane Society International, an international division of The Humane Society of the United States, ninety percent of the marine life caught in the nets along the Australian beaches are harmless and not those that the government states are its intended targets (they state that their intended targets are great whites, tigers, and bulls).[13] The Humane Society International found that more than half of the marine animals captured in the nets (animals like dolphins, turtles, whales, and other nonthreatening sharks) are killed as a result.[14] How can we be okay with this?

The truth is that marine conservationists, and average Australians alike, are not okay with it. Marine conservationists have called on Australia to use other safety measures that they already have in place, such as alert systems and drone surveillance, as an alternative for the deadly nets.[15] With these harmless technologies already implemented, there is simply no need for the harmful shark nets across the continent. In a poll conducted in which Australians were asked about the continent's widespread use of shark nets, eighty-three percent of New South Wales residents stated that they understand that the ocean is the shark's home and that it is the responsibility of humans to steer clear of any potential danger when encroaching on the shark's rightful space (not the other way around).[16] Despite pleas to forego this incredibly harmful and unethical practice (particularly in regions where non-lethal and harmless technologies are already implemented), shark culling continues to exist to this day.

This is amazing when you consider not only how unethical shark nets are, but also how ineffective they are. The nets in New South Wales only stretch 150 meters, meaning that sharks can quite easily swim above and around them.[17] Statistics show that sixty-five percent of shark attacks in New South Wales have taken place at beaches with shark nets engaged.[18] Associate Professor Laurie Laurenson of Deaken University has said of shark nets:

> '[They] have no statistical impact on the number of shark attacks. In fact, they may actually have a contra effect, making us "feel" safer and behave with less caution than we should – as well as unnecessarily killing sharks and other marine life.'[19]

While the intended targets often steer clear of the nets specifically designed to catch them, other innocent marine life suffers the consequences. Mother Ocean Freediving found that 100 percent of the dolphins inadvertently caught in the nets during the 2022/2023 season drowned before they could be released.[20] The New South Wales government has even strictly prohibited people from assisting in the rescue of an entangled animal.[21]

Shark culling programs in New South Wales are horrifying, but in fact, it is Queensland that operates the largest shark culling program across all of Australia, having killed more than 50,000 sharks since its culling program began in the early 1960s.[22] A primary technique used in Queensland to capture and kill sharks is the deployment of drum lines. Drum lines are baited hooks that are attached to a buoy as well as an anchor. In some rather graphic and disturbing pictures I have seen, the sharks that 'take the bait' end up with a hook pierced through their skulls. These drum lines are placed far away from the shore, outside of the range where bathers typically swim. To that end, the use of drum lines feels particularly unnecessary and heinous.

You'll recall that KwaZulu-Natal, South Africa, was the site of one of the more 'modern day' strings of shark attacks that we reviewed in Chapter Ten. As a result of the 'Black December' shark attacks between 1957 and 1958, KwaZulu-Natal also implemented the use of shark nets and drum lines along its beaches. Since the start of their shark culling program, more than 30,000 sharks have been killed with thousands of other marine animals – like turtles, rays, and dolphins – dying as innocent bycatch.

With today's technology, this brutal killing practice is simply not necessary. There are other ways to mitigate the risk of shark attacks by implementing safe and effective tools like drones, alarm systems, tagging and tracking practices, shark listening devices, safety education, and more.

If the shark culling practices described above bother you as much as they bother me, there are several petitions you can sign to support the end of shark nets and other unethical shark killing practices. I have provided information about where you can find these petitions on the Resources page at the end of the book.

It is alarming to read the way that sharks are perceived and mistreated in various parts of the world. What is perhaps even more alarming is that we have Hollywood to 'thank' for much of this negative perception.

Beyond *Jaws*, though certainly *Jaws* is the most popular and most well-known, 109 films featuring sharks between the years of 1958 and 2019 portrayed a whopping ninety-six percent of them in a way that was threatening to humans.[23] Professor Brianna Le Busque of the University of South Australia conducted an in-depth analysis of films featuring sharks over a more than sixty-year span and found this alarming statistic. Further, of the movie posters for these films she reviewed, she found that more than half of them featured great white sharks, with bull sharks as a close runner-up, and that seventy-five percent of these posters showed sharks with their teeth exposed (presumably, in a menacing manner).[24]

Given these statistics, is it any surprise that the average American is under the assumption that all sharks are dangerous, that they intend to kill you, and that an encounter with a shark is more likely to occur than not? Given these statistics, it is any surprise that a 2015 study found that fifty-one percent of Americans are scared of sharks and that another thirty-eight percent of Americans are terrified to swim in the ocean for fear of an attack by a shark?[25] Films like *Jaws* have given the false perception that simply stepping foot into the ocean comes with the high probability of being attacked by a shark when the odds of being attacked by a shark are realistically only one in 11.5 million.

In all actuality, humans are a greater threat to sharks than sharks are to us. Somewhere between the blurry line of fact and fiction, humanity's relationship with sharks has been redefined, leading humans to become the predators and sharks to become the prey. Every year, 100 million sharks are killed by humans, making more than thirty percent of shark species endangered and venturing on extinction.[26] This means that more than one-third of all species of sharks are currently facing an 'extinction crisis.'[27] According to author William McKeever in his book titled *Emperors of the Deep*, sharks are currently facing 'the greatest threat in their entire 450-million-year history.'[28]

Beyond the thoughtless killing of sharks in the immediate wake of *Jaws*, conducted by people hoping to bring home a trophy – even beyond the violent killing of sharks through inhumane culling efforts – are sharks that are killed every single day for much more mundane reasons: they are killed in order to make products for consumers. The most obvious product made from sharks is shark fin soup, a celebratory dish is Southeast Asian cultures. Approximately seventy-three million sharks are finned every single year in order to make shark fin soup.[29] Unbelievably, this soup only requires the fin of the shark; after the shark is finned, the rest of its body is simply discarded. The act of finning a shark is brutal and ruthless: the shark is captured, its fins are cut off (often while the shark is still alive), and then it is unconscionably thrown back into the ocean where it is left to slowly bleed to death.

Most people assume that, so long as they do not consume shark fin soup (or other meals made from shark meat), they are free of shark products. But this is unfortunately not true. Sharks are used in a vast array of products such as garden fertilizer, anti-aging creams, skin lotions, deodorants, hair products, makeup products, medicines and supplements, leather bags and shoes, vaccines, sunscreens, and more.[30] It is not always obvious that the product you are using contains shark. In fact, oftentimes, sharks are mislabeled as other fish in a long list of ingredients written in fine print, all in an attempt to persuade the consumer otherwise.[31]

One of the largest byproducts of sharks is squalene (or squalane) which is an oil used in many cosmetic products such as lotions, makeup, lip balms, sunscreens, and more. Squalene/squalane is primarily derived from one of two sources: 1) plants; or 2) shark liver. In 2015, a study was conducted into the beauty industry's use of shark products and found that one in five moisturizing creams contained squalene from sharks.[32] The vast majority of beauty companies, however, have massively shifted their sourcing in the last ten years, moving away from animal products to more plant-based sources.

Shark cartilage is also sourced for an array of medicines and supplements including those that treat illnesses such as eczema, shingles, and psoriasis.[33]

This cartilage can be found in both pill and powder products at various stores worldwide.[34]

And finally, and perhaps most alarming to many American readers, is the use of sharks for their meat, something that is becoming increasingly popular throughout the states. Contrary to popular belief, shark meat is not illegal in the United States. There are certain regulations around acquiring shark meat in the US – for example, finning is illegal, as is the killing of endangered shark species – but otherwise, eating shark at a seafood restaurant or picking up shark meat at a local deli is not only legal, but becoming more and more popular by the day.

The greatest threat to sharks today is overfishing. Overfishing is the act of taking fish faster than they can reproduce and, by default, causing the population of said fish to rapidly decline. Sharks face a particular threat to overfishing given the fact that sharks reproduce at a much slower rate than many other types of fish. Most sharks (roughly seventy percent) are viviparous, meaning that they give birth to live young. As opposed to the other thirty percent of sharks that are oviparous and lay eggs, viviparous sharks take much longer to reproduce as they grow a full-length infant in the womb. For some viviparous sharks, it can take up to two years to fully produce and birth their young.[35] This is in stark contrast to bass, the most popular marine animal for fishing, which can reproduce (from start to finish) in as little as three weeks! Given the lengthy process of reproduction for sharks, it is no wonder that shark populations are so vulnerable to overfishing.

Sharks quite literally keep the entire marine ecosystem intact. Without sharks, the marine ecosystem will become critically imbalanced. Sharks are apex predators, meaning that they are at the top of the food chain without any natural predators of their own. Further, this means that sharks are responsible for maintaining and regulating the population of other marine life. Sharks are known to prey upon sick or injured animals and, therefore, naturally balance the ocean out and make it a healthier and more biodiverse environment for other marine life to live. Without sharks, other marine animals that prey on fish consumed by humans will go unchecked and the fish supply that humans have come to rely upon will suffer. Sharks are, without exaggeration, absolutely vital to maintaining the health and balance of our current marine ecosystem.

So, what are we doing now to protect sharks? What are the people that recognize that sharks are indeed the victims, and not the villains, doing to ensure the world is not one day void of these vital components to the ocean's ecosystem?

Identified by some of the largest shark conservationist organizations in the world, the following list is considered to be the most important set of objectives in relation to shark conservation:

1) Responsible management of fisheries;
2) Protection of species and extinction prevention; and
3) Identification of shark areas.

One of the biggest ways to help conserve and preserve sharks is to ensure that fisheries abide by the law and are sourcing marine life in a way that is both sustainable and legal.[36]

The Shark Conservation Fund (SCF) has already taken huge strides in making this objective a reality. In 2022, the SCF campaigned and received an agreement at the Convention on International Trade in Endangered Species (CITES) to regulate the global trade on a number of shark species.[37] This agreement is truly monumental as it ensures that the bulk of shark that is sourced and traded will be regulated by CITES Appendix II which holds fisheries to a legal and sustainable standard. The SCF continues to work with local governments that are implementing CITES regulations to ensure the regulations are rolled out correctly and followed appropriately. They also provide overall help in achieving the greater goal of decreasing the mass reduction of sharks that the world has witnessed in the last several decades.

Beyond regulating fisheries to prohibit the overfishing of sharks, the SCF is also working to conserve sixty-five specific species of sharks that are at a threatening level of endangerment. Regulating overfishing only goes so far if the sharks you are trying to protect are already extinct. That is why the SCF has a specific focus and attention on these endangered species of sharks, working to make it illegal to fish for them, and striving to enhance their current environments.

Finally, the SCF is striving to identify at least fifty areas where sharks can be secured to grow and thrive. This means placing limitations on shark catch in these select locations which will, in turn, allow for the shark population there to repopulate and rebuild the ocean's natural ecosystem.

But the single greatest thing we as humans can do to save sharks? The answer is rather simple: we can change our perception of them. If we were to recognize that sharks are not man-eating monsters with an appetite for human blood, but rather, apex predators that maintain our very way of life, the world might start to look a lot different. If we were to begin to respect sharks for the majestic – albeit sometimes terrifying – creatures that they are, that respect could then extend to their environments and the order we must maintain if we want to preserve and conserve these wonderful species. If we could let go of the fear that *Jaws* – and, before it, the misconceptions that arose out of the 1916 shark attacks – instilled within us, then we might be able to also let go of the harmful misinformation and general disrespect that is weaponized to destroy millions of sharks every single year.

The author of *Jaws*, Peter Benchley, later acknowledged the misinformation spread about sharks because of his book and, subsequently, the movie. He stated that there is no such thing as a rogue shark with a taste for human blood and that he regretted portraying sharks in such a way that would perpetuate this falsehood. In a 2000 article for *National Geographic*, Benchley stated:

> 'Considering the knowledge accumulated about sharks in the last 25 years, I couldn't possibly write *Jaws* today…not in good conscience anyway. Back then, it was generally accepted that great whites were anthropophagus (they ate people) by choice. Now we know that almost every shark attack on a human is an accident: A shark mistakes a human for its normal prey.'[38]

In the years following the release of *Jaws*, Benchley went scuba diving in Costa Rica and was met with a horrific sight: all across the bottom of the ocean, he spotted the corpses of finned sharks.[39] Between this harrowing experience and the other alarming responses the world had to *Jaws*, Benchley stated that he regretted any contribution he may have made to the killing of sharks. He said that if he were to write the book all over again, the shark, which had been portrayed in the novel – and later, in the movie – as the villain, would instead 'have to be written as the victim, for worldwide, sharks are much more oppressed than the oppressors.'[40] Following these realizations, Benchley spent the rest of his life as a fervent advocate of ocean conservation. His website features an entire section titled 'Save the Sharks' with information about organizations you can join or contribute to that are making a difference in shark conservation (a list of these organizations can be found on the Resources page at the end of this book).

I hope that in reading this book, you have grown to appreciate sharks in all their capacity. I hope that you can appreciate them as dangerous and sometimes unpredictable creatures in the same turn that you can appreciate them as majestic and necessary creatures that quite literally hold the fabric of the ocean together. While the first half of this book thoroughly discussed the violence that sharks can enact on humans, I hope the second half of this book reminded you that the ocean is their home and that we are to respect it if we want to not only keep all our limbs, but also, keep our very way of life.

My heart aches for each and every one of the families impacted by the attacks that destroyed the Jersey Shore that fateful summer in 1916. I ache for the families that took a much-needed vacation, a routine swim, or a normal play date at the creek and came back with one family member less. It's not right and it's not fair. You don't expect to go on a family vacation and return home days later to plan a funeral. I will never blame any one of the victims of the 1916 shark attacks for the way in which they tragically lost their lives. We genuinely did not know better at the time about the capacity of sharks, and the behavior of the shark (or sharks) involved in the 1916 attacks is something that continues to boggle experts to this day.

We do know better now though. We know what a shark can do when we enter its home. We know that the force of a shark's bite can quite literally take the leg off a human and what was originally meant to be a leisurely swim can end in a tragic fatality.

But we also know better now about the odds of this happening. We know that the likelihood of a shark attack is one in 11.5 million and that something as ridiculous as a coconut falling from a tree is far more likely to kill you than an encounter with a shark. Though researchers disagree as to why sharks bite humans in the first place, we know that there is evidence to support both the theory that sharks bite due to mistaken identity or that they bite simply as a way of exploring their world. In summary, sharks rarely mean to bite humans with the intent of harming them.

We know now that speculation, misinformation, and the sensationalism of false news stories and Hollywood blockbusters have led to the misconception that sharks are man-killers with a taste for human flesh. Shocking headlines and gory scenes sell papers and movie tickets. Unfortunately, they also have a propensity to inform people's opinions. Like I said before, 'A lie once told remains a lie, but a lie told a thousand times becomes the truth.'

We know now that sharks are at a severe risk of extinction. We know that humans kill millions upon millions of sharks every single year through horrifying practices such as culling and finning, and that sharks are killed and used for products ranging from lip balms to eczema relief creams. We know that the shark population is particularly vulnerable to overfishing and that, if we're not careful, our children and our children's children may live in a world where several sharks species no longer exist.

And finally, we know now the critical importance that sharks have to our ecosystem and our very way of life. The world does not continue to exist as it currently does without the existence of sharks in our waters.

I implore you to take sharks seriously for the wild animals that they are, respect their territory and environment, and steer clear of certain activities and regions that may make you more susceptible to an attack. You may have noticed earlier in the book that anytime I used the phrase 'shark-infested' waters, I placed quotations around the term. This is because there is no such thing as 'shark-infested' waters. The ocean is their home. They are simply living in it. I implore you to respect sharks for the gorgeous creatures that they are, and I urge you, if you feel so inclined, to review the Resources page at the end of this book to find ways that you can conserve and preserve sharks for the many generations to come.

Prior to extensively studying the shark attacks of 1916, I had perhaps an unhealthy fear of sharks, spurred on by the sensationalism of *Jaws* and the mass misinformation about these alleged man-eating killers lurking just beneath the ocean's surface. Since studying these events and sharks in more detail, I would say I now have a healthy fear of them. I respect them, I want to protect them and their environment, and I trust that the average shark would not intend to kill me if we happened upon one another during some sea bathing. I have dedicated time and donated money to many of the organizations listed on the Resources page and intend to continue to put my words and my money behind supporting sharks and their livelihood in the days to come. But, given that healthy fear that I have of sharks (and the fact that, over the course of my extensive research for this book, I have now viewed far too many pictures of shark teeth and shark attack injuries), you can rest assured that I will not be sea bathing any time soon.

# Epilogue

# The Fiftieth Anniversary of *Jaws*

It may be hard for some to believe that the year 2025 marks the fiftieth anniversary of the movie *Jaws*. For many of us, we grew up in a post-*Jaws* world in which we were raised to fear sharks. For some, that fear was raised to the level of exacting some sort of revenge on innocent sharks through inhumane killing and culling. But for most, it simply meant perpetuating harmful stereotypes about the ocean's apex predator.

As we have already established, *Jaws* did this. *Jaws* set into motion the misconceptions about sharks that had long existed. But what we have yet to discuss are the more positive impacts of the movie and the way that it has served as somewhat of a bonding experience for millions upon millions of people worldwide.

People love *Jaws*. The film has acquired somewhat of a cult following. It has inspired three sequels, *Jaws 2*, *Jaws 3-D*, and *Jaws: The Revenge* (though we won't talk about those. They were not directed by Steven Spielberg and, though they did rather well at the box office, were not received well in the long run). The love for this film has inspired massive amounts of merchandise, video games, a musical, and even theme park rides at Universal Studios Florida and Universal Studios Japan. The location where the movie was filmed, Martha's Vineyard, Massachusetts, has since been dubbed 'Jaws Island.'[1] Various tourism agencies host *Jaws* tours where they take you around the island and show you iconic spots from the film.[2] Martha's Vineyard also hosted, for several years, the 'Jaws Fest' which was a weekend-long event that included an array of *Jaws*-themed activities, including tours and a screening of the movie.[3]

Perhaps one of the most cultural legacies of *Jaws* is 'an entire industry and television programming' that it birthed which includes Discovery Channel's Shark Week and National Geographic's Shark Fest.[4]

In July of 1988, Discovery Channel, an American cable channel, premiered for the first time what would become known as an annual, week-long series of shark-related programs called Shark Week. For more than thirty years now, Shark Week has aired every single year in the month of July or August and has garnered an audience of millions across seventy-two countries. In 2023 alone, Shark Week pulled in more than twenty-two million viewers.[5] Shark Week has now become the longest-running cable television programming event in history![6] With hosts ranging from John Cena to Jason Momoa to Dwayne 'The Rock' Johnson, Shark Week continues to be a cultural phenomenon that keeps people that love sharks – and even, people that are generally indifferent towards sharks – coming back year after year. Shark Week has an interesting hold on viewers, garnering viewership from people who otherwise do not frequent the Discovery Channel. In an extensive content analysis of Shark Week conducted by Lisa Whitenack, it was found that, in 2020, thirty-seven percent of the people that tuned into the Discovery Channel for Shark Week had not watched the Discovery Channel at all in the month prior.[7] It's no wonder the Discovery Channel has continued to air Shark Week every year for the last thirty-plus years.

Shark Week has certainly not done much to squash the misconceptions and misinformation surrounding sharks. In fact, some of the greatest criticism leveled against Shark Week is the way in which it misconstrues – and in some instances, downright lies – about sharks and their behaviors, all for the sake of entertainment and views. Many of the so-called 'experts' serving as commentators for the various programs have questionable certifications with the channel even labeling some of them as 'Dr' when they do not hold doctorates at all.[8] Additionally, a handful of Shark Week shows are not of an informative, documentary nature. Despite presenting itself as a factual documentary with supposedly supporting evidence that the long-extinct Megalodon still exists, *Megalodon: The Monster Shark Lives* featured blatant lies and showed false photographs and alleged encounters with the creature.[9] Despite this – or perhaps, because of it – *Megalodon: The Monster Shark Lives* continues to rank as the most-watched show featured during Shark Week with an estimated 4.8 million views. Although Megalodons have been extinct for approximately three million years, seventy-nine percent of respondents walked away from viewing *Megalodon: The Monster Shark Lives* with the belief that Megalodons are very much still alive today.

The 2022 study conducted by Whitenack also found that, of 201 shows featured for Shark Week, seventy-four percent referenced negative connotations about sharks with titles including words like 'bite,' 'attack,' and 'deadly.'[10] And, to no surprise, the most featured species of shark during Shark Week is, of course, the great white, with significant neglect paid to the more than 500 other shark species known to man.[11]

The shark fever that *Jaws* instilled in millions of people continues to thrive with the biggest fans of the film eagerly gearing up for the fiftieth anniversary. It is still unclear exactly how the event will be celebrated. In fact, some fans have expressed their 'underwhelming' feelings about the current plans in place.[12] At the time of writing this book, Martha's Vineyard has announced a *Jaws* exhibition at the local museum, a meet-and-greet with Jeffrey Voorhees (the actor that played Alex Kintner in the movie, the young boy that dies in arguably the most heartbreaking death to occur in the film), and a local baseball game.[13] Die-hard fans are expecting more from the event, including a hopeful appearance from Steven Spielberg. From what I gather in the fan clubs online, there is optimism that the plans that Martha's Vineyard has announced thus far are just a 'first wave' of information with many more exciting announcements to come. *The Daily Jaws*, a website dedicated to following and reporting on all news related to *Jaws*, is a great hub for information about the upcoming celebration. They suggest that, if you are interested in following any news or updates about the fiftieth anniversary, you follow the hashtag #JAWS50 online.

At this time, there are at least two documentaries in production that are set to be released in 2025 in honor of the fiftieth anniversary. In an exclusive announcement, *Deadline* reported that National Geographic – as part of their annual Shark Fest programming – will be releasing a documentary with the working title of 'Jaws @ 50.' The documentary is to be produced in partnership with Steven Spielberg's Amblin Documentaries and Nedland Media.[14] It will include behind-the-scenes footage of the filming of the movie as well as new interviews. Additionally, the documentary is meant to draw attention to conservation efforts. With the documentary, they hope to change the focus on sharks as man-eating creatures to viewing them as 'awe-inspiring creatures' instead.[15] The documentary is set to stream on Disney+ and Hulu.

A rival documentary was announced only days after the *Deadline* exclusive. From Newen Connect and directed by French filmmakers Olivier Bonnard and Antoine Coursat, a documentary titled 'Jaws: Making a Splash in Hollywood' will also take a behind-the-scenes look at the film with a specific focus on how *Jaws* quite literally changed the Hollywood landscape and established our modern-day understanding of blockbuster films.[16]

For all the shortcomings and misconceptions that *Jaws* has perpetuated (all acknowledged by the book's author, Peter Benchley), it certainly has become a cultural phenomenon with a devoted following. People love *Jaws*. And, by default, the love of the film has led many to have greater appreciation and respect for sharks. According to the Whitenack study, there is evidence that supports the theory that 'respondents who are Shark Week viewers tend to display higher levels of knowledge about sharks and tendency to believe shark conservation is urgent compared to survey respondents who have not watched Shark Week.'[17]

And, for that, we do have *Jaws* to thank.

However you choose to celebrate the fifty-year anniversary, might I suggest you begin by checking out the Resources page of this book? Stay safe in the waters. And save the sharks.

# Resources

**Safeguard the Seas**  (www.safeguardtheseas.org)
A non-profit company that produces books and films to educate the public about the threats to the ocean.

**The #SHARKFREE Campaign**  (www.robstewartsharkwaterfoundation.org)
#SHARKFREE is a campaign to keep sharks out of our products, so we can produce pressure on their populations and save them from extinction

**Sharks4Kids**  (www.sharks4kids.com)
The goal of Sharks4Kids is to create a new generation of shark advocates through access to a dynamic range of educational materials. Curriculum, videos and activities will allow teachers to integrate shark education into their science programs on an introductory, intermediate or advanced level. Students can access coloring pages, activities and info sheets to satisfy their own curiosity about sharks. Photos and videos from scientists and conservationists bring an exciting element into the classroom and show students the beauty of the ocean

**Shark Trust**  (www.sharktrust.org)
Our mission is to safeguard a future for sharks, skates and rays through positive change. We achieve this through science, education, influence and action.

**World Wildlife Fund**  (www.worldwidlife.org)
Our mission is to build a future in which people live in harmony with nature. To deliver this mission, we work to conserve and restore biodiversity, the web that supports all life on Earth; to reduce humanity's environmental footprint; and to ensure the sustainable use of natural resources to support current and future generations.

**Shark Stewards**  (www.sharkstewards.org)
Shark Stewards saves endangered sharks and rays sharks from overfishing and the wildlife trade, and protecting marine habitat.

**Shark Angels**  (www.sharkangels.org)
Shark Angels is a shark conservation organization that turns fear into fascination and passion into action. Shark Angels around the world are coming together to focus on areas we can make a real difference – for sharks, the oceans and our planet. By leading through example, we inspire others to take action and protect sharks, their future, and one another.

**Shark Conservation Fund**  (www.sharkconservationfund.org)

The Shark Conservation Fund (SCF) is a collaboration of philanthropists dedicated to solving the global shark and ray crisis. Our goal is to halt the overexploitation of the world's sharks and rays, prevent extinctions, reverse population declines, and restore imperiled species through strategic and catalytic grantmaking.

**Saving the Blue**   (www.savingtheblue.org)
Saving the Blue aims to recover and restore a variety of threatened marine species, including sharks, while connecting people to ocean wildlife.

**Organizations Listed on Peter Benchley's Website:**

**Environment Defense Fund**   (www.edf.org)
Guided by science and economics, and committed to climate justice, we work in the places, on the projects and with the people that can make the biggest difference.

**Beneath the Waves**   (www.beneaththewaves.org)
Beneath The Waves is dedicated to promoting ocean health and using science and technology to catalyze ocean policy. We are broad in our approach, but we focus our work on protecting threatened species, establishing protected areas, and creating nature-based solutions to climate change.

**Blue Frontier**   (www.bluefront.org)
Blue Frontier builds the solution-oriented citizen engagement needed to protect our ocean, coasts and the communities, both human and wild that depend on them

**Conservation International**   (www.conservation.org)
Conservation International is a global organization that works to protect nature and its benefits for humanity. Learn about their science, finance, partnership and innovation strategies to secure forests, oceans and nature-positive economies.

(Descriptions for all organizations and campaigns were pulled verbatim from their respective websites.)

# Notes

**Chapter One**
1. "Shark Attack File." *International Shark Attack File*, Florida Museum of Natural History, www.sharkattackfile.net.
2. "Shark Attack File." *International Shark Attack File*.
3. Stevens, John D. *Sharks*. Facts on File Publications, 1987.
4. Stevens, *Sharks*.
5. Ball, Jessica. "Historical Art Paints a Picture of Past Shark Abundance." *Hakai Magazine*, 6 Mar. 2018, https://hakaimagazine.com/features/historical-art-paints-picture-past-shark-abundance/#:~:text=Herodotus's%20account%20that%20shark%20attacks,of%20a%20great%20white%20shark.
6. "The Fiji Myth of Dakuwaqa, the Shark God." *The Kid Should See This*, 25 Oct. 2021, https://thekidshouldseethis.com/post/fiji-myth-dakuwaqa-shark-god-animation.
7. "Shark Reef Marine Reserve." *Fiji Shark Dive*, https://www.fijisharkdive.com/shark-reef-marine-reserve/#:~:text=Shark%20Reef%20Marine%20Reserve%20was,Adventure%20Divers%20and%20disbursed%20monthly.
8. "Cultural Significance of Sharks." *HawaiiActivities.com*, https://www.hawaiiactivities.com/travelguide/cultural-significance-sharks/#:~:text=Some%20species%20of%20sharks%2C%20like,between%20humans%20and%20the%20gods.
9. Bush, Evan. "U.S. Takes Aim at Global Shark Fin Trade." *NBC News*, 6 Jan. 2023, https://www.nbcnews.com/science/science-news/us-takes-aim-global-shark-fin-trade-rcna68369.
10. Galati, Peter. "Sharks and the Navy: From 'Shark Lore' to 'Shark Chaser'—The United States Navy's Quest for a Shark Repellant and Its Impact on Shark Science." *The Saber and Scroll Journal*.
11. Kroll, Michael. "The Sinking of the USS Indianapolis Triggered the Worst Shark Attack in History." *Smithsonian Magazine*, 7 Aug. 2013, https://www.smithsonianmag.com/history/sinking-uss-indianapolis-triggered-worst-shark-attack-history-25715092/#:~:text=Sharks%20were%20drawn%20in%20by,group%2C%20ideally%20toward%20its%20center.
12. Kroll, "The Sinking of the USS Indianapolis Triggered the Worst Shark Attack in History."
13. Kroll, "The Sinking of the USS Indianapolis Triggered the Worst Shark Attack in History."
14. Galati, Peter. "Sharks and the Navy: From 'Shark Lore' to 'Shark Chaser'—The United States Navy's Quest for a Shark Repellant and Its Impact on Shark Science." *The Saber and Scroll Journal*.
15. Capuzzo, Michael. *Close to Shore: A True Story of Terror in an Age of Innocence*. Broadway Books, 2001.

16. "Why We're So Terrified of the Unknown." *BBC Worklife*, 22 Oct. 2021, www.bbc.com/worklife/article/20211022-why-were-so-terrified-of-the-unknown.
17. "Why We're So Terrified of the Unknown", *BBC Worklife*.
18. "Why We're So Terrified of the Unknown", *BBC Worklife*.
19. "10 Common Things That Are Far More Dangerous Than the Things You Actually Fear." *Listverse*, 23 Mar. 2015, https://listverse.com/2015/03/23/10-common-things-that-are-far-more-dangerous-than-the-things-you-actually-fear/#:~:text=Rest%20assured%3A%20You%20probably%20won,rails%20sometimes%20make%20things%20worse.
20. Skomal, Greg. *Shark Handbook.* Simon and Schuster, 2014.
21. McKeever, William. *Emperors of the Deep: Sharks--The Ocean's Most Mysterious, Most Misunderstood, and Most Important Guardians.* HarperCollins, 2019.
22. McKeever, *Emperors of the Deep.*
23. Skomal, Greg. *Shark Handbook.* Simon and Schuster, 2014.
24. Kaplan, Sarah. "Your Sense of Smell Is More Powerful than You Think." *The Washington Post*, 11 May 2017, https://www.washingtonpost.com/news/speaking-of-science/wp/2017/05/11/your-sense-of-smell-is-more-powerful-than-you-think/.
25. "How Far Can Sharks Smell Blood?" *Field & Stream*, www.fieldandstream.com/survival/how-far-can-sharks-smell-blood.
26. "Shark Science." *Shark Trust*, www.sharktrust.org/shark-science.
27. Fernicola, Richard G. *Twelve Days of Terror: Inside the Shocking 1916 New Jersey Shark Attacks.* Rowman & Littlefield, 2016.
28. Fernicola, *Twelve Days of Terror.*
29. Berman, Mark. "Shark Week: 7 Things Way More Likely to Kill You Than Sharks." *USA Today*, 24 July 2017, https://www.usatoday.com/story/news/nation-now/2017/07/24/shark-week-7-things-way-more-likely-kill-you-than-sharks/506115001/#:~:text=Lightning%20strike,3%2C748%2C067%20for%20a%20shark%20attack.
30. "Shark Attack vs. Other Causes of Death." *PETA*, https://www.peta.org/features/shark-attack-vs-other-causes-of-death/.
31. "Shark Attack vs. Other Causes of Death." *PETA*.
32. "What's More Likely to Kill You Than a Shark?" *Gili Shark Conservation*, https://www.gilisharkconservation.com/whats-more-likely-to-kill-you-than-a-shark/.
33. "Ipsos Study: Sharks Terrify Half of Americans (51%), with Many (38%) Scared to Swim in the Ocean Because of Them." *Ipsos*, www.ipsos.com/en-us/sharks-half-51-americans-are-absolutely-terrified-them-and-many-38-scared-swim-ocean-because-them.
34. "Shark Attack Incident Log." *International Shark Attack File*, Florida Museum of Natural History, www.sharkattackfile.net/incidentlog.htm.
35. "Shark Attack Incident Log," *International Shark Attack File.*
36. Encyclopaedia Britannica. "White Shark." *Encyclopaedia Britannica*, 2023, https://www.britannica.com/animal/white-shark.
37. Fernicola, Richard G. *Twelve Days of Terror: Inside the Shocking 1916 New Jersey Shark Attacks.* Rowman & Littlefield, 2016.
38. Skomal, Greg. *Shark Handbook.* Simon and Schuster, 2014.
39. Skomal, *Shark Handbook.*
40. "Scarlet Billows." *Order of the Jackalope*, https://order-of-the-jackalope.com/scarlet-billows/.

41. "Scarlet Billows," *Order of the Jackalope*.
42. Heyer, Patricia and Robert. *Shark Attacks of the Jersey Shore: A History*. Arcadia Publishing, 2020.
43. Science Bulletin, vol. 3, no. 1, *Brooklyn Institute of Arts and Sciences*, 1909, pp. 28–29. Internet Archive, https://archive.org/details/sciencebulletin0301broouoft/page/28/mode/2up

**Chapter Two**
1. Capuzzo, Michael. *Close to Shore: A True Story of Terror in an Age of Innocence*. Broadway Books, 2001.
2. "Travel Advisory: Beach Vacationers Beware." *Los Angeles Times*, 28 June 1992, www.latimes.com/archives/la-xpm-1992-06-28-tr-1725-story.html.
3. "The History of How We Got Paid Vacation in the US." *Fast Company*, www.fastcompany.com/90220227/the-history-of-how-we-got-paid-vacation-in-the-us.
4. "Ford Model T." *Heritage Society*, www.heritagesociety.org/ford-model-t#:~:text=Henry%20Ford's%20revolutionary%20advancements%20in,often%20cost%20%242000%2D%243000.
5. "Ford Model T," *Heritage Society*.
6. "Ford's Assembly Line Starts Rolling." *History, A&E Television Network*s, www.history.com/this-day-in-history/fords-assembly-line-starts-rolling.
7. Lay, M. G., and James E. Vance. *Ways of the World: A History of the World's Roads and of the Vehicles That Used Them*. Rutgers University Press, 1992.
8. Bureau of the Census. Historical Statistics of the United States: Colonial Times to 1970. Table Q398. Washington, DC: U.S. Government Printing Office, 1976. Bureau of the Census. Statistical Abstract of the United States: 2012. Washington, DC: U.S. Government Printing Office, 2011, pp. 1064–1068.
9. Cocks, Catherine. *Doing the Town: The Rise of Urban Tourism in the United States, 1850–1915*. University of California Press, 2001.
10. "Travel Advisory: Beach Vacationers Beware." *Los Angeles Times*, 28 June 1992, www.latimes.com/archives/la-xpm-1992-06-28-tr-1725-story.html.
11. "The Hotel Business in America Has a Long and Sometimes Even Illustrious History." *The Baltimore Sun*, 16 Oct. 1994, www.baltimoresun.com/1994/10/16/the-hotel-business-in-america-has-a-long-and-sometimes-even-illustrious-history/.
12. https://www.britannica.com/biography/Jonas-Salk
13. "Paralysis Kills 22 More Babies in New York City." The New York Times, 8 July 1916.
14. Fortieth Annual Report of the Department of Health of the State of New Jersey, 1916. *Trenton, NJ: State Gazette Publishing Co., Printers*, 1916.
15. Fortieth Annual Report of the Department of Health of the State of New Jersey, 1916, *Gazette Publishing Co., Printers*.
16. Fortieth Annual Report of the Department of Health of the State of New Jersey, 1916, *Gazette Publishing Co., Printers*.
17. Risse, George B. "Epidemics and History: Ecological Perspectives." And AIDS: The Burden of History, edited by Elizabeth Fee and Dorothy M. Fox, *University of California Press*, 1988. Risse GB (1988). *Fee E, Fox DM* (eds.).
18. Fortieth Annual Report of the Department of Health of the State of New Jersey, 1916, *Gazette Publishing Co., Printers*.

19. Fortieth Annual Report of the Department of Health of the State of New Jersey, 1916, *Gazette Publishing Co., Printers.*
20. Fortieth Annual Report of the Department of Health of the State of New Jersey, 1916, *Gazette Publishing Co., Printers.*
21. Capuzzo, Michael. *Close to Shore: A True Story of Terror in an Age of Innocence.* Broadway Books, 2001.
22. Fernicola, Richard. G. *Twelve Days of Terror: Inside the Shocking 1916 New Jersey Shark Attacks.* Rowman & Littlefield, 2016.
23. Vecchione, Maria. "Robert Engle of the Engleside Hotel Remembered." *Asbury Park Press*, 20 May 2015, www.app.com/story/news/local/southern-ocean-county/2015/05/20/robert-engle-engleside-hotel/27640509/.
24. Sinnott, Eileen. "Robert Engle and the Engleside Hotel." *Asbury Park Press*, 20 May 2015, www.app.com/story/news/local/southern-ocean-county/2015/05/20/robert-engle-engleside-hotel/27640509/.
25. Capuzzo, Michael. *Close to Shore: A True Story of Terror in an Age of Innocence.* Broadway Books, 2001.
26. Fortieth Annual Report of the Department of Health of the State of New Jersey, 1916. *Trenton, NJ: State Gazette Publishing Co., Printers*, 1916.
27. Fernicola, Richard. G. *Twelve Days of Terror: Inside the Shocking 1916 New Jersey Shark Attacks.* Rowman & Littlefield, 2016.
28. Fernicola, *Twelve Days of Terror.*
29. Capuzzo, Michael. *Close to Shore: A True story of Terror in an Age of Innocence.* Broadway Books, 2001.
30. Capuzzo, *Close to Shore.*
31. Fernicola, Richard. G. *Twelve Days of Terror: Inside the Shocking 1916 New Jersey Shark Attacks.* Rowman & Littlefield, 2016.
32. Capuzzo, Michael. *Close to Shore: A True Story of Terror in an Age of Innocence.* Broadway Books, 2001.
33. Fernicola, Richard. G. *Twelve Days of Terror: Inside the Shocking 1916 New Jersey Shark Attacks.* Rowman & Littlefield, 2016.
34. Fernicola, *Twelve Days of Terror.*
35. Fernicola, *Twelve Days of Terror.*
36. "Dies after attack by fish." *New York Times*, 3 Jul 1916.
37. Capuzzo, Michael. *Close to Shore: A True Story of Terror in an Age of Innocence.* Broadway Books, 2001.
38. Capuzzo, *Close to Shore.*
39. "Bathers Need Have No Fear of Sharks: Lousy Fish Expert Declares One That Killed Swimmer May Have Sought To Attack Dog." *Philadelphia Public Ledger.*

## Chapter Three

1. "10 Best New Jersey Beach Towns." *Travel + Leisure*, 12 June 2023, www.travelandleisure.com/best-new-jersey-beach-towns-8675718.
2. Fernicola, Richard. G. *Twelve Days of Terror: Inside the Shocking 1916 New Jersey Shark Attacks.* Rowman & Littlefield, 2016.
3. Capuzzo, Michael. *Close to Shore: A True Story of Terror in an Age of Innocence.* Broadway Books, 2001.
4. "Shark Kills Bather off Jersey Beach; Bites Off Both Legs of a Youth." *The New York Times*, 7 July 1916,

## Notes 173

5. *Asbury Park Evening Press*, July 1916.
6. Capuzzo, Michael. *Close to Shore: A True Story of Terror in an Age of Innocence.* Broadway Books, 2001.
7. Fernicola, Richard. G. *Twelve Days of Terror: Inside the Shocking 1916 New Jersey Shark Attacks.* Rowman & Littlefield, 2016.
8. Capuzzo, Michael. *Close to Shore: A True Story of Terror in an Age of Innocence.* Broadway Books, 2001.
9. Fernicola, Richard. G. *Twelve Days of Terror: Inside the Shocking 1916 New Jersey Shark Attacks.* Rowman & Littlefield, 2016.
10. Heyer, Patricia, and Robert Heyer. *Shark Attacks of the Jersey Shore: A History.* Arcadia Publishing, 2020.
11. McCormick, Harold. W. *Shadows in the Sea: The Sharks, Skates and Rays.* Chilton Book Company, 1963.
12. Capuzzo, Michael. *Close to Shore: A True Story of Terror in an Age of Innocence.* Broadway Books, 2001.
13. "New Jersey Shark Attacks of 1916." *Disaster History*, https://elephant-clavichord-ny49.squarespace.com/disaster/new-jersey-shark-attacks-of-1916
14. "New Jersey Shark Attacks of 1916," *Disaster History*.
15. Fernicola, Richard. G. *Twelve Days of Terror: Inside the Shocking 1916 New Jersey Shark Attacks.* Rowman & Littlefield, 2016.
16. Science Bulletin, vol. 3, no. 1, *Brooklyn Institute of Arts and Sciences*, 1909, pp. 28–29. Internet Archive, https://archive.org/details/sciencebulletin0301broouoft/page/28/mode/2up
17. Science Bulletin, *Brooklyn Institute of Arts and Sciences.*
18. Laffaye, Horace A. *Polo in the United States: A History.* McFarland, 2011.
19. Capuzzo, Michael. *Close to Shore: A True Story of Terror in an Age of Innocence.* Broadway Books, 2001.
20. Capuzzo, *Close to Shore.*
21. Mountford, Kent, PhD, and Richard G. Fernicola, MD. "Earliest Recorded Human Death from a Shark Encounter in North America." *Bay Journal*, self-published, 1 May 2023, https://www.bayjournal.com/earliest-recorded-human-death-from-a-shark-encounter-in-north-america/pdf_841f17e8-e4fb-11ed-bb11-b70c80a07d1d.html.
22. Science Bulletin, vol. 3, no. 1, *Brooklyn Institute of Arts and Sciences*, 1909, pp. 28–29. Internet Archive, https://archive.org/details/sciencebulletin0301broouoft/page/28/mode/2up
23. Science Bulletin, *Brooklyn Institute of Arts and Sciences.*
24. "NETS AND ARMED MOTORBOATS TO PROTECT BATHERS: BELIEVED PRECAUTION TAKEN WILL ASSURE ABSOLUTE SAFETY TO BATHERS ALONG NORTH SHORE." *Asbury Park Press*, 7 July 1916.
25. Capuzzo, Michael. *Close to Shore: A True Story of Terror in an Age of Innocence.* Broadway Books, 2001.
26. Fernicola, Richard. G. *Twelve Days of Terror: Inside the Shocking 1916 New Jersey Shark Attacks.* Rowman & Littlefield, 2016.
27. "New Jersey Shark Attacks of 1916." *Disaster History*, https://elephant-clavichord-ny49.squarespace.com/disaster/new-jersey-shark-attacks-of-1916
28. Capuzzo, Michael. *Close to Shore: A True Story of Terror in an Age of Innocence.* Broadway Books, 2001.

29. "New Jersey Shark Attacks of 1916." *Disaster History*, https://elephant-clavichord-ny49.squarespace.com/disaster/new-jersey-shark-attacks-of-1916
30. Capuzzo, Michael. *Close to Shore: A True Story of Terror in an Age of Innocence*. Broadway Books, 2001.
31. Fernicola, Richard. G. *Twelve Days of Terror: Inside the Shocking 1916 New Jersey Shark Attacks*. Rowman & Littlefield, 2016.
32. Heyer, Patricia and Robert. *Shark Attacks of the Jersey Shore: A History*. Arcadia Publishing, 2020.

**Chapter Four**
1. "Popular Jersey Shore Resort Rapidly Filling with Visitors." *The New York Times*, June 9, 1912.
2. "10 Best New Jersey Beach Towns." Travel + Leisure, 12 June 2023, www.travelandleisure.com/best-new-jersey-beach-towns-8675718.
3. Capuzzo, Michael. *Close to Shore: A True Story of Terror in an Age of Innocence*. Broadway Books, 2001.
4. "Shark." *Chronicling America: Historic American Newspapers*, 8 July 1916, www.chroniclingamerica.loc.gov/lccn/sn83045211/1916-07-08/ed-1/seq-2/.
5. "New Jersey Shark Attacks of 1916." *Disaster History*, https://elephant-clavichord-ny49.squarespace.com/disaster/new-jersey-shark-attacks-of-1916
6. "New Jersey Shark Attacks of 1916," *Disaster History*.
7. "New Jersey Shark Attacks of 1916," *Disaster History*.
8. "Shark drives Hughes' nephew from sea beach." *New York Tribune*, 11 July 1916.
9. "New Jersey Shark Attacks of 1916." *Disaster History*, https://elephant-clavichord-ny49.squarespace.com/disaster/new-jersey-shark-attacks-of-1916
10. Capuzzo, Michael. *Close to Shore: A True Story of Terror in an Age of Innocence*. Broadway Books, 2001.
11. Fernicola, Richard. G. *Twelve Days of Terror: Inside the Shocking 1916 New Jersey Shark Attacks*. Rowman & Littlefield, 2016.
12. "Jersey Shore Shark Attacks of 1916." *Chondrichthyes Wiki*, https://chondrichthyes.fandom.com/wiki/Jersey_Shore_shark_attacks_of_1916
13. Fernicola, Richard. G. *Twelve Days of Terror: Inside the Shocking 1916 New Jersey Shark Attacks*. Rowman & Littlefield, 2016.
14. Fernicola, *Twelve Days of Terror*.
15. McCormick, Harold W. *Shadows in the Sea: The Sharks, Skates and Rays*. Chilton Book Company, 1963.
16. Heyer, Patricia, and Robert Heyer. *Shark Attacks of the Jersey Shore: A History*. Arcadia Publishing, 2020.
17. Savolaine, John Allan. *Stanley Fisher: Shark Attack Hero of a Bygone Age*. 48 Hour Books, 2016.
18. Fernicola, Richard. G. *Twelve Days of Terror: Inside the Shocking 1916 New Jersey Shark Attacks*. Rowman & Littlefield, 2016.
19. "Profile of Matawan Borough, New Jersey." *United States Census Bureau*, https://data.census.gov/profile/Matawan_borough,_New_Jersey?g=160XX00US3444520
20. "Shark Kills 2 Bathers, Maims 1 Near New York; Swims Ten Miles from Sea Through Matawan Creek." *The New York Times*, 13 July 1916,
21. Fernicola, Richard. G. *Twelve Days of Terror: Inside the Shocking 1916 New Jersey Shark Attacks*. Rowman & Littlefield, 2016.

22. Savolaine, John Allan. *Stanley Fisher: Shark Attack Hero of a Bygone Age.* 48 Hour Books, 2016.
23. Heyer, Patricia and Robert. *Shark Attacks of the Jersey Shore: A History.* Arcadia Publishing, 2020.
24. Capuzzo, Michael. *Close to Shore: A True Story of Terror in an Age of Innocence.* Broadway Books, 2001.
25. Heyer, Patricia and Robert. *Shark Attacks of the Jersey Shore: A History.* Arcadia Publishing, 2020.
26. Fernicola, Richard. G. *Twelve Days of Terror: Inside the Shocking 1916 New Jersey Shark Attacks.* Rowman & Littlefield, 2016.
27. Heyer, Patricia and Robert. *Shark Attacks of the Jersey Shore: A History.* Arcadia Publishing, 2020.
28. "The Sight That Stopped a Nation." *The Philadelphia Inquirer*, 18 July 1916.
29. Fernicola, Richard. G. *Twelve Days of Terror: Inside the Shocking 1916 New Jersey Shark Attacks.* Rowman & Littlefield, 2016.
30. "New Jersey Shark Attacks of 1916." *Disaster History*, https://elephant-clavichord-ny49.squarespace.com/disaster/new-jersey-shark-attacks-of-1916
31. Capuzzo, Michael. *Close to Shore: A True Story of Terror in an Age of Innocence.* Broadway Books, 2001.
32. Fernicola, Richard. G. *Twelve Days of Terror: Inside the Shocking 1916 New Jersey Shark Attacks.* Rowman & Littlefield, 2016.
33. *The Matawan Journal*, July 1916.
34. Savolaine, John Allan. *Stanley Fisher: Shark Attack Hero of a Bygone Age.* 48 Hour Books, 2016.
35. Fernicola, Richard. G. *Twelve Days of Terror: Inside the Shocking 1916 New Jersey Shark Attacks.* Rowman & Littlefield, 2016.
36. Fernicola, *Twelve Days of Terror.*
37. Fernicola, *Twelve Days of Terror.*
38. Fernicola, *Twelve Days of Terror.*
39. Savolaine, John Allan. *Stanley Fisher: Shark Attack Hero of a Bygone Age.* 48 Hour Books, 2016.
40. Savolaine, *Stanley Fisher.*
41. Fernicola, Richard. G. *Twelve Days of Terror: Inside the Shocking 1916 New Jersey Shark Attacks.* Rowman & Littlefield, 2016.
42. Heyer, Patricia and Robert. *Shark Attacks of the Jersey Shore: A History.* Arcadia Publishing, 2020.
43. Fernicola, Richard. G. *Twelve Days of Terror: Inside the Shocking 1916 New Jersey Shark Attacks.* Rowman & Littlefield, 2016.
44. Heyer, Patricia and Robert. *Shark Attacks of the Jersey Shore: A History.* Arcadia Publishing, 2020.
45. Fernicola, Richard. G. *Twelve Days of Terror: Inside the Shocking 1916 New Jersey Shark Attacks.* Rowman & Littlefield, 2016.
46. "Saturday, July 15 – Matawan." *Matawan Historical Society*, https://matawanhistoricalsociety.org/saturday-july-15-matawan/
47. Savolaine, John Allan. *Stanley Fisher: Shark Attack Hero of a Bygone Age.* 48 Hour Books, 2016.
48. "Shark Attack Anniversary." Matawan Historical Society, https://matawanhistoricalsociety.org/shark-attack-anniversary/

## Chapter Five

1. "Cliffwood Beach, NJ Demographics." *Census Dots*, www.censusdots.com/race/cliffwood-beach-nj-demographics.
2. Fernicola, Richard. G. *Twelve Days of Terror: Inside the Shocking 1916 New Jersey Shark Attacks*. Rowman & Littlefield, 2016.
3. Fernicola, *Twelve Days of Terror*.
4. Heyer, Patricia and Robert. *Shark Attacks of the Jersey Shore: A History*. Arcadia Publishing, 2020.
5. Fernicola, Richard. G. *Twelve Days of Terror: Inside the Shocking 1916 New Jersey Shark Attacks*. Rowman & Littlefield, 2016.
6. Heyer, Patricia and Robert. *Shark Attacks of the Jersey Shore: A History*. Arcadia Publishing, 2020.

## Chapter Six

1. Capuzzo, Michael. *Close to Shore: A True Story of Terror in an Age of Innocence*. Broadway Books, 2001.
2. Capuzzo, *Close to Shore*.
3. Capuzzo, *Close to Shore*.
4. "Many See Sharks, But All Get Away: Matawan's Population, with Weapons and Dynamite, Seek Man-Eater That Killed Two." *The New York Times*, July 14, 1916.
5. Capuzzo, Michael. *Close to Shore: A True Story of Terror in an Age of Innocence*. Broadway Books, 2001.
6. Fernicola, Richard. G. *Twelve Days of Terror: Inside the Shocking 1916 New Jersey Shark Attacks*. Rowman & Littlefield, 2016.
7. Capuzzo, Michael. *Close to Shore: A True Story of Terror in an Age of Innocence*. Broadway Books, 2001.
8. *The Sunday Star*, July 23, 1916.
9. Fernicola, Richard. G. *Twelve Days of Terror: Inside the Shocking 1916 New Jersey Shark Attacks*. Rowman & Littlefield, 2016.
10. Fernicola, *Twelve Days of Terror*.
11. Fernicola, *Twelve Days of Terror*.
12. *The New York Times*, July 1916.
13. *The New York Times*, July 1916.
14. "Scarlet Billows." *Order of the Jackalope*, https://order-of-the-jackalope.com/scarlet-billows/
15. Fernicola, Richard. G. *Twelve Days of Terror: Inside the Shocking 1916 New Jersey Shark Attacks*. Rowman & Littlefield, 2016.
16. Fernicola, Twelve Days of Terror.
17. Fernicola, Twelve Days of Terror.
18. Fernicola, Twelve Days of Terror.
19. Capuzzo, Michael. *Close to Shore: A True Story of Terror in an Age of Innocence*. Broadway Books, 2001.
20. *The New York Times*, 18 July 1916.
21. Fernicola, Richard. G. *Twelve Days of Terror: Inside the Shocking 1916 New Jersey Shark Attacks*. Rowman & Littlefield, 2016.
22. "Scarlet Billows." *Order of the Jackalope*, https://order-of-the-jackalope.com/scarlet-billows/
23. "Scarlet Billows," *Order of the Jackalope*.

24. Fernicola, Richard. G. *Twelve Days of Terror: Inside the Shocking 1916 New Jersey Shark Attacks*. Rowman & Littlefield, 2016.
25. Fernicola, *Twelve Days of Terror*.
26. "Harlem Man In Tiny Boat Kills a 7 ½ Foot Man-Eating Shark." *The Home News*. July 19, 1916.
27. "TWO MEN IN TINY BOAT CATCH KILLER SHARK, BEAT IT TO DEATH AFTER SHARK TANGLES ITSELF IN DRIFT NET…PART OF BOY'S SHIN TAKEN FROM LARGE FISH CAUGHT NEAR CITY." *Bronx Home News*. 19 July 1916.
28. "TWO MEN IN TINY BOAT CATCH KILLER SHARK," *Bronx Home News*.
29. "TWO MEN IN TINY BOAT CATCH KILLER SHARK," *Bronx Home News*.
30. Fernicola, Richard. G. *Twelve Days of Terror: Inside the Shocking 1916 New Jersey Shark Attacks*. Rowman & Littlefield, 2016.
31. Capuzzo, Michael. *Close to Shore: A True Story of Terror in an Age of Innocence*. Broadway Books, 2001.

## Chapter Seven

1. "U-Boats: The First Weapon of War to Terrorize the Seas." *History, A&E Television Networks*, www.history.com/news/u-boats-world-war-i-germany.
2. "U-boat." *Encyclopaedia Britannica*, www.britannica.com/technology/U-boat.
3. "U-Boats: The First Weapon of War to Terrorize the Seas." *History, A&E Television Networks*, www.history.com/news/u-boats-world-war-i-germany.
4. "UNARMED GERMAN SUBMARINE WITH MERCHANDISE CARGO NOW LIES NEAR BALTIMORE." *The Sun*, 10 July 1916.
5. Wilson, Woodrow. *Final Address in Support of the League of Nations*. Archived 11 July 2014, at the Wayback Machine, www.AmericanRhetoric.com.
6. "Anti-German Hysteria." *Historical Marker Database*, www.hmdb.org/m.asp?m=134945.
7. "Yale University Manuscripts and Archives Collections." *Yale University Library Digital Collections*, https://elischolar.library.yale.edu/cgi/viewcontent.cgi?article=1021&context=mssa_collections
8. Krammer, Arnold. *Undue Process: The Untold Story of America's German Alien Internees*. Rowman & Littlefield, 1997.
9. *Collinsville Advertiser*, 29 December 1917.
10. Stehman, Peter. *Patriotic Murder: A World War I Hate Crime for Uncle Sam*. Lincoln, NE: Potomac Books, 2018.
11. Stehman, *Patriotic Murder*.
12. Schwartz, E. A. "The Lynching of Robert Prager, the United Mine Workers, and the Problems of Patriotism in 1918." *Journal of the Illinois State Historical Society*, vol. 95, no. 4, 2002.
13. "Sharks and Submarines." *The New York Times*, 15 July 1916.
14. *The New York Times*, 18 July 1916.
15. Fernicola, Richard. G. *Twelve Days of Terror: Inside the Shocking 1916 New Jersey Shark Attacks*. Rowman & Littlefield, 2016.
16. "When New Yorkers Lived Knee-Deep in Trash." *Collectors Weekly*, www.collectorsweekly.com/articles/when-new-yorkers-lived-knee-deep-in-trash/.
17. "When New Yorkers Lived Knee-Deep in Trash," *Collectors Weekly*.

18. "A Brief History of New York City Recycling." *Weill Cornell Medicine Sustainability*, www.sustainability.weill.cornell.edu/waste-management-recycling/brief-history-new-york-city-recycling/.
19. "On the Jersey Shore, a Summer to Forget." *The New York Times*, 2 Sept. 1988.
20. "Monarch Populations Rebound, but It's Still a Long Journey to Recovery." *Mongabay News*, 31 Jan. 2023, www.news.mongabay.com/2023/01/monarch-populations-rebound-but-its-still-a-long-journey-to-recovery/.
21. McCormick, Harold. W. *Shadows in the Sea: The Sharks, Skates and Rays*. Chilton Book Company, 1963.
22. Murphy, Robert Cushman, and John Treadwell Nichols. "The Shark Situation in the Waters About New York." *Brooklyn Museum Quarterly*, vol. 3, no. 4, Oct. 1916, pp. 203-210.
23. Murphy, "The Shark Situation in the Waters About New York."
24. Fernicola, Richard. G. *Twelve Days of Terror: Inside the Shocking 1916 New Jersey Shark Attacks*. Rowman & Littlefield, 2016.
25. "The Relative Risk of Shark Attacks to Humans: More People Mean More Attacks." *Florida Museum of Natural History*, www.flmnh.ufl.edu/fish/sharks/isaf/moreattacks.htm.
26. Murphy, Robert Cushman, and John Treadwell Nichols. "The Shark Situation in the Waters About New York." *Brooklyn Museum Quarterly*, vol. 3, no. 4, Oct. 1916, pp. 203-210.

**Chapter Eight**
1. "Shark." *Chronicling America: Historic American Newspapers*, 8 July 1916, www.chroniclingamerica.loc.gov/lccn/sn83045211/1916-07-08/ed-1/seq-2/.
2. Murphy, Robert Cushman, and John Treadwell Nichols. "The Shark Situation in the Waters About New York." *Brooklyn Museum Quarterly*, vol. 3, no. 4, Oct. 1916, pp. 203-210.
3. Murphy, "The Shark Situation in the Waters About New York."
4. Ellis, Richard. *Book of Sharks*. Facts on File, 1991.
5. Fernicola, Richard. G. *Twelve Days of Terror: Inside the Shocking 1916 New Jersey Shark Attacks*. Rowman & Littlefield, 2016.
6. McKeever, William. *Emperors of the Deep: Sharks--The Ocean's Most Mysterious, Most Misunderstood, and Most Important Guardians*. HarperCollins, 2019.
7. "How close do sharks come to shore? Study from Mass. shark experts holds an answer." *MassLive*, Advance Local Media LLC, 19 July 2023, https://www.masslive.com/capecod/2023/07/how-close-do-sharks-come-to-shore-study-from-mass-shark-experts-holds-an-answer.html.
8. "Carcharhinus Plumbeus (Sandbar Shark)." *Florida Museum*, University of Florida, www.floridamuseum.ufl.edu/discover-fish/species-profiles/carcharhinus-plumbeus/.
9. McKeever, *Emperors of the Deep*.

**Chapter Nine**
1. Lynch, Jennifer. "Why Do Sharks Bite People?" *Psychology Today*, 6 Mar. 2023, www.psychologytoday.com/intl/blog/animal-minds/202303/why-do-sharks-bite-people.
2. "International Shark Attack File." Florida Museum, www.floridamuseum.ufl.edu/shark-attacks/.

3. McKeever, William. *Emperors of the Deep: Sharks--The Ocean's Most Mysterious, Most Misunderstood, and Most Important Guardians*, 2019.
4. McKeever, *Emperors of the Deep*.
5. "ISAF Case Classifications." *Florida Museum*, www.floridamuseum.ufl.edu/shark-attacks/about/isaf-case-classifications/.
6. "Yearly Worldwide Shark Attack Summary." *Florida Museum*, www.floridamuseum.ufl.edu/shark-attacks/yearly-worldwide-summary/.
7. "Yearly Worldwide Shark Attack Summary," *Florida Museum*.
8. "Yearly Worldwide Shark Attack Summary," *Florida Museum*.
9. "Yearly Worldwide Shark Attack Summary," *Florida Museum*.
10. Maxouris, Christina. "3 Shark Attacks Were Reported in Florida over the Weekend." CNN, 5 Aug. 2019, www.cnn.com/2019/08/05/us/florida-3-shark-attacks-trnd/index.html.
11. "Yearly Worldwide Shark Attack Summary." *Florida Museum*, www.floridamuseum.ufl.edu/shark-attacks/yearly-worldwide-summary/.
12. "Hippos: Aggressive and Deadly but Also Vital to Africa's Ecosystems." *Animals Asia*, 13 Apr. 2021, www.animalsasia.org/us/media/news/news-archive/hippos-aggressive-and-deadly-but-also-vital-to-africas-ecosystems.html.
13. "Vector-Borne Diseases." *World Health Organization (WHO)*, 2020. www.who.int/en/news-room/fact-sheets/detail/vector-borne-diseases.
14. "Menstruation and Shark Attacks: Is There an Increased Risk?" *Florida Museum*, www.floridamuseum.ufl.edu/shark-attacks/reduce-risk/menstruation/.
15. "Shark Bites Consistent with Recent Trends, with Small Spike in Fatalities." Florida Museum, www.floridamuseum.ufl.edu/science/shark-bites-consistent-with-recent-trends-with-small-spike-in-fatalities/#:~:text=Despite%20the%20increase%2C%20the%20number,the%20water%2C%E2%80%9D%20Naylor%20said.
16. Capuzzo, Michael. *Close to Shore: A True Story of Terror in an Age of Innocence*. Broadway Books, 2001.
17. "Shark Attack Victim's Family Shares Touching Tribute." *Sun Herald*, 15 July 2023, www.sunherald.com/entertainment/article278274698.html.
18. Cooke, Melanie. "Summer of the shark". *The Guardian*, 5 Sept. 2001. https://www.theguardian.com/theguardian/2001/sep/05/features11.g23
19. "'Summer of the Shark' in 2001: More Hype than Fact, New Numbers Show." *University of Florida News Archive*, 27 Feb. 2002, https://news.ufl.edu/archive/2002/02/summer-of-the-shark-in-2001-more-hype-than-fact-new-numbers-show.html
20. "Summer of the Shark," *University of Florida News Archive*.
21. "Summer of the Shark," *University of Florida News Archive*.
22. "Understanding Misinformation and Its Impact." *American Psychological Association*, www.apa.org/topics/journalism-facts/misinformation-belief-action.
23. Stossel, John. *Give Me a Break: How I Exposed Hidden Evils in America and Learned to Love the Real World*. New York, Random House, 2004.

## Chapter Ten
1. "The Truth About the 9 Shark Attacks Known as Black December." *The Daily Jaws*, https://thedailyjaws.com/blog/the-truth-about-the-9-shark-attacks-known-as-black-december

2. "South Africa Shark Attack File." *Stop Shark Cage Diving*, Web Archive, 3 May 2012, https://web.archive.org/web/20120503092351/http://www.stopsharkcagediving.com/south_africa_shark_attack_file.htm
3. "What Was the Black December of 1957?" *Getaway*, www.getaway.co.za/travel/travel-ideas/what-was-the-black-december-of-1957/.
4. "South Africa Shark Attack File." *Stop Shark Cage Diving*, Web Archive, 3 May 2012, https://web.archive.org/web/20120503092351/http://www.stopsharkcagediving.com/south_africa_shark_attack_file.htm
5. "South Africa Shark Attack File," *Stop Shark Cage Diving*.
6. "South Africa Shark Attack File," *Stop Shark Cage Diving*.
7. "South Africa Shark Attack File," *Stop Shark Cage Diving*.
8. "South Africa Shark Attack File," *Stop Shark Cage Diving*.
9. "South Africa Shark Attack File," *Stop Shark Cage Diving*.
10. "South Africa Shark Attack File," *Stop Shark Cage Diving*.
11. "Shark Attacks - Historical Accounts." *Shark Research Institute*, Web Archive, 12 Apr. 2010, https://web.archive.org/web/20100412072644/http://www.shark.co.za/hist2.htm
12. Heyer, Patricia, and Robert Heyer. *Shark Attacks of the Jersey Shore: A History.* Arcadia Publishing, 2020.
13. Heyer, *Shark Attacks of the Jersey Shore: A History.*
14. Heyer, *Shark Attacks of the Jersey Shore: A History.*
15. Heyer, *Shark Attacks of the Jersey Shore: A History.*
16. Heyer, *Shark Attacks of the Jersey Shore: A History.*
17. Heyer, *Shark Attacks of the Jersey Shore: A History.*
18. Heyer, *Shark Attacks of the Jersey Shore: A History.*
19. "Shark Attacks." *Pravda*, 23 Dec. 2010, https://english.pravda.ru/hotspots/116042-shark_attacks/
20. "Shark Attacks," *Pravda*.
21. "Shark Attacks," *Pravda*.
22. "Shark Attacks," *Pravda*.
23. Tisdall, Simon. "Shark Attacks in Sharm El Sheikh, Egypt." *The Guardian*, 3 Dec. 2010, www.theguardian.com/world/2010/dec/03/shark-attacks-sharm-el-sheikh-egypt.
24. "Shark Attack Incident Log." International Shark Attack File, *Florida Museum of Natural History*, www.sharkattackfile.net/incidentlog.htm.
25. Tisdall, Simon. "Tourist Killed in Sharm El Sheikh Shark Attack." *The Guardian*, 5 Dec. 2010, www.theguardian.com/world/2010/dec/05/tourist-killed-sharm-shark-attack.
26. "Diving Continues as Experts Investigate." *Divernet*, 22 Sept. 2002, www.divernet.com/home_diving_news/692022/diving_continues_as_experts_investigate.html.
27. "Shark Bites Man off Sullivan's." *Moultrie News, The Post and Courier*, 19 July 2021, www.postandcourier.com/moultrie-news/news/shark-bites-man-off-sullivan-s/article_f0838c12-750f-528d-8549-2e45a9cd266f.html.
28. "Girl Injured in Reported Shark Attack at Ocean Isle Thursday." *StarNewsOnline*, 11 June 2015, www.starnewsonline.com/story/news/2015/06/11/girl-injured-in-reported-shark-attack-at-ocean-isle-thursday/30981541007/.
29. Harris, Paul. "Holidaymakers Return to North Carolina Beach After Double Shark Attack." *The Guardian,* 16 June 2015, www.theguardian.com/environment/2015/jun/16/holidaymakers-return-to-north-carolina-beach-after-double-shark-attack.

30. Harris, "Holidaymakers Return to North Carolina Beach After Double Shark Attack."
31. McCarthy, Michael. "Fourth Shark Attack in North Carolina." The Guardian, 25 June 2015, www.theguardian.com/us-news/2015/jun/25/fourth-shark-attack-north-carolina.
32. McCarthy, "Fourth Shark Attack in North Carolina."
33. "Shark Attack Reported in Outer Banks." *WTKR*, 26 June 2015, https://www.wtkr.com/2015/06/26/shark-attack-reported-in-outer-banks.
34. "Shark Bites Reported in Beaufort County Waters." *The Island Packet*, www.islandpacket.com/news/local/community/beaufort-news/article33693867.html.
35. "Second Shark Attack in Two Days Reported on Hatteras." *Island Free Press*, 27 June 2015, https://islandfreepress.org/outer-banks-news/06272015-secondsharkattackintwodaysreportedonhatteras/
36. "Young Boy Bitten by Shark off Isle of Palms." *Count on 2,* www.counton2.com/news/young-boy-bitten-by-shark-off-isle-of-palms/.
37. Fantz, Ashley, and Ed Payne. "North Carolina Shark Attack Victims Face Long Recoveries." *CNN*, 1 July 2015, www.cnn.com/2015/07/01/us/north-carolina-shark-attack/index.html.
38. Fantz, "North Carolina Shark Attack Victims Face Long Recoveries."
39. Fantz, "North Carolina Shark Attack Victims Face Long Recoveries."
40. Fantz, "North Carolina Shark Attack Victims Face Long Recoveries."
41. Degener, Richard. "1916 Shark Attacks: The Day the Terror Began." Asbury Park Press, 1 July 2016, www.app.com/story/news/history/2016/07/01/1916-shark-attacks-day-terror-began/86484828/.

**Chapter Eleven**
1. "Shark-Scared, Crowd Lets Bather Drown." *Asbury Park Press*, 25 July 1916.
2. "Shark-Scared, Crowd Lets Bather Drown," *Asbury Park Press*.
3. Murphy, Robert Cushman, and John Treadwell Nichols. "The Shark Situation in the Waters About New York." *Brooklyn Museum Quarterly*, vol. 3, no. 4, Oct. 1916.
4. *Scientific American* Magazine, 1916.
5. Murphy, Robert Cushman, and John Treadwell Nichols. "The Shark Situation in the Waters About New York." *Brooklyn Museum Quarterly*, vol. 3, no. 4, Oct. 1916.
6. Capuzzo, Michael. *Close to Shore: A True Story of Terror in an Age of Innocence*. Broadway Books, 2001.
7. *The New York Times*, 18 July 1916.
8. *The New York Times*, 18 July 1916.
9. Heyer, Patricia and Robert. *Shark Attacks of the Jersey Shore: A History*. Arcadia Publishing, 2020.
10. Heyer, *Shark Attacks of the Jersey Shore*.
11. Capuzzo, Michael. *Close to Shore: A True Story of Terror in an Age of Innocence*. Broadway Books, 2001.
12. McCormick, Harold. W. *Shadows in the Sea: The Sharks, Skates and Rays*. Chilton Book Company, 1963.
13. McCormick, *Shadows in the Sea*.
14. "The Electoral Vote: Total 531, Necessary to a Choice 266." *The New York Times*, 9 Nov. 1916

15. Fowler, David. "Shark Attacks and the Political Science of 1916." *Vox*, 19 Aug. 2022, https://www.vox.com/future-perfect/23279012/shark-attack-1916-woodrow-wilson-political-science-achen-bartels-fowler-hall.
16. Fowler, Anthony, and Andrew B. Hall. "Blind Retrospection: Why Shark Attacks Are Bad For Democracy". *Center for the Study of Democratic Institutions, Vanderbilt University*, May 2013, www.vanderbilt.edu/csdi/research/CSDI_WP_05-2013.pdf.
17. Fowler, "Blind Retrospection."

**Chapter Twelve**
1. Wilgoren, Jodi. "Scientists Say Frenzy Over Shark Attacks Is Unwarranted." *The New York Times*, 5 Sept. 2001.
2. "Corrections." *The New York Times*, 8 Sept. 2001,
3. "About Peter Benchley." *Peter Benchley*, www.peterbenchley.com/about-peter-benchley.
4. Barber, Nicholas. "The True Story of Jaws." *BBC Culture*, British Broadcasting Corporation, 13 July 2016, https://www.bbc.com/culture/article/20160713-the-true-story-of-jaws.
5. "A Wilder View: Impact of 'Jaws' Endures Beyond the Silver Screen." *KPAX News*, www.kpax.com/news/a-wilder-view/a-wilder-view-impact-of-jaws-endures-beyond-the-silver-screen#:~:text=Charles%20Vansant%2C%20a%20young%20man,life%20research%20and%20conservation%20efforts.
6. Sharf, Zack. "How 'Jaws' Forever Changed the Modern Blockbuster and Made Steven Spielberg a Household Name." *IndieWire, Penske Media Corporation*, www.indiewire.com/features/general/jaws-modern-blockbuster-steven-spielberg-1201844390/#:~:text=Made%20for%20less%20than%20$9,the%20box%20office%20in%201975.
7. "Jaws: The Groundbreaking Summer Blockbuster That Changed Hollywood and Summer Vacations Forever." Cinephilia & Beyond, https://cinephiliabeyond.org/jaws-groundbreaking-summer-blockbuster-changed-hollywood-summer-vacations-forever/.
8. "Think Sharks Are Scary? Blame Hollywood, New Study Suggests." *Mongabay News*, 20 Sept. 2021, https://news.mongabay.com/2021/09/if-you-think-sharks-are-scary-blame-hollywood-new-study-suggests/.
9. Neff, Christopher. *The Jaws Effect: How Movie Narratives Are Used to Influence Policy Responses to Shark Bites in Western Australia*. 2012.
10. "134 Non-Target Animals, Including Turtles and Dolphins, Killed by NSW Shark Nets This Season." *Humane Society International (HSI) Australia*, www.hsi.org.au/blog/134-non-target-animals-including-turtles-and-dolphins-killed-by-nsw-shark-nets-this-season/.
11. "Shark Nets." *Australian For Dolphins*, www.afd.org.au/shark-nets/.
12. "Shark Nets." *Shark Angels*, www.sharkangels.org/shark-nets/.
13. Harris, Paul. "More Than 90% of Marine Animals Caught in NSW Shark Nets Over Summer Were Non-Target Species." *The Guardian*, 30 Apr. 2024, www.theguardian.com/environment/2024/apr/30/more-than-90-of-marine-animals-caught-in-nsw-shark-nets-over-summer-were-non-target-species.
14. Harris, "More than 90% of Marine Animals Caught in NSW Shark Nets Over Summer Were Non-Target Species."

15. "134 Non-Target Animals, Including Turtles and Dolphins, Killed by NSW Shark Nets This Season." *Humane Society International (HSI) Australia*, www.hsi.org.au/blog/134-non-target-animals-including-turtles-and-dolphins-killed-by-nsw-shark-nets-this-season/.
16. "134 Non-Target Animals, Including Turtles and Dolphins, Killed by NSW Shark Nets This Season," *Humane Society International (HSI) Australia*.
17. "Shark Nets." *Australian For Dolphins*, www.afd.org.au/shark-nets/.
18. Morris, Jessica. "Shark Nets – Death Traps For Marine Animals." *HSI.org.au*, 8 Dec. 2016, archived from the original on 2 Oct. 2018. https://hsi.org.au/blog/shark-nets-death-traps-for-marine-animals/
19. "Shark Attacks: Time for Perspective." *Deakin University*, www.deakin.edu.au/research/research-news-and-publications/articles/shark-attacks-time-for-perspective.
20. "Shark Nets." *Australian For Dolphins*, www.afd.org.au/shark-nets/.
21. Eddie, Rachel. "Threat to Cut Shark Nets if Government Fails to Act." *The New Daily*, 9 Jan. 2018, www.thenewdaily.com.
22. "Aussie Shark Population Is in Staggering Decline." *News.com.au*, 19 Dec. 2024, www.news.com.au/technology/science/animals/aussie-shark-population-is-staggering-decline/news-story/49e910c828b6e2b735d1c68e6b2c956e.
23. "Think Sharks Are Scary? Blame Hollywood, New Study Suggests." *Mongabay News*, 20 Sept. 2021, https://news.mongabay.com/2021/09/if-you-think-sharks-are-scary-blame-hollywood-new-study-suggests/
24. "Think Sharks Are Scary? Blame Hollywood, New Study Suggests," *Mongabay News*.
25. "Ipsos Study: Sharks Terrify Half of Americans (51%), with Many (38%) Scared to Swim in the Ocean Because of Them." *Ipsos*, www.ipsos.com/en-us/sharks-half-51-americans-are-absolutely-terrified-them-and-many-38-scared-swim-ocean-because-them.
26. "Sharks Before and After Jaws." *JSTOR Daily*, https://daily.jstor.org/sharks-before-and-after-jaws/
27. "Shark Science." Shark Trust, www.sharktrust.org/shark-science.
28. McKeever, William. *Emperors of the Deep: Sharks--The Ocean's Most Mysterious, Most Misunderstood, and Most Important Guardians.* HarperCollins, 2019.
29. "Sharks." *WildAid*, www.wildaid.org/programs/sharks/#:~:text=Fins%20from%20up%20to%2073,shark%20fin%20soup%20each%20year.
30. "Products Containing Sharks." *Rob Stewart Sharkwater Foundation*, www.robstewartsharkwaterfoundation.org/articles/products-containing-sharks.
31. "Products Containing Sharks," *Rob Stewart Sharkwater Foundation*.
32. "Eco-Friendly Makeup." *IDEAS For Us*, https://ideasforus.org/eco-friendly-makeup/.
33. "Products Containing Sharks." *Rob Stewart Sharkwater Foundation*, www.robstewartsharkwaterfoundation.org/articles/products-containing-sharks.
34. "Products Containing Sharks," *Rob Stewart Sharkwater Foundation*.
35. Skomal, Greg. *Shark Handbook.* Simon and Schuster, 2014.
36. "Fisheries Management Reform." *Shark Conservation Fund*, www.sharkconservationfund.org/fisheries-management-reform/.
37. "Fisheries Management Reform," *Shark Conservation Fund*.
38. Benchley, Peter. "Great White Sharks." *National Geographic*, Apr. 2000.

39. McKeever, William. *Emperors of the Deep: Sharks--The Ocean's Most Mysterious, Most Misunderstood, and Most Important Guardians.* HarperCollins, 2019.
40. Shoard, Catherine. "Why the Author of Jaws Wished He Never Wrote It." *Boston.com*, 19 June 2015, www.boston.com/culture/entertainment/2015/06/19/why-the-author-of-jaws-wished-he-never-wrote-it/.

## Epilogue

1. "Jaws on Martha's Vineyard." *MVY*, www.mvy.com/jaws-on-marthas-vineyard/#:~:text=The%20Jaws%20Effect:,%22Jaws%20Island%E2%80%9D%20since%20then.
2. "Jaws on Martha's Vineyard," MVY.
3. "Jaws on Martha's Vineyard," MVY.
4. "How Jaws Influenced Shark Perception." Shark Stewards, https://sharkstewards.org/how-jaws-influenced-shark-perception/.
5. Waxman, Olivia B. "The History of Shark Week: How It Became a Summer Sensation." *Time*, 28 July 2023, https://time.com/6996703/shark-week-history/
6. Fetters, Ashley. "The Evolution of Shark Week, Pop-Culture Leviathan." *The Atlantic*, 13 Aug. 2012, www.theatlantic.com. Archived from the original on 8 Aug. 2013.
7. Whitenack, Lisa B., et al. "A Content Analysis of 32 Years of Shark Week Documentaries." *PLOS ONE*, vol. 17, no. 11, 2022, https://pmc.ncbi.nlm.nih.gov/articles/PMC9632781/.
8. Whitenack, "A Content Analysis of 32 Years of Shark Week Documentaries."
9. Willingham, Val. "Discovery's Shark Week Kicks Off with Controversial 'Megalodon' Program." *CNN*, 7 Aug. 2013, www.cnn.com/2013/08/07/showbiz/tv/discovery-shark-week-megalodon/.
10. Whitenack, Lisa B., et al. "A Content Analysis of 32 Years of Shark Week Documentaries." *PLOS ONE*, vol. 17, no. 11, 2022, https://pmc.ncbi.nlm.nih.gov/articles/PMC9632781/.
11. Whitenack, "A Content Analysis of 32 Years of Shark Week Documentaries."
12. "Fans Hopeful Underwhelming Jaws 50th Anniversary Announcement Is Just First Wave." *The Daily Jaws*, https://thedailyjaws.com/news/fans-hopeful-underwhelming-jaws-50th-anniversary-announcement-is-just-first-wave.
13. "Fans Hopeful Underwhelming Jaws 50th Anniversary Announcement Is Just First Wave," *The Daily Jaws*.
14. D'Alessandro, Anthony. "'Jaws' 50th Anniversary Feature Documentary in the Works at National Geographic." *Deadline*, 21 June 2024, https://deadline.com/2024/06/jaws-50th-anniversary-feature-documentary-national-geographic-steven-spielberg-1235980526/
15. D'Alessandro, "'Jaws' 50th Anniversary Feature Documentary in the Works at National Geographic."
16. D'Alessandro, Anthony. "Dueling 'Jaws' Documentaries in Works: 'Jaws: Making a Splash in Hollywood' & 'Jaws 50.'" *Deadline*, 12 July 2024, https://deadline.com/2024/07/dueling-jaws-documentaries-in-works-jaws-making-a-splash-in-hollywood-jaws-50-1235998408/
17. Whitenack, Lisa B., et al. "A Content Analysis of 32 Years of Shark Week Documentaries." *PLOS ONE*, vol. 17, no. 11, 2022, https://pmc.ncbi.nlm.nih.gov/articles/PMC9632781/.

# Bibliography

**Books and Historical Documents:**
Benchley, Peter. "Great White Sharks." *National Geographic*, Apr. 2000
Benchley, Peter. Jaws. *Doubleday*, 1974.
Bureau of the Census. Historical Statistics of the United States: Colonial Times to 1970. Table Q398. Washington, DC: *U.S. Government Printing Office*, 1976.
Bureau of the Census. Statistical Abstract of the United States: 2012. Washington, DC: *U.S. Government Printing Office*, 2011.
Capuzzo, Michael. Close to Shore: A True Story of Terror in an Age of Innocence. *Broadway Books*, 2001.
Chapman, Blake. Shark Attacks: Myths, Misunderstandings and Human Fear. *CSIRO Publishing*, 2017.
Cocks, Catherine. Doing the Town: The Rise of Urban Tourism in the United States, 1850–1915. *University of California Press*, 2001.
Coppleson, V. M. Shark Attack. *A. H. & A. W. Reed*, 1962.
Ellis, Richard, and John E. McCosker. Great White Shark: The Definitive Look at the Most Terrifying Creature of the Ocean. *Scholastic*, 1991.
Ellis, Richard. Book of Sharks. *Facts on File*, 1991.
Fernicola, Richard G. Twelve Days of Terror: Inside the Shocking 1916 New Jersey Shark Attacks. *Rowman & Littlefield*, 2016.
Fortieth Annual Report of the Department of Health of the State of New Jersey, 1916. Trenton, NJ: *State Gazette Publishing Co., Printers*, 1916.
Francis, Beryl. "Before and After 'Jaws': Changing Representations of Shark Attacks." *The Great Circle*, 2012.
Galati, Peter. "Sharks and the Navy: From 'Shark Lore' to 'Shark Chaser'—The United States Navy's Quest for a Shark Repellant and Its Impact on Shark Science." *The Saber and Scroll Journal*.
Healy, J. B. Unspeakable Horror: The Deadliest Shark Attacks in Maritime History. *Skyhorse*, 2017.
Heyer, Patricia, and Robert Heyer. Shark Attacks of the Jersey Shore: A History. *Arcadia Publishing*, 2020.
Krammer, Arnold. Undue Process: The Untold Story of America's German Alien Internees. *Rowman & Littlefield*, 1997.
Laffaye, Horace A. Polo in the United States: A History. *McFarland*, 2011.
Lay, M. G., and James E. Vance. Ways of the World: A History of the World's Roads and of the Vehicles That Used Them. *Rutgers University Press*, 1992.
Le Busque, B., and C. Litchfield. "Sharks on Film: An Analysis of How Shark-Human Interactions Are Portrayed in Films." *Human Dimensions of Wildlife*, 2021.

MacCormick, Alex. Shark Attacks: Terrifying True Accounts of Shark Attacks Worldwide. *Macmillan*, 1998.
Maniguet, Xavier. The Jaws of Death. *Macmillan*, 1991.
McCormick, Harold W. Shadows in the Sea: The Sharks, Skates and Rays. *Chilton Book Company*, 1963.
McKeever, William. *Emperors of the Deep: Sharks--The Ocean's Most Mysterious, Most Misunderstood, and Most Important Guardians.* HarperCollins, 2019.
Müller, Johannes, and Jacob Henle. Systematische Beschreibung der Plagiostomen. *Veit und comp*, 1841.
Murphy, Robert Cushman, and John Treadwell Nichols. "The Shark Situation in the Waters About New York." *Brooklyn Museum Quarterly*, vol. 3, no. 4, Oct. 1916.
Neff, Christopher. *The Jaws Effect: How Movie Narratives Are Used to Influence Policy Responses to Shark Bites in Western Australia.* 2012.
Risse, George B. "Epidemics and History: Ecological Perspectives." AIDS: The Burden of History, edited by Elizabeth Fee and Dorothy M. Fox, *University of California Press*, 1988.
Savolaine, John Allan. Stanley Fisher: Shark Attack Hero of a Bygone Age. *48 Hour Books*, 2016.
Schwartz, E. A. "The Lynching of Robert Prager, the United Mine Workers, and the Problems of Patriotism in 1918." *Journal of the Illinois State Historical Society*, 2002.
Science Bulletin, vol. 3, no. 1, *Brooklyn Institute of Arts and Sciences*, 1909.
Skomal, Greg. Shark Handbook. *Simon and Schuster*, 2014.
Stehman, Peter. Patriotic Murder: A World War I Hate Crime for Uncle Sam. *Potomac Books*, 2018.
Stevens, John D. Sharks. *Facts on File Publications*, 1987.
Stossel, John. Give Me a Break: How I Exposed Hidden Evils in America and Learned to Love the Real World. New York, *Random House*, 2004.

**Newspapers and Media Outlets:**
*Asbury Park Evening Post*
*Asbury Park Press*
*Asbury Park Evening Press*
*Barre Evening News*
*Bridgewater Courier-News*
*Bristol Daily Courier*
*Brooklyn Daily Eagle*
*Butler Citizen*
*Chambersburg Public Opinion*
*Collinsville Advertisers*
*Connellsville Daily Courier*
*Harrisburg Daily Independent*
*Matawan Journal*
*New Castle (PA) News*
*New York Evening World*
*New York Sun*
*New York Tribune*

*Passaic Daily News*
*Paterson Morning Call*
*Perth Amboy Evening News*
*Philadelphia Inquirer*
*Philadelphia Public Ledger*
*Reading Times*
*Rochester Democrat and Chronicle*
*The Bronx Home News*
*The New York Times*
*The Sun*
*Trenton Evening Times*
*Wilkes-Barre Evening News*
*Wilmington News Journal*
*York Daily*

**Documentaries:**
Shark Terror: The Real Jaws. Directed by Reelz TV, Reelz, 2015.
In Search of History: The Shark Attack 1916. Directed by The History Channel, 2005.

**Websites:**
"'Summer of the Shark' in 2001: More Hype than Fact, New Numbers Show." *University of Florida News Archive*, 27 Feb. 2002, www.archive.news.ufl.edu/articles/2002/02/summer-of-the-shark-in-2001-more-hype-than-fact-new-numbers-show.html.
"10 Best New Jersey Beach Towns." *Travel + Leisure*, 12 June 2023, www.travelandleisure.com/best-new-jersey-beach-towns-8675718.
"10 Common Things That Are Far More Dangerous Than the Things You Actually Fear." *Listverse*, 23 Mar. 2015, www.listverse.com/2015/03/23/10-common-things-that-are-far-more-dangerous-than-the-things-you-actually-fear/.
"100 Years Ago This Month: Sharks." *Historical Research Update*, www.historicalresearchupdate.com/research-tips/100-years-ago-this-month-sharks/.
"134 Non-Target Animals, Including Turtles and Dolphins, Killed by NSW Shark Nets This Season." *Humane Society International (HSI) Australia*, www.hsi.org.au/blog/134-non-target-animals-including-turtles-and-dolphins-killed-by-nsw-shark-nets-this-season/.
"1912 Presidential Election." *270toWin*, www.270towin.com/1912_Election/.
"1916 Presidential Election." *270toWin*, www.270towin.com/1916_Election/.
"1916 Shark Attack." *Matawan Historical Society*, www.matawanhistoricalsociety.org/1916-shark-attack/.
"A Brief History of New York City Recycling." *Weill Cornell Medicine Sustainability*, www.sustainability.weill.cornell.edu/waste-management-recycling/brief-history-new-york-city-recycling/.
"A Wilder View: Impact of 'Jaws' Endures Beyond the Silver Screen." *KPAX News*, www.kpax.com/news/a-wilder-view/a-wilder-view-impact-of-jaws-endures-beyond-the-silver-screen#:~:text=Charles%20Vansant%2C%20a%20young%20man,life%20research%20and%20conservation%20efforts.

"About Peter Benchley." *Peter Benchley*, www.peterbenchley.com/about-peter-benchley.

"Ancient Sharks." *Micronesian Conservation Coalition*, www.micronesianconservation.org/jen-page-2/.

"Anti-German Hysteria." *Historical Marker Database*, www.hmdb.org/m.asp?m=134945.

"Anti-German Sentiment." *Wikipedia*, 19 Dec. 2024, www.en.wikipedia.org/wiki/Anti-German_sentiment.

"Aussie Shark Population Is in Staggering Decline." *News.com.au*, 19 Dec. 2024, www.news.com.au/technology/science/animals/aussie-shark-population-is-staggering-decline/news-story/49e910c828b6e2b735d1c68e6b2c956e.

"Black December." *Wikipedia*, 19 Dec. 2024, www.en.wikipedia.org/wiki/Black_December.

"Carcharhinus Plumbeus (Sandbar Shark)." *Florida Museum*, University of Florida, www.floridamuseum.ufl.edu/discover-fish/species-profiles/carcharhinus-plumbeus/.

"Cliffwood Beach, NJ Demographics." *Census Dots*, www.censusdots.com/race/cliffwood-beach-nj-demographics.

"Cultural Significance of Sharks." *HawaiiActivities.com*, https://www.hawaiiactivities.com/travelguide/cultural-significance-sharks/#:~:text=Some%20species%20of%20sharks%2C%20like,between%20humans%20and%20the%20gods.

"Diving Continues as Experts Investigate." *Divernet*, 22 Sept. 2002, www.divernet.com/home_diving_news/692022/diving_continues_as_experts_investigate.html.

"Eco-Friendly Makeup." *IDEAS For Us*, www.ideasforus.org/eco-friendly-makeup/.

"Fans Hopeful Underwhelming Jaws 50th Anniversary Announcement Is Just First Wave." *The Daily Jaws*, www.thedailyjaws.com/news/fans-hopeful-underwhelming-jaws-50th-anniversary-announcement-is-just-first-wave.

"Fisheries Management Reform." *Shark Conservation Fund*, www.sharkconservationfund.org/fisheries-management-reform/.

"Ford Model T." *Heritage Society*, www.heritagesociety.org/ford-model-t#:~:text=Henry%20Ford's%20revolutionary%20advancements%20in,often%20cost%20%242000%2D%243000.

"Ford's Assembly Line Starts Rolling." *History, A&E Television Networks*, www.history.com/this-day-in-history/fords-assembly-line-starts-rolling.

"Girl Injured in Reported Shark Attack at Ocean Isle Thursday." *StarNewsOnline*, 11 June 2015, www.starnewsonline.com/story/news/2015/06/11/girl-injured-in-reported-shark-attack-at-ocean-isle-thursday/30981541007/.

"Hippos: Aggressive and Deadly but Also Vital to Africa's Ecosystems." *Animals Asia*, 13 Apr. 2021, www.animalsasia.org/us/media/news/news-archive/hippos-aggressive-and-deadly-but-also-vital-to-africas-ecosystems.html.

"History of Asbury Park." *Atlantic Highlands Historical Society*, www.aphistoricalsociety.org/history/.

"How a Century of Fear Turned Deadly for Sharks." *Florida Museum*, www.floridamuseum.ufl.edu/science/how-a-century-of-fear-turned-deadly-for-sharks/.

"How a Summer of Shark Attacks in 1916 Became the Real-Life 'Jaws.'" *All That's Interesting*, www.allthatsinteresting.com/shark-attacks-1916.

"How close do sharks come to shore? Study from Mass. shark experts holds an answer." *MassLive*, Advance Local Media LLC, 19 July 2023, https://www.masslive.com/capecod/2023/07/how-close-do-sharks-come-to-shore-study-from-mass-shark-experts-holds-an-answer.html.

"How Far Can Sharks Smell Blood?" *Field & Stream*, www.fieldandstream.com/survival/how-far-can-sharks-smell-blood.

"How Jaws Influenced Shark Perception." *Shark Stewards*, www.sharkstewards.org/how-jaws-influenced-shark-perception/

"How Many Sharks Are in the Ocean?" *Wonderopolis*, www.wonderopolis.org/wonder/how-many-sharks-are-in-the-ocean#:~:text=There%20could%20be%20a%20billion,of%20sharks%20in%20the%20world.

"International Shark Attack File." *Florida Museum*, www.floridamuseum.ufl.edu/shark-attacks/.

"Ipsos Study: Sharks Terrify Half of Americans (51%), with Many (38%) Scared to Swim in the Ocean Because of Them." *Ipsos*, www.ipsos.com/en-us/sharks-half-51-americans-are-absolutely-terrified-them-and-many-38-scared-swim-ocean-because-them.

"ISAF Case Classifications." *Florida Museum*, www.floridamuseum.ufl.edu/shark-attacks/about/isaf-case-classifications/.

"Jaws on Martha's Vineyard." *MVY*, www.mvy.com/jaws-on-marthas-vineyard/#:~:text=The%20Jaws%20Effect:,%22Jaws%20Island%E2%80%9D%20since%20then.

"Jaws: The Groundbreaking Summer Blockbuster That Changed Hollywood and Summer Vacations Forever." *Cinephilia & Beyond*, www.cinephiliabeyond.org/jaws-groundbreaking-summer-blockbuster-changed-hollywood-summer-vacations-forever/.

"Jersey Shore Shark Attacks of 1916." *Bionity.com*, www.bionity.com/en/encyclopedia/Jersey_Shore_shark_attacks_of_1916.html.

"Jersey Shore Shark Attacks of 1916." *Chondrichthyes Wiki*, www.wchondrichthyes.fandom.com/wiki/Jersey_Shore_shark_attacks_of_1916.

"Jonas Salk." *Encyclopaedia Britannica*, www.britannica.com/biography/Jonas-Salk.

"July 6, 1916 – Jersey Shore." *Today in History*, 6 July 2021, www.todayinhistory.blog/2021/07/06/july-6-1916-jersey-shore/.

"Matawan Man-Eater: The 1916 New Jersey Shark Attacks." *Hushed Up History*, www.husheduphistory.com/post/122810518008/matawan-man-eater-the-1916-new-jersey-shark.

"Matawan Shark Attack: A Deadly Day in 1916." *Yesterday's America*, https://yesterdaysamerica.com/matawan-shark-attack-a-deadly-day-in-1916/.

"Menstruation and Shark Attacks: Is There an Increased Risk?" *Florida Museum*, www.floridamuseum.ufl.edu/shark-attacks/reduce-risk/menstruation/.

"Monarch Populations Rebound, but It's Still a Long Journey to Recovery." *Mongabay News*, 31 Jan. 2023, www.news.mongabay.com/2023/01/monarch-populations-rebound-but-its-still-a-long-journey-to-recovery/.

"New Jersey 'Man-Eater' Shark Attacks of 1916." *ReefQuest Centre for Shark Research*, www.elasmo-research.org/education/topics/saf_nj_maneater.htm.

"New Jersey Shark Attack File (NJSAF)." *Shark Files*, www.sharkfiles.org/njsaf.

"New Jersey Shark Attacks of 1916." *Disaster History*, www.elephant-clavichord-ny49.squarespace.com/disaster/new-jersey-shark-attacks-of-1916.

"Our Work." *Shark Trust*, www.sharktrust.org/our-work.

"Products Containing Sharks." *Rob Stewart Sharkwater Foundation*, www.robstewartsharkwaterfoundation.org/articles/products-containing-sharks.

"Profile of Matawan Borough, New Jersey." *United States Census Bureau*, www.data.census.gov/profile/Matawan_borough,_New_Jersey?g=160XX00US3444520.

"Real-Life Horror: Matawan, New Jersey." *Grafiklit*, 24 Oct. 2011, www.grafiklit.wordpress.com/2011/10/24/real-life-horror-matawan-new-jersey/.

"Saturday, July 15 – Matawan." *Matawan Historical Society*, www.matawanhistoricalsociety.org/saturday-july-15-matawan/.

"Scarlet Billows." *Order of the Jackalope*, www.order-of-the-jackalope.com/scarlet-billows/.

"Second Shark Attack in Two Days Reported on Hatteras." *Island Free Press*, 27 June 2015, www.islandfreepress.org/outer-banks-news/06272015-secondsharkattackintwodaysreportedonhatteras/.

"Shark Attack Anniversary." *Matawan Historical Society*, www.matawanhistoricalsociety.org/shark-attack-anniversary/.

"Shark Attack File." *International Shark Attack File, Florida Museum of Natural History*, www.sharkattackfile.net.

"Shark Attack Incident Log." *International Shark Attack File, Florida Museum of Natural History*, www.sharkattackfile.net/incidentlog.htm.

"Shark Attack Reported in Outer Banks." *WTKR*, 26 June 2015, https://www.wtkr.com/2015/06/26/shark-attack-reported-in-outer-banks.

"Shark Attack Victim's Family Shares Touching Tribute." *Sun Herald*, 15 July 2023, www.sunherald.com/entertainment/article278274698.html.

"Shark Attack vs. Other Causes of Death." *PETA*, https://www.peta.org/features/shark-attack-vs-other-causes-of-death/.

"Shark Attacks - Historical Accounts." *Shark Research Institute*, Web Archive, 12 Apr. 2010, www.web.archive.org/web/20100412072644/http://www.shark.co.za/hist2.htm.

"Shark Attacks vs. Other Causes of Death." *PETA*, www.peta.org/features/shark-attack-vs-other-causes-of-death/.

"Shark Attacks." *Florida Museum of Natural History, University of Florida*, https://www.floridamuseum.ufl.edu/shark-attacks/.

"Shark Attacks." *Pravda*, 23 Dec. 2010, www.english.pravda.ru/hotspots/116042-shark_attacks/.

"Shark Attacks: Time for Perspective." *Deakin University*, www.deakin.edu.au/research/research-news-and-publications/articles/shark-attacks-time-for-perspective.

"Shark Bites Consistent with Recent Trends, with Small Spike in Fatalities." *Florida Museum*, www.floridamuseum.ufl.edu/science/shark-bites-consistent-with-recent-trends-with-small-spike-in-fatalities/#:~:text=Despite%20the%20increase%2C%20the%20number,the%20water%2C%E2%80%9D%20Naylor%20said.

"Shark Bites Man off Sullivan's." *Moultrie News, The Post and Courier*, 19 July 2021, www.postandcourier.com/moultrie-news/news/shark-bites-man-off-sullivan-s/article_f0838c12-750f-528d-8549-2e45a9cd266f.html.

"Shark Bites Reported in Beaufort County Waters." *The Island Packet*, www.islandpacket.com/news/local/community/beaufort-news/article33693867.html.

"Shark Myths vs. Facts." *Oceana USA*, www.usa.oceana.org/shark-myths-vs-facts/.

"Shark Nets." *Australian For Dolphins*, www.afd.org.au/shark-nets/.

"Shark Nets." *Shark Angels*, www.sharkangels.org/shark-nets/.

"Shark Science." *Shark Trust*, www.sharktrust.org/shark-science.

"Shark Senses." *Shark Trust*, www.sharktrust.org/shark-senses.

"Shark." *Chronicling America: Historic American Newspapers*, 8 July 1916, www.chroniclingamerica.loc.gov/lccn/sn83045211/1916-07-08/ed-1/seq-2/.

"Shark." *The Day Book*, 13 July 1916, www.chroniclingamerica.loc.gov/lccn/sn83045487/1916-07-13/ed-1/seq-8/

"Sharks and Humans: A Love-Hate Story." *Smithsonian Ocean*, www.ocean.si.edu/ocean-life/sharks-rays/sharks-and-humans-love-hate-story/.

"Sharks Before and After Jaws." *JSTOR Daily*, www.daily.jstor.org/sharks-before-and-after-jaws/.

"Sharks." *WildAid*, www.wildaid.org/programs/sharks/#:~:text=Fins%20from%20up%20to%2073,shark%20fin%20soup%20each%20year.

"Sharks: A Case Study in Misunderstood Predators." *Lamont-Doherty Earth Observatory*, www.ldeo.columbia.edu/edu/eesj/casestudies/shark.html.

"Shark Reef Marine Reserve." *Fiji Shark Dive*, https://www.fijisharkdive.com/shark-reef-marine-reserve/#:~:text=Shark%20Reef%20Marine%20Reserve%20was,Adventure%20Divers%20and%20disbursed%20monthly.

"South Africa Shark Attack File." *Stop Shark Cage Diving*, Web Archive, 3 May 2012, www.web.archive.org/web/20120503092351/http://www.stopsharkcagediving.com/south_africa_shark_attack_file.htm.

"The Fiji Myth of Dakuwaqa, the Shark God." *The Kid Should See This*, 25 Oct. 2021, https://thekidshouldseethis.com/post/fiji-myth-dakuwaqa-shark-god-animation.

"The History of How We Got Paid Vacation in the US." *Fast Company*, www.fastcompany.com/90220227/the-history-of-how-we-got-paid-vacation-in-the-us.

"The Hotel Business in America Has a Long and Sometimes Even Illustrious History." *The Baltimore Sun*, 16 Oct. 1994, www.baltimoresun.com/1994/10/16/the-hotel-business-in-america-has-a-long-and-sometimes-even-illustrious-history/.

"The Jersey Shore Shark Attacks of 1916." *The Daily Jaws*, www.thedailyjaws.com/blog/the-jersey-shore-shark-attacks-of-1916.

"The Truth About the 9 Shark Attacks Known as Black December." *The Daily Jaws*, www.thedailyjaws.com/blog/the-truth-about-the-9-shark-attacks-known-as-black-december.

"Think Sharks Are Scary? Blame Hollywood, New Study Suggests." *Mongabay News*, 20 Sept. 2021, www.news.mongabay.com/2021/09/if-you-think-sharks-are-scary-blame-hollywood-new-study-suggests/.

"Travel Advisory: Beach Vacationers Beware." *Los Angeles Times*, 28 June 1992, www.latimes.com/archives/la-xpm-1992-06-28-tr-1725-story.html.

"U-boat." *Encyclopaedia Britannica*, www.britannica.com/technology/U-boat.

"U-Boats: The First Weapon of War to Terrorize the Seas." *History, A&E Television Networks*, www.history.com/news/u-boats-world-war-i-germany.

"Understanding Misinformation and Its Impact." *American Psychological Association*, www.apa.org/topics/journalism-facts/misinformation-belief-action.

"Vector-Borne Diseases." *World Health Organization (WHO)*, www.who.int/en/news-room/fact-sheets/detail/vector-borne-diseases.

"What Makes People So Afraid of Sharks?" *CBS News*, www.cbsnews.com/news/what-makes-people-so-afraid-of-sharks-jaws-scientists/.

"What Was the Black December of 1957?" *Getaway*, www.getaway.co.za/travel/travel-ideas/what-was-the-black-december-of-1957/.

"What's More Likely to Kill You Than a Shark?" *Gili Shark Conservation*, www.gilisharkconservation.com/whats-more-likely-to-kill-you-than-a-shark/.

"When New Yorkers Lived Knee-Deep in Trash." *Collectors Weekly*, www.collectorsweekly.com/articles/when-new-yorkers-lived-knee-deep-in-trash/.

"Why Do Sharks Bite People?" *Save Our Seas Foundation*, www.saveourseas.com/worldofsharks/why-do-sharks-bite-people.

"Why Do Sharks Bite People?" *Save Our Seas Foundation*, www.saveourseas.com/worldofsharks/why-do-sharks-bite-people.

"Why We're So Terrified of the Unknown." *BBC Worklife*, 22 Oct. 2021, www.bbc.com/worklife/article/20211022-why-were-so-terrified-of-the-unknown.

"Yale University Manuscripts and Archives Collections." *Yale University Library Digital Collections*, www.elischolar.library.yale.edu/cgi/viewcontent.cgi?article=1021&context=mssa_collections.

"Yearly Worldwide Shark Attack Summary." *Florida Museum*, www.floridamuseum.ufl.edu/shark-attacks/yearly-worldwide-summary/.

"Young Boy Bitten by Shark off Isle of Palms." *Count on 2*, www.counton2.com/news/young-boy-bitten-by-shark-off-isle-of-palms/.

"The Relative Risk of Shark Attacks to Humans: More People Mean More Attacks." *Florida Museum of Natural History*, www.flmnh.ufl.edu/fish/sharks/isaf/moreattacks.htm.

Ball, Jessica. "Historical Art Paints a Picture of Past Shark Abundance." *Hakai Magazine*, 6 Mar. 2018, https://hakaimagazine.com/features/historical-art-paints-picture-past-shark-abundance/#:~:text=Herodotus's%20account%20that%20shark%20attacks,of%20a%20great%20white%20shark.

Barber, Nicholas. "The True Story of Jaws." *BBC Culture*, British Broadcasting Corporation, 13 July 2016, https://www.bbc.com/culture/article/20160713-the-true-story-of-jaws.

Berman, Mark. "Shark Week: 7 Things Way More Likely to Kill You Than Sharks." *USA Today*, 24 July 2017, https://www.usatoday.com/story/news/nation-now/2017/07/24/shark-week-7-things-way-more-likely-kill-you-than-sharks/506115001/#:~:text=Lightning%20strike,3%2C748%2C067%20for%20a%20shark%20attack.

Bush, Evan. "U.S. Takes Aim at Global Shark Fin Trade." *NBC News*, 6 Jan. 2023, https://www.nbcnews.com/science/science-news/us-takes-aim-global-shark-fin-trade-rcna68369.

Cooke, Melanie. "Summer of the shark". *The Guardian*, 5 Sept. 2001. https://www.theguardian.com/theguardian/2001/sep/05/features11.g23

D'Alessandro, Anthony. "'Jaws' 50th Anniversary Feature Documentary in the Works at National Geographic." *Deadline*, 21 June 2024, www.deadline.com/2024/06/jaws-50th-anniversary-feature-documentary-national-geographic-steven-spielberg-1235980526/.

D'Alessandro, Anthony. "Dueling 'Jaws' Documentaries in Works: 'Jaws: Making a Splash in Hollywood' & 'Jaws 50.'" *Deadline*, 12 July 2024, www.deadline.com/2024/07/dueling-jaws-documentaries-in-works-jaws-making-a-splash-in-hollywood-jaws-50-1235998408/.

Eddie, Rachel. "Threat to Cut Shark Nets if Government Fails to Act." *The New Daily*, 9 Jan. 2018, www.thenewdaily.com.

Encyclopaedia Britannica. "White Shark." *Encyclopaedia Britannica*, 2023, https://www.britannica.com/animal/white-shark.

Fantz, Ashley, and Ed Payne. "North Carolina Shark Attack Victims Face Long Recoveries." *CNN*, 1 July 2015, www.cnn.com/2015/07/01/us/north-carolina-shark-attack/index.html.

Fetters, Ashley. "The Evolution of Shark Week, Pop-Culture Leviathan." *The Atlantic*, 13 Aug. 2012, www.theatlantic.com. Archived from the original on 8 Aug. 2013.

Fowler, Anthony, and Andrew B. Hall. "Blind Retrospection: Why Shark Attacks Are Bad For Democracy". *Center for the Study of Democratic Institutions, Vanderbilt University*, May 2013, www.vanderbilt.edu/csdi/research/CSDI_WP_05-2013.pdf.

Fowler, David. "Shark Attacks and the Political Science of 1916." *Vox*, 19 Aug. 2022, https://www.vox.com/future-perfect/23279012/shark-attack-1916-woodrow-wilson-political-science-achen-bartels-fowler-hall.

Griggs, Brandon. "The Myth of the Shark: How Sharks Became the Ocean's Most Feared Predator." *The Verge*, 26 July 2017, www.theverge.com/2017/7/26/15998676/sharks-myths-history-culture.

Halliday, Claire. "Academics Identify 'The Jaws Effect' in World-First UniSA Study." *EducationDaily*, 24 Nov. 2023, https://educationdaily.au/general/academics-jaws-effect-unisa-study-9051/.

Harris, Paul. "Holidaymakers Return to North Carolina Beach After Double Shark Attack." *The Guardian*, 16 June 2015, www.theguardian.com/environment/2015/jun/16/holidaymakers-return-to-north-carolina-beach-after-double-shark-attack.

Harris, Paul. "More Than 90% of Marine Animals Caught in NSW Shark Nets Over Summer Were Non-Target Species." *The Guardian*, 30 Apr. 2024, www.theguardian.com/environment/2024/apr/30/more-than-90-of-marine-animals-caught-in-nsw-shark-nets-over-summer-were-non-target-species.

Kaplan, Sarah. "Your Sense of Smell Is More Powerful than You Think." *The Washington Post*, 11 May 2017, https://www.washingtonpost.com/news/speaking-of-science/wp/2017/05/11/your-sense-of-smell-is-more-powerful-than-you-think/.

Kroll, Michael. "The Sinking of the USS Indianapolis Triggered the Worst Shark Attack in History." *Smithsonian Magazine*, 7 Aug. 2013, https://www.smithsonianmag.com/history/sinking-uss-indianapolis-triggered-worst-shark-attack-history-25715092/#:~:text=Sharks%20were%20drawn%20in%20by,group%2C%20ideally%20toward%20its%20center.

Levin, Sarah. "Animals More Likely to Kill You than Sharks." *Treehugger*, 23 Oct. 2019, www.treehugger.com/animals-more-likely-to-kill-you-than-sharks-4864195.

Lombardo, Christy. "Jersey Shore Shark Attacks of 1916: Caroline White Shark Brings Back Memories." *NorthJersey.com*, 5 July 2020, www.northjersey.com/story/news/new-jersey/2020/07/05/jersey-shore-shark-attacks-of-1916-caroline-white-shark-brings-back-memories/5365588002/.

Lynch, Jennifer. "Why Do Sharks Bite People?" *Psychology Today*, 6 Mar. 2023, www.psychologytoday.com/intl/blog/animal-minds/202303/why-do-sharks-bite-people.

Maxouris, Christina. "3 Shark Attacks Were Reported in Florida over the Weekend." *CNN*, 5 Aug. 2019, www.cnn.com/2019/08/05/us/florida-3-shark-attacks-trnd/index.html.

Maycock, Sophie. "45 Years of the Jaws Effect." *Sophie Maycock Shark Speak*, 16 June 2020, www.sophiemaycocksharkspeak.com/post/45-years-of-the-jaws-effect-1.

Maycock, Sophie. "The Shark, The Myth, The Legend." *Sophie Maycock Shark Speak*, 1 Sept. 2020, www.sophiemaycocksharkspeak.com/post/the-shark-the-myth-the-legend.

McCarthy, Michael. "Fourth Shark Attack in North Carolina." *The Guardian*, 25 June 2015, www.theguardian.com/us-news/2015/jun/25/fourth-shark-attack-north-carolina.

Morris, Jessica. "Shark Nets – Death Traps For Marine Animals." www.*HSI.org.au*, 8 Dec. 2016, archived from the original on 2 Oct. 2018. https://hsi.org.au/blog/shark-nets-death-traps-for-marine-animals/

Morris, Kiona. "Steven Spielberg Regrets How Jaws Impacted Real-World Sharks." *Smithsonian Magazine*, 6 Oct. 2015, www.smithsonianmag.com/smart-news/steven-spielberg-regrets-how-jaws-impacted-real-world-sharks-180981335/.

Mountford, Kent, PhD, and Richard G. Fernicola, MD. "Earliest Recorded Human Death from a Shark Encounter in North America." *Bay Journal*, self-published, 1 May 2023, https://www.bayjournal.com/earliest-recorded-human-death-from-a-shark-encounter-in-north-america/pdf_841f17e8-e4fb-11ed-bb11-b70c80a07d1d.html.

Pappas, Stephanie. "7 Mysteries About Sharks." *Live Science*, 27 June 2016, www.livescience.com/55235-7-mysteries-about-sharks.html.

Schneider, Mary. "History Book: Shark Attacks Panicked Public 100 Years Ago." *Reading Eagle*, 13 July 2016, www.readingeagle.com/2016/07/13/history-book-shark-attacks-panicked-public-100-years-ago/.

Sharf, Zack. "How 'Jaws' Forever Changed the Modern Blockbuster and Made Steven Spielberg a Household Name." *IndieWire*, Penske Media Corporation, www.indiewire.com/features/general/jaws-modern-blockbuster-steven-spielberg-1201844390/#:~:text=Made%20for%20less%20than%20$,the%20box%20office%20in%201975.

Shoard, Catherine. "Why the Author of Jaws Wished He Never Wrote It." *Boston.com*, 19 June 2015, www.boston.com/culture/entertainment/2015/06/19/why-the-author-of-jaws-wished-he-never-wrote-it/.

Sinnott, Eileen. "Robert Engle and the Engleside Hotel." *Asbury Park Press*, 20 May 2015, www.app.com/story/news/local/southern-ocean-county/2015/05/20/robert-engle-engleside-hotel/27640509/.

Tisdall, Simon. "Shark Attacks in Sharm El Sheikh, Egypt." *The Guardian*, 3 Dec. 2010, www.theguardian.com/world/2010/dec/03/shark-attacks-sharm-el-sheikh-egypt.

Tisdall, Simon. "Tourist Killed in Sharm El Sheikh Shark Attack." *The Guardian*, 5 Dec. 2010, www.theguardian.com/world/2010/dec/05/tourist-killed-sharm-shark-attack.

Vecchione, Maria. "Robert Engle of the Engleside Hotel Remembered." *Asbury Park Press*, 20 May 2015, www.app.com/story/news/local/southern-ocean-county/2015/05/20/robert-engle-engleside-hotel/27640509/.

Waxman, Olivia B. "The History of Shark Week: How It Became a Summer Sensation." *Time*, 28 July 2023, www.time.com/6996703/shark-week-history/.

Whitenack, Lisa B., et al. "A Content Analysis of 32 Years of Shark Week Documentaries." *PLOS ONE*, 2022, https://pmc.ncbi.nlm.nih.gov/articles/PMC9632781/.

Willingham, Val. "Discovery's Shark Week Kicks Off with Controversial 'Megalodon' Program." *CNN*, 7 Aug. 2013, www.cnn.com/2013/08/07/showbiz/tv/discovery-shark-week-megalodon/.

Wilson, Woodrow. Final Address in Support of the League of Nations. Archived 11 July 2014, at the Wayback Machine, www.AmericanRhetoric.com.

# Index

9/11, 23
"bite and wait", 33
"hit-and-run", 14, 113
"Jaws effect", the, 151–2
19th Amendment, the, 144
2015–2016 El Nino, 134
2020 coronavirus pandemic, 26, 28
2020 pandemic, 26, 28, 144

Academy Awards, 150
Allen, Tom, 144
al-Qaeda, 123
American Film Institute, 150
American Museum of Natural History, 19, 45, 85
American Psychological Assocation, 123
Amity, Long Island, 147
Anderson Basket Factory, 57
Anderson, Chris, 41
Apex predator, 163
Arbogast, Jessie, 22
Asbury Avenue Beach, 52
Asbury Park, 52, 56, 73, 136–7, 140
Asbury Park Hotel, 73
Asbury Park, New Jersey, xvi
assembly line, 23
asymptomatic, 24, 28
Atlantic Highlands, 21, 37
Atlantic Ocean, 40, 54, 93, 96, 104–5
Aumakua, 4
Avon Beach on Hatteras Island, North Carolina, 183

Bacharach, Isaac, 79
Badenhorst, Nicholaas, 126,
Bangudja, 4
Barnum & Bailey Circus, xvii, 81
Barry, Vernon James, 126

Batten, Mary, 144
Battle of the Somme, 74
Bayonne, New Jersey, xvi, 52, 81
Beach Haven, New Jersey, xviii, xix, 22, 28–32, 35, 37–40, 43, 55, 88, 99, 101–2, 149
Bees, 118
Benchley, Peter, xviii, 147–9, 159–60, 166
Bergman, Larry, 133
Best Music (Score), 150
Bester, Fay Jones, 127
Black December, xviii, 125, 130, 154
Boat Bites (ISAF Category Type), 116
Brodeur, John, 128
Bronx Home News, xvii, 82–84
Brooklyn Museum, xvi, 45, 82,
Brooklyn Museum Quarterly, xvi, 98, 102, 138
Brooklyn Museum Science Bulletin, xvi, 45
brown shark, 18, 107, 142
Brown, David, 149
Bruder, Charles, xvi, 40–3, 47–8, 51, 92, 120, 128
bull shark, 16, 103–4, 106–8, 122, 155
Bureau of Fisheries, 79, 102
Burgess, George, x, 31, 99, 116, 120, 123, 132, 134–5
Burlew, George "Red", 58–61
Bycatch, 152, 154

Cable, Russell, 49
Cape May, 21, 37, 44
Capuzzo, Michael, ix, 8, 21, 31, 37, 44, 96, 139, 141, 145
Carcharhinus leucas, 16,18
Carcharias taurus
Carcharodon carcharias, 15
Carden, GL, 75

Cartan, Johnson, 58
Cartan, Rensselaer "Renny", 55, 58
Carter, Esterbrook, xvi, 53
Cartilage, 6, 11 156, 157
cartilaginous skeleton, 11
Cassiopeia, 3
Central Powers, the, xvii, 143
Ceto, 3
Chamber of Diving and Watersports (Egypt), 131
Chung, Richard, 129–30
Cliffwood, New Jersey, xvi, 69, 71
Clua, Eric, 114
Cole, John, 48
Collinsville, Illinois, 91
Colohan, Dennis, 52–3
Coney Island, 53, 74
Convention on International Trade in Endangered Species of Wild Fauna and Flora (CITES), the, 158
Cooley, Herbert, 70
Copley, John Singleton, 5
Cornell, John, 42
Cottrell, Thomas, 54–5, 70, 81, 103
Cows, 118

Dakuwaqa, 4
Danvers, Massachusetts, 67
Dengue, 118
Depth charges, 127
dermal denticles, 11
Deutschland, xvi, 88, 92–3, 143
Discovery Channel, xviii, 164
Dog, XIX, 32, 38, 57, 119–20
Dogs, 57, 118, 120
Doubleday, 148
Doubtful (ISAF Category Type), 116
Drum lines, 128, 154
Dunk Brothers Coal and Coke Company, 91
Dunn, Joseph, xvi, 69, 71, 81–2, 104–5
Dunn, Michael, 69 105–6, 121
Dwarf lanternshark, 152

Ecosystem, 157–9, 161
Ellis, Richard, ix, 103, 144
Emmons, Jr., Levi, 56

Enemy Alien Control Program, 90
Engle, Robert, 29, 37,
Engleside Hotel, xix, xx, 29, 31, 34, 37
Essex & Sussex (E & S), 40, 42–4, 79
Everingham, Benjamin, xvi, 52
Everton, John, 33

Fernicola, Richard, ix, 31, 44, 49, 58, 78–9, 95, 98, 136, 141, 145
Field, Edwin, 62
Fielder, James Fairman, 75
Finning, 157-7, 161
First World War, xv, xvii, 28, 74, 88–90, 92, 94, 124, 143–7
Fisher, Stanley, xvi, 58–66, 69, 82, 104, 109, 114, 121
Fitkin Hospital, 128
Florida Museum of Natural History, 117
Florida Program for Shark Research, 117
Ford Motor Company, 22–3
Ford, Henry, 22–3

Galeocerdo cuvier, 17
gills, 12
Global Shark Attack File, 14, 131
great white shark, xviii, 8, 13, 15–6, 45–6, 85, 101–8, 120, 139, 144, 147–8, 151–2, 155, 165
Green, Allan, 126
Gulf Stream, 94–5, 108

Harding, Samuel, 137
Harker, Amos, 52
Henderson, Arris, 62, 77
Herodotus, xv, 3
Hippopotamus, 118
Hoffman, Gertrude, 74
Horses, 118
Hourihan, Jerry, 69
Hughes, Charles Evan, xvi, 53, 142
Hunting Island, South Carolina, 133

infantile paralysis, 25–6
infant paralysis, 25
influenza pandemic, xvii, 144
International Shark Attack File (ISAF), 116–7, 119, 123, 132

Internment of German Americans, xvii, 90, 92
Ischia, Italy, xv, 4
Isle of Palms, South Carolina, 134

Jaws, the book, xviii, 145, 147–8, 159–60, 166
Jaws, the film, xviii, 14–5, 105–6, 150–2, 155–6, 163, 166

Karridene, KwaZulu-Natal, South Africa, 125
Kauhuhu, 4
Ketcham, John, 53
Killer whale (orca), 48
Koliy, Viktor, 131
KwaZulu-Natal Sharks Board, 128
KwaZulu-Natal, South Africa, xviii, 125, 127, 154

Lake Pontchartrain, Louisiana, 15
Langdon Beach, 122
Lefferts, Jacob, 70
Leonidas of Tarentum, xv, 3
Little Egg Harbor, New Jersey, 18
Livers, 12
Long Beach Island, 21, 29, 53
Lucas, Frederic, xvi, 19, 45, 49, 85, 97, 141
Lucerne, Switzerland, 43
Lusitania, xv, 88

MaKakatana River, 126
Malaria, 118
Margate, KwaZulu-Natal, South Africa, 126
Martha's Vineyard, Massachusetts, 163, 165
Martsinko, Olga, 130
Matawan Creek, xvi, 54–6, 58–9, 63, 66, 69, 72, 74, 76–7, 81–2, 101, 103–7
Matawan Historical Society, x, 66, 68, 105
Matawan, New Jersey, xvi
McAdoo, William, 43, 79
McCormick, Harold W, 144
McCosker, John, 144
McDonald, Thomas, 129
McKeever, William, 116, 155

Medical waste, 96–7, 104
Meehan, James, 38
Menstruating, 119,
Meyer, Carl, 114
Migration, 94, 97, 134
Mistaken Identity Hypothesis (MIH), 13, 113. 161
Model T, 23
Monmouth Memorial Hospital, x, 62
Montauk, Long Island, 148
Mosquitoes, 118
Mother Ocean Freediving, 154
Muller, Johannes, xv, 6
Mulsoff, John, 55
Murphy, John, 82
Murphy, Robert, xvi, xvii, 45, 85, 97, 102, 139

National Geographic, 159, 165
Natural Exploration Hypothesis, 114, 118
Naylor, Gavin, 117
Neff, Christopher, 151–2
New Jersey Shark Attack File (NJSAF), 71
New Smyrna Beach, Florida, 117
New South Wales, Australia, 152–4
New York, 22, 27, 30, 45–6, 52, 54, 69, 82, 84, 94–6, 104, 111, 123
New York City, 25–6, 44, 95–6, 99, 123
Nichols, Agusta Fisher, 65
Nichols, John, xvi, xvii, 45, 47–9, 77–8, 85, 97–9, 102, 139
No Assignment Could Be Made, 116
Nolan, Henry, 40
North Atlantic City, 19
North Carolina, 122
Not Confirmed (ISAF Category Type), 117

Oak Island, North Carolina, 133
Ocean City, New Jersey, 129
Ocean dumping, 95–6
Ocean Isle Beach, North Carolina, 133
Ocracoke Island, North Carolina, 134
Oelrichs Reward, 46
Oelrichs, Hermann, xv, 46
O'Hara, Albert "Ally", 58
OJ Simpson, 124

olfactory bulb, 13
Ott, Alexander, xx, 32–4
Overfishing, 132, 157–8, 161, 167
Oviparous, 157

Painting, Julia, 126
Patterson Chamber of Commerce, 78
Pensacola, Florida, 122
Pentagon, 123
Plumer, David, 44
Plutarch, xv, 3
Polio, 24–6, 28
polio epidemic, xvi, 24–6, 30, 95, 98, 108
poliomyelitis, 24
Port Edward, KwaZulu-Natal, South Africa, 126–7
Porter, Norman, 128
Poseidon, 3
Prager, Robert, xvii, 91–2
Prinsloo, Derryck Garth, 126
Provoked Bites (ISAF Category Type), 116
Public Aquaria (ISAF Category Type), 116

Queensland, Australia, 152, 154

Raritan Bay, 54, 56, 82, 84–5, 101,104
Rashad, Mohamed,131
Red Sea, the, 130–1
Reproduce, 157
Reproduction, 157
Reproductive, 94
revolver dentition, 12, 16
Reynolds, George, 61
Richard, Thomas, 53
Robbins Reef Yacht Club, 52
Roinestad, Kurtis, x, 57, 67–8, 97, 105, 141
Roosevelt, Theodore, 142
Rose Hill Cemetary, 65–6

Safety nets, xx, 49, 75, 127
Saint Helena Island, South Carolina, 133
Saint Peter's Hospital, 61, 71
Salem Village, Massachusetts, 67
Salem Witch Trials, 67
Salem, Massachusetts, 67
Salk, Jonas, 24

sand bar shark, 15, 18, 106–7
Sanitation, 74, 95
Savolaine, Allan, ix, x, 64–5, 68, 141
Scavenge (ISAF Category Type), 116
Schauffler, William, 42
Schleisser, Michael, xvi, 81–5, 101, 104
Scientific American (magazine), 139
Scottburgh, KwaZulu-Natal South Africa, 126
Sea bathing, 98, 162
Sea Bright, New Jersey, 71, 140
Sea Girt, New Jersey, 128–9
Seaside Park, New Jersey, 129
Seiffert, Renate, 131,
sense of smell, 12–3, 119
Shadow Lawn, 28, 51
Shark Conservation Fund (SCF), the, 158–9, 168
Shark control, 152
Shark culling, 152–4
Shark Fest, 163, 165
Shark fin soup, 156
Shark meshing, 152
Shark nets, 128, 152–4
Shark Week, xviii, 163–6
Sharm el-Sheikh, Egypt, xviii, 130–2
Shore Memorial Hospital,130
Siegel, John H, 91
Sinai Peninsula, 130
Smith, Arthur, 58
Smith, Hugh, 47, 141
Snakes, 118
South Africa Shark Attack File, 126
South Carolina, xviii, 132–4
Spanish flu, the, xvii, 144
Spanish-American War, 62
Spiders, 118
Spielberg, Steven, 149, 163, 165
Spring Lake, New Jersey, xvi, 39–40, 42, 44, 53–5, 101, 128
Spyhopping, 106
Squalane, 156
Squalene, 156
staten Island, New York, 19
Steel nets, 79
Steel netting, 52, 140

Stillwell, Lester, xvi, 56–9, 61–3, 66, 68–9, 82, 104, 109, 114, 120–1
Stolyarova, Yludmila, 130
Sullivan's Island, South Carolina, 132
Summer of the Shark, xviii, 121–4
Surf City, North Carolina, 133
Swordfish, 47, 85
Systematische Beschreibung der Plagiostomen, xv, 6

Taft, William Howard Taft, 22
Taylor, Ron, 144
Taylor, Sheridan, 33
Taylor, Valerie, 144
The Humane Society International, 152–3
The Humane Society of the United States, 152
The Matawan Alliance, 68
Thompson, Daniel, 141
Thorne, Edwin, 142
Tice, Bart, 56
tiger shark, 15–7
Tourniquet, 34, 61, 128–9
Tourniquets, 41
Treaty of Versailles, 144
Trishkin, Yevgeniy, 131
Trout, William, 42
Tuckerton Railroad, 22
Tuckerton Railroad/Beach Haven Express, 30
Twin Towers, 123

U-boat, xv, xvi, 92–3, 143
U-boats, 87–8, 92–3, 108

Unprovoked Bites (ISAF Category Type), 116
US Coast Guard, 48, 53, 75, 79
US Coastguard, 122
Uvongo, KwaZulu-Natal, South Africa, 126–7

Vaccine, 24
Van Brunt, William, 75
Van Cleaf, Harry, 63
Vansant, Charles Epting, xvi, xix, xx, 29, 31, 34, 38, 47, 74, 109, 120
Vansant, Eugene, xix, 29–31, 34, 38
Viviparous, 157

Warner, EF, 81
Washington, DC, 75, 123, 143
Watson and the Shark, 5
Waves, North Carolina, 134
Webster, Donald, 126
Wherley, Robert, 125
White, George, 41
Willis, Herbert, 35
Wilson, Woodrow, xvi, xvii, 28, 51, 53, 79, 89, 142–3
World Trade Center, 123
Wyckoff dock, 56, 70

Zanuck, Richard D, 149,
Zimmerman Telegram, the, 143
Zimmerman, Arthur, xvii

Dear Reader,

We hope you have enjoyed this book, but why not share your views on social media? You can also follow our pages to see more about our other products: facebook.com/penandswordbooks or follow us on X @penswordbooks

You can also view our products at www.pen-and-sword.co.uk (UK and ROW) or www.penandswordbooks.com (North America).

To keep up to date with our latest releases and online catalogues, please sign up to our newsletter at: www.pen-and-sword.co.uk/newsletter

If you would like a printed catalogue with our latest books, then please email: enquiries@pen-and-sword.co.uk or telephone: 01226 734555 (UK and ROW) or email: uspen-and-sword@casematepublishers.com or telephone: (610) 853-9131 (North America).

We respect your privacy and we will only use personal information to send you information about our products.

Thank you!